Understanding Basic Music Theory

Collection edited by:
Catherine Schmidt-Jones

Understanding Basic Music Theory

Collection edited by:

Catherine Schmidt-Jones

By:

Catherine Schmidt-Jones

Russell Jones

(Authors listed in the order their modules appear)

Online:

<http://cnx.org/content/col10363/1.3/ >

C O N N E X I O N S

Rice University, Houston, Texas

Table of Contents

Introduction[1]

Although it is significantly expanded from "Introduction to Music Theory", this course still covers only the bare essentials of music theory. Music is a very large subject, and the advanced theory that students will want to pursue after mastering the basics will vary greatly. A trumpet player interested in jazz, a vocalist interested in early music, a pianist interested in classical composition, and a guitarist interested in world music, will all want to delve into very different facets of music theory; although, interestingly, if they all become very well-versed in their chosen fields, they will still end up very capable of understanding each other and cooperating in musical endeavors. The final section of this course does include a few challenges that are generally not considered "beginner level" musicianship, but are very useful in just about every field and genre of music.

The main purpose of the course, however, is to explore basic music theory so thoroughly that the interested student will then be able to easily pick up whatever further theory is wanted. Music history and the physics of sound are included to the extent that they shed light on music theory. Students who find the section on acoustics (The Physical Basis) uninteresting may skip it at first, but should then go back to it when they begin to want to understand why musical sounds work the way they do. Remember, the main premise of this course is that a better understanding of where the basics come from will lead to better and faster comprehension of more complex ideas.

It also helps to remember, however, that music theory is a bit like grammar. Languages are invented by the people who speak them, who tend to care more about what is easy and what makes sense than about following rules. Later, experts study the best speakers and writers in order to discover how they use language. These language theorists then make up rules that clarify grammar and spelling and point out the relationships between words. Those rules are only guidelines based on patterns discovered by the theoreticians, which is why there are usually plenty of "exceptions" to every rule. Attempts to develop a new language by first inventing the grammar and spelling never seem to result in a language that people find useful.

Music theory, too, always comes along after a group of composers and performers have already developed a musical tradition. Theoreticians then study the resulting music and discover good ways of explaining it to the audience and to other composers and performers. So sometimes the answer to "Why is it that way?" is simply "that's what is easiest for the performer", or "they borrowed that from an earlier music tradition".

In the case of music, however, the answers to some "why"s can be found in the basic physics of sound, so the pivotal section of this course is an overview of acoustics as it pertains to music. Students who are already familiar with notation and basic musical definitions can skip the first sections and begin with this introduction to the physical basis of music. Adults who have already had some music instruction should be able to work through this course with or without a teacher; simply use the opening sections to review any concepts that are unclear or half-forgotten. Young students and beginning musicians should go through it with a teacher, in either a classroom or lesson setting.

There is, even within the English-speaking world, quite a variety of music teaching traditions,

---

[1]This content is available online at <http://cnx.org/content/m13685/1.6/>.

which sometimes use different terms for the same concepts. The terms favored in this course are mostly those in common use in the U.S., but when more than one system of terms is widely used, the alternatives are mentioned.

Chapter 1

Notation

1.1 Pitch

1.1.1 The Staff[1]

People were talking long before they invented writing. People were also making music long before anyone wrote any music down. Some musicians still play "by ear" (without written music), and some music traditions rely more on improvisation and/or "by ear" learning. But written music is very useful, for many of the same reasons that written words are useful. Music is easier to study and share if it is written down. Western music (Section 2.8) specializes in long, complex pieces for large groups of musicians singing or playing parts exactly as a composer intended. Without written music, this would be too difficult. Many different types of music notation have been invented, and some, such as tablature[2], are still in use. By far the most widespread way to write music, however, is on a **staff**. In fact, this type of written music is so ubiquitous that it is called **common notation**.

1.1.1.1 The Staff

The **staff** (plural **staves**) is written as five horizontal parallel lines. Most of the notes (Section 1.2.1) of the music are placed on one of these lines or in a space in between lines. Extra **ledger lines** may be added to show a note that is too high or too low to be on the staff. Vertical **bar lines** divide the staff into short sections called **measures** or **bars**. A **double bar line**, either heavy or light, is used to mark the ends of larger sections of music, including the very end of a piece, which is marked by a heavy double bar.

---

[1]This content is available online at <http://cnx.org/content/m10880/2.9/>.

[2]"Reading Guitar Tablature" <http://cnx.org/content/m11905/latest/>

The Staff

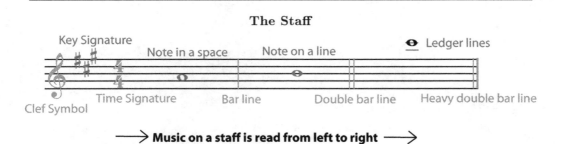

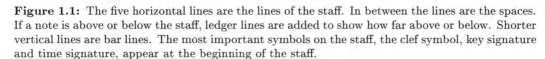

Figure 1.1: The five horizontal lines are the lines of the staff. In between the lines are the spaces. If a note is above or below the staff, ledger lines are added to show how far above or below. Shorter vertical lines are bar lines. The most important symbols on the staff, the clef symbol, key signature and time signature, appear at the beginning of the staff.

Many different kinds of symbols can appear on, above, and below the staff. The notes (Section 1.2.1) and rests (Section 1.2.2) are the actual written music. A note stands for a sound; a rest stands for a silence. Other symbols on the staff, like the clef (Section 1.1.2) symbol, the key signature (Section 1.1.4), and the time signature (Section 1.2.3), tell you important information about the notes and measures. Symbols that appear above and below the music may tell you how fast it goes (tempo (Section 1.2.8) markings), how loud it should be (dynamic (Section 1.3.1) markings), where to go next (repeats (Section 1.2.9), for example) and even give directions for how to perform particular notes (accents (pg 57), for example).

Other Symbols on the Staff

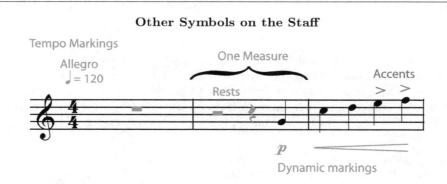

Figure 1.2: The bar lines divide the staff into short sections called bars or measures. The notes (sounds) and rests (silences) are the written music. Many other symbols may appear on, above, or below the staff, giving directions for how to play the music.

1.1.1.2 Groups of staves

Staves are read from left to right. Beginning at the top of the page, they are read one staff at a time unless they are connected. If staves should be played at the same time (by the same person or by different people), they will be connected at least by a long vertical line at the left hand side. They may also be connected by their bar lines. Staves played by similar instruments or voices, or staves that should be played by the same person (for example, the right hand and left hand of a piano part) may be grouped together by braces or brackets at the beginning of each line.

Groups of Staves

Figure 1.3: (b) When many staves are to be played at the same time, as in this orchestral score, the lines for similar instruments - all the violins, for example, or all the strings - may be marked with braces or brackets.

1.1.2 Clef[3]

1.1.2.1 Treble Clef and Bass Clef

The first symbol that appears at the beginning of every music staff (Section 1.1.1) is a **clef symbol**. It is very important because it tells you which note (Section 1.2.1) (A, B, C, D, E, F, or G) is found on each line or space. For example, a **treble clef** symbol tells you that the second line from the bottom (the line that the symbol curls around) is "G". On any staff, the notes are always arranged so that the next letter is always on the next higher line or space. The last note letter, G, is always followed by another A.

Treble Clef

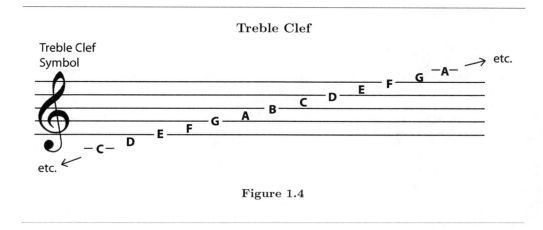

Figure 1.4

A **bass clef** symbol tells you that the second line from the top (the one bracketed by the symbol's dots) is F. The notes are still arranged in ascending order, but they are all in different places than they were in treble clef.

Bass Clef

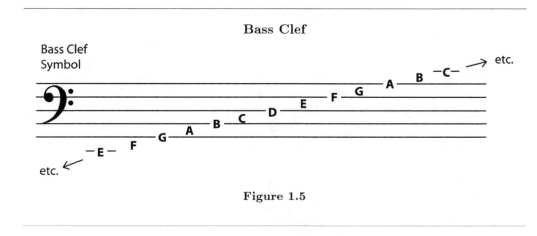

Figure 1.5

---

[3]This content is available online at <http://cnx.org/content/m10941/2.15/>.

1.1.2.2 Memorizing the Notes in Bass and Treble Clef

One of the first steps in learning to read music in a particular clef is memorizing where the notes are. Many students prefer to memorize the notes and spaces separately. Here are some of the most popular mnemonics used.

Treble clef lines:
"Every Good Boy Does Fine"
or
"Every Good Boy Deserves Fudge"

Treble clef spaces spell "FACE"

(a)

Bass clef lines:
"Good Boys Do Fine Always"
or
"Good Boys Deserve Fudge Always"

Bass clef spaces:
"All Cows Eat Grass"

(b)

Figure 1.6: You can use a word or silly sentence to help you memorize which notes belong on the lines or spaces of a clef. If you don't like these ones, you can make up your own.

1.1.2.3 Moveable Clefs

Most music these days is written in either bass clef or treble clef, but some music is written in a **C clef**. The C clef is moveable: whatever line it centers on is a middle C (pg 120).

C Clefs

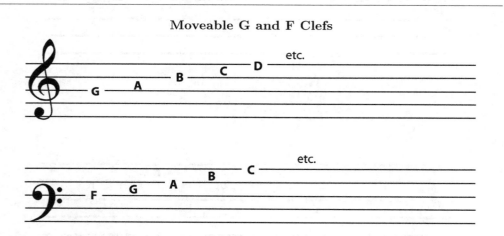

Figure 1.7: All of the notes on this staff are middle C.

The bass and treble clefs were also once moveable, but it is now very rare to see them anywhere but in their standard positions. If you do see a treble or bass clef symbol in an unusual place, remember: treble clef is a **G clef**; its spiral curls around a G. Bass clef is an **F clef**; its two dots center around an F.

Moveable G and F Clefs

Figure 1.8: It is rare these days to see the G and F clefs in these nonstandard positions.

Much more common is the use of a treble clef that is meant to be read one octave below the written pitch. Since many people are uncomfortable reading bass clef, someone writing music that is meant to sound in the region of the bass clef may decide to write it in the treble clef so that it is easy to read. A very small "8" at the bottom of the treble clef symbol means that the notes should sound one octave lower than they are written.

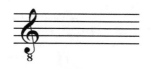

Figure 1.9: A small "8" at the bottom of a treble clef means that the notes should sound one octave lower than written.

1.1.2.4 Why use different clefs?

Music is easier to read and write if most of the notes fall on the staff and few ledger lines (pg 3) have to be used.

Figure 1.10: These scores show the same notes written in treble and in bass clef. The staff with fewer ledger lines is easier to read and write.

The G indicated by the treble clef is the G above middle C (pg 120), while the F indicated by the bass clef is the F below middle C. (C clef indicates middle C.) So treble clef and bass clef together cover many of the notes that are in the range (Section 2.7) of human voices and of most instruments. Voices and instruments with higher ranges usually learn to read treble clef, while voices and instruments with lower ranges usually learn to read bass clef. Instruments with ranges that do not fall comfortably into either bass or treble clef may use a C clef or may be transposing instruments[4].

---

[4]"Transposing Instruments" <http://cnx.org/content/m10672/latest/>

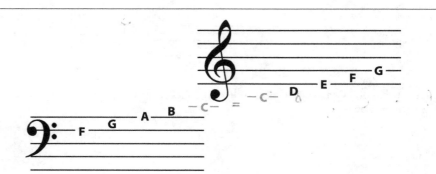

Figure 1.11: Middle C is above the bass clef and below the treble clef; so together these two clefs cover much of the range of most voices and instruments.

Exercise 1.1:

Write the name of each note below the note on each staff in Figure 1.12.

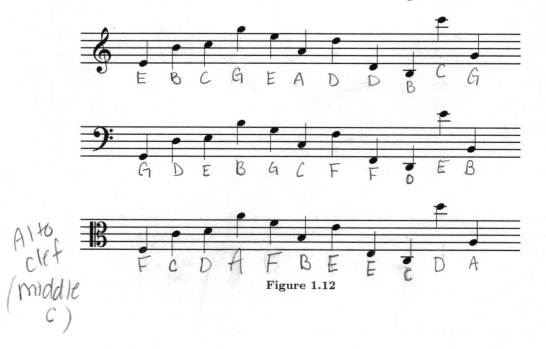

Figure 1.12

(*Solution to Exercise 1.1 on p. 63.*)

Exercise 1.2:

Choose a clef in which you need to practice recognizing notes above and below the staff in Figure 1.13. Write the clef sign at the beginning of the staff, and then write the correct note names below each note.

Figure 1.13

(Solution to Exercise 1.2 on p. 64.)

Exercise 1.3:

Figure 1.14 gives more exercises to help you memorize whichever clef you are learning. You may print these exercises as a PDF worksheet[5] if you like.

[5]http://cnx.org/content/m10941/latest/ClefWorksheet.pdf

Clef Practice

Practice writing your clef symbol on this staff. Write at least eight clef symbols

Write the letter names of the lines in your staff: Write the letter names of the spaces:

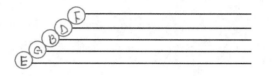   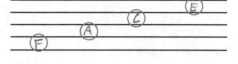

Write the letter names of the three ledger lines below
and the three ledger lines above your staff.

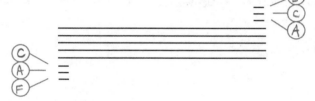

Write your clef symbol at the beginning of this line.
Then write the correct letter name above each note.

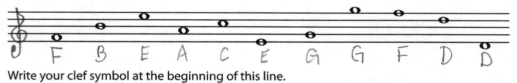

Write your clef symbol at the beginning of this line.
Then write a note in the staff for each letter below the staff.

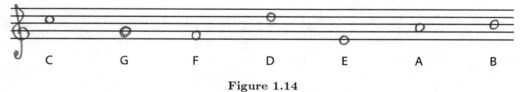

Figure 1.14

(Solution to Exercise 1.3 on p. 64.)

1.1.3 Pitch: Sharp, Flat, and Natural Notes[6]

The **pitch** of a note is how high or low it sounds. Pitch depends on the frequency (Section 3.1.4) of the fundamental[7] sound wave of the note. The higher the frequency of a sound wave, and the shorter its wavelength (Section 3.1.4), the higher its pitch sounds. But musicians usually don't want to talk about wavelengths and frequencies. Instead, they just give the different pitches different letter names: A, B, C, D, E, F, and G. These seven letters name all the **natural** notes (on a keyboard, that's all the white keys) within one octave. (When you get to the eighth natural note, you start the next octave (Section 4.1) on another A.)

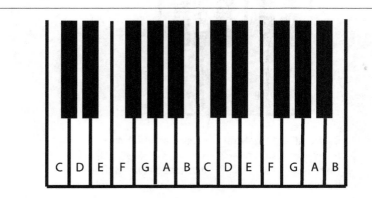

Figure 1.15: The natural notes name the white keys on a keyboard.

But in Western (Section 2.8) music there are twelve notes in each octave that are in common use. How do you name the other five notes (on a keyboard, the black keys)?

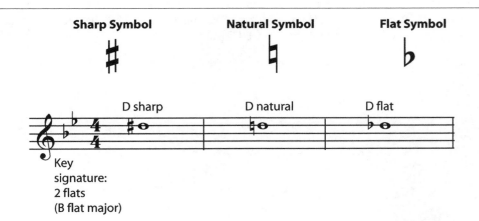

Figure 1.16: Sharp, flat, and natural signs can appear either in the key signature (Section 1.1.4), or right in front of the note that they change.

[6]This content is available online at <http://cnx.org/content/m10943/2.9/>.

[7]"Harmonic Series" <http://cnx.org/content/m11118/latest/#p1c>

A **sharp sign** means "the note that is one half step (Section 4.2) higher than the natural note". A **flat sign** means "the note that is one half step lower than the natural note". Some of the natural notes are only one half step apart, but most of them are a whole step (Section 4.2) apart. When they are a whole step apart, the note in between them can only be named using a flat or a sharp.

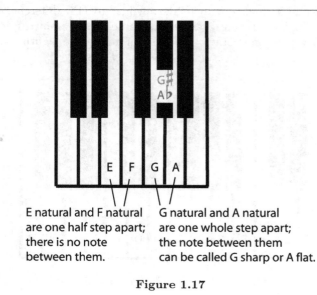

E natural and F natural are one half step apart; there is no note between them.

G natural and A natural are one whole step apart; the note between them can be called G sharp or A flat.

Figure 1.17

Notice that, using flats and sharps, any pitch can be given more than one note name. For example, the G sharp and the A flat are played on the same key on the keyboard; they sound the same. You can also name and write the F natural as "E sharp"; F natural is the note that is a half step higher than E natural, which is the definition of E sharp. Notes that have different names but sound the same are called enharmonic (Section 1.1.5) notes.

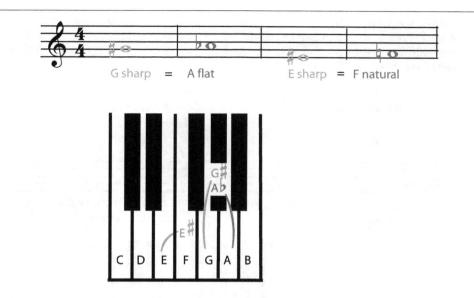

Figure 1.18: G sharp and A flat sound the same. E sharp and F natural sound the same.

Sharp and flat signs can be used in two ways: they can be part of a key signature (Section 1.1.4), or they can mark accidentals. For example, if most of the C's in a piece of music are going to be sharp, then a sharp sign is put in the "C" space at the beginning of the staff (Section 1.1.1), in the key signature. If only a few of the C's are going to be sharp, then those C's are marked individually with a sharp sign right in front of them. Pitches that are not in the key signature are called **accidentals**.

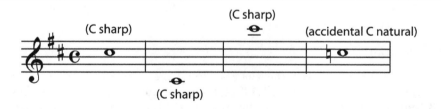

Figure 1.19: When a sharp sign appears in the C space in the key signature, all C's are sharp unless marked as accidentals.

A note can also be double sharp or double flat. A **double sharp** is two half steps (one whole step) higher than the natural note; a **double flat** is two half steps (a whole step) lower. Triple, quadruple, etc. sharps and flats are rare, but follow the same pattern: every sharp or flat raises or lowers the pitch one more half step.

Using double or triple sharps or flats may seem to be making things more difficult than they need to be. Why not call the note "A natural" instead of "G double sharp"? The answer is that, although A natural and G double sharp are the same pitch, they don't have the same function within a particular chord or a particular key. For musicians who understand some music theory (and that includes most performers, not just composers and music teachers), calling a note "G double sharp" gives important and useful information about how that note functions in the chord (Chords) and in the progression of the harmony (Section 5.5).

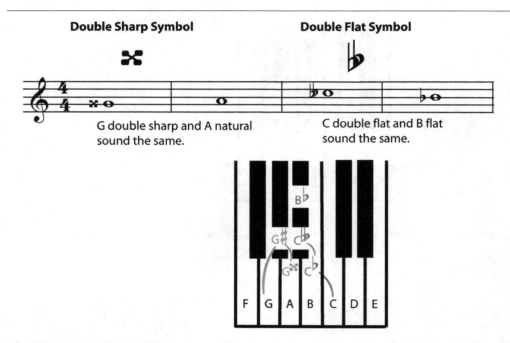

Figure 1.20: Double sharps raise the pitch by two half steps (one whole step). Double flats lower the pitch by two half steps (one whole step).

1.1.4 Key Signature[8]

The key signature comes right after the clef (Section 1.1.2) symbol on the staff (Section 1.1.1). It may have either some sharp (Section 1.1.3) symbols on particular lines or spaces, or some flat (Section 1.1.3) symbols, again on particular lines or spaces. If there are no flats or sharps listed after the clef symbol, then the key signature is "all notes are natural".

In common notation, clef and key signature are the only symbols that normally appear on every staff. They appear so often because they are such important symbols; they tell you what note is on each line and space of the staff. The clef tells you the letter name of the note (A, B, C, etc.), and the key tells you whether the note is sharp, flat or natural.

---

[8]This content is available online at <http://cnx.org/content/m10881/2.11/>.

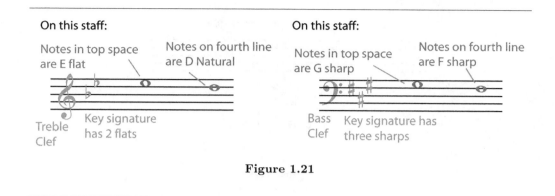

Figure 1.21

The **key signature** is a list of all the sharps and flats in the key (Section 4.3) that the music is in. *When a sharp (or flat) appears on a line or space in the key signature, all the notes on that line or space are sharp (or flat), and all other notes with the same letter names in other octaves are also sharp (or flat).*

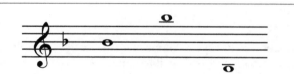

Figure 1.22: This key signature has a flat on the "B" line, so all of these B's are flat.

The sharps or flats always appear in the same order in all key signatures. This is the same order in which they are added as keys get sharper or flatter. For example, if a key (G major or E minor) has only one sharp, it will be F sharp, so F sharp is always the first sharp listed in a sharp key signature. The keys that have two sharps (D major and B minor) have F sharp and C sharp, so C sharp is always the second sharp in a key signature, and so on. *The order of sharps is: F sharp, C sharp, G sharp, D sharp, A sharp, E sharp, B sharp. The order of flats is the reverse of the order of sharps: B flat, E flat, A flat, D flat, G flat, C flat, F flat.* So the keys with only one flat (F major and D minor) have a B flat; the keys with two flats (B flat major and G minor) have B flat and E flat; and so on. The order of flats and sharps, like the order of the keys themselves, follows a circle of fifths (Section 4.7).

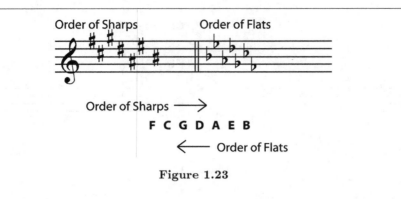

Figure 1.23

If you do not know the name of the key of a piece of music, the key signature can help you find out. Assume for a moment that you are in a major key (Section 4.3). If the key contains sharps, the name of the key is one half step (Section 4.2) higher than the last sharp in the key signature. If the key contains flats, the name of the key signature is the name of the second-to-last flat in the key signature.

Example 1.1:

Figure 1.24 demonstrates quick ways to name the (major) key simply by looking at the key signature. In flat keys, the second-to-last flat names the key. In sharp keys, the note that names the key is one half step above the final sharp.

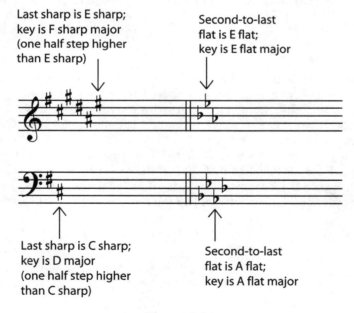

Figure 1.24

The only major keys that these rules do not work for are C major (no flats or sharps) and F major (one flat). It is easiest just to memorize the key signatures for these two very common keys. If you want a rule that also works for the key of F major, remember that the second-to-last flat is always a perfect fourth (pg 140) higher than (or a perfect fifth lower than) the final flat. So you can also say that the name of the key signature is a perfect fourth lower than the name of the final flat.

Figure 1.25: The key of C major has no sharps or flats. F major has one flat.

If the music is in a minor key, it will be in the relative minor (Section 4.4.3) of the major key for that key signature. You may be able to tell just from listening (see Major Keys and Scales (Section 4.3)) whether the music is in a major or minor key. If not, the best clue is to look at the final chord (Chords). That chord (and often the final note of the melody, also) will usually name the key.

Exercise 1.4:

Write the key signatures asked for in Figure 1.26 and name the major keys that they represent.

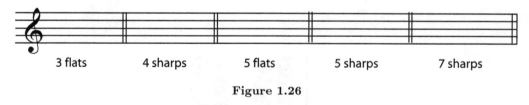

Figure 1.26

(Solution to Exercise 1.4 on p. 67.)

1.1.5 Enharmonic Spelling[9]

1.1.5.1 Enharmonic Notes

In common notation (Section 1.1.1), any note can be sharp, flat, or natural (Section 1.1.3). A sharp symbol raises the pitch (Section 1.1.3) (of a natural note) by one half step (Section 4.2); a flat symbol lowers it by one half step.

---

[9]This content is available online at <http://cnx.org/content/m11641/1.9/>.

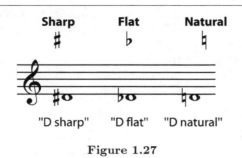

Figure 1.27

Why do we bother with these symbols? There are twelve pitches available within any octave (Section 4.1). We could give each of those twelve pitches its own name (A, B, C, D, E, F, G, H, I, J, K, and L) and its own line or space on a staff. But that would actually be fairly inefficient, because most music is in a particular key (Section 4.3). And music that is in a major (Section 4.3) or minor (Section 4.4) key will tend to use only seven of those twelve notes. So music is easier to read if it has only lines, spaces, and notes for the seven pitches it is (mostly) going to use, plus a way to write the occasional notes that are not in the key.

This is basically what common notation does. There are only seven note names (A, B, C, D, E, F, G), and each line or space on a staff (Section 1.1.1) will correspond with one of those note names. To get all twelve pitches using only the seven note names, we allow any of these notes to be sharp, flat, or natural. Look (Figure 1.28) at the notes on a keyboard.

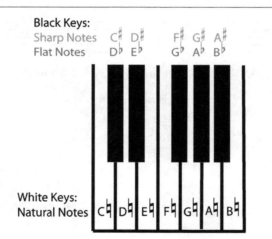

Figure 1.28: Seven of the twelve possible notes in each octave (Section 4.1) are "natural" notes.

Because most of the natural notes are two half steps apart, there are plenty of pitches that you can only get by naming them with either a flat or a sharp (on the keyboard, the "black key" notes). For example, the note in between D natural and E natural can be named either D sharp or E flat. These two names look very different on the staff, but they are going to sound exactly the same, since you play both of them by pressing the same black key on the piano.

Figure 1.29: D sharp and E flat look very different when written in common notation, but they sound exactly the same when played on a piano.

This is an example of **enharmonic spelling**. Two notes are **enharmonic** if they sound the same on a piano but are named and written differently.

Exercise 1.5:

Name the other enharmonic notes that are listed above the black keys on the keyboard in Figure 1.28. Write them on a treble clef staff. If you need staff paper, you can print out this PDF file[10]   *(Solution to Exercise 1.5 on p. 67.)*

But these are not the only possible enharmonic notes. Any note can be flat or sharp, so you can have, for example, an E sharp. Looking at the keyboard (Figure 1.28) and remembering that the definition of sharp is "one half step higher than natural", you can see that an E sharp must sound the same as an F natural. Why would you choose to call the note E sharp instead of F natural? Even though they sound the same, E sharp and F natural, as they are actually used in music, are different notes. (They may, in some circumstances, also sound different; see below (Section 1.1.5.4).) Not only will they look different when written on a staff, but they will have different functions within a key and different relationships with the other notes of a piece of music. So a composer may very well prefer to write an E sharp, because that makes the note's place in the harmonies of a piece more clear to the performer. (Please see Triads (Section 5.1), Beyond Triads (Section 5.4), and Harmonic Analysis (Section 5.5) for more on how individual notes fit into chords and harmonic progressions.)

In fact, this need (to make each note's place in the harmony very clear) is so important that double sharps and double flats have been invented to help do it. A double sharp is two half steps (one whole step (Section 4.2)) higher than the natural note. A double flat is two half steps lower than the natural note. Double sharps and flats are fairly rare, and triple and quadruple flats even rarer, but all are allowed.

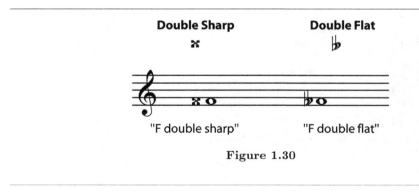

Figure 1.30

[10]http://cnx.org/content/m11641/latest/staffpaper1.pdf

Exercise 1.6:

Give at least one enharmonic spelling for the following notes. Try to give more than one. (Look at the keyboard (Figure 1.28) again if you need to.)

1.E natural

2.B natural

3.C natural

4.G natural

5.A natural

(Solution to Exercise 1.6 on p. 67.)

1.1.5.2 Enharmonic Keys and Scales

Keys and scales can also be enharmonic. Major keys, for example, always follow the same pattern of half steps and whole steps. (See Major Keys and Scales (Section 4.3). Minor keys also all follow the same pattern, different from the major scale pattern; see Minor Keys (Section 4.4).) So whether you start a major scale on an E flat, or start it on a D sharp, you will be following the same pattern, playing the same piano keys as you go up the scale. But the notes of the two scales will have different names, the scales will look very different when written, and musicians may think of them as being different. For example, most instrumentalists would find it easier to play in E flat than in D sharp. In some cases, an E flat major scale may even sound slightly different from a D sharp major scale. (See below (Section 1.1.5.4).)

Figure 1.31: The E flat major and D sharp major scales sound the same on the piano, although they look very different. If this surprises you, look again at the piano keyboard (Figure 1.28) and find the notes that you would play for each scale.

Since the scales are the same, D sharp major and E flat major are also **enharmonic keys**. Again, their key signatures will look very different, but music in D sharp will not be any higher or lower than music in E flat.

Enharmonic Keys

Figure 1.32: The key signatures for E flat and D sharp look very different, but would sound the same on a keyboard.

Exercise 1.7:

Give an enharmonic name and key signature for the keys given in Figure 1.33. (If you are not well-versed in key signatures (Section 1.1.4) yet, pick the easiest enharmonic spelling for the key name, and the easiest enharmonic spelling for every note in the key signature. Writing out the scales may help, too.)

Figure 1.33

(Solution to Exercise 1.7 on p. 68.)

1.1.5.3 Enharmonic Intervals and Chords

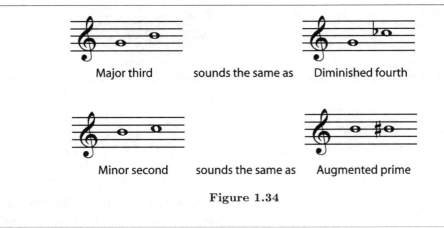

Figure 1.34

Chords (Chords) and intervals (Section 4.5) also can have enharmonic spellings. Again, it is important to name a chord or interval as it has been spelled, in order to understand how it fits into the rest of the music. A C sharp major chord means something different in the key of D than a D flat major chord does. And an interval of a diminished fourth means something different than an interval of a major third, even though they would be played using the same keys on a piano. (For practice naming intervals, see Interval (Section 4.5). For practice naming chords, see Naming Triads (Section 5.2) and Beyond Triads (Section 5.4). For an introduction to how chords function in a harmony, see Beginning Harmonic Analysis (Section 5.5).)

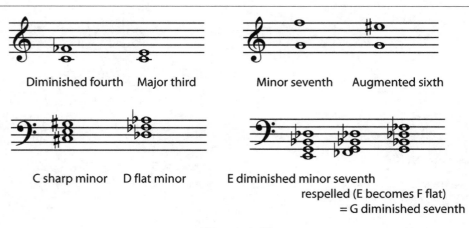

Figure 1.35

1.1.5.4 Enharmonic Spellings and Equal Temperament

All of the above discussion assumes that all notes are tuned in equal temperament (Section 6.2.3.2). Equal temperament has become the "official" tuning system for Western music (Section 2.8). It is easy to use in pianos and other instruments that are difficult to retune (organ, harp, and xylophone, to name just a few), precisely because enharmonic notes sound exactly the same. But voices and instruments that can fine-tune quickly (for example violins, clarinets, and trombones) often move away from equal temperament. They sometimes drift, consciously or unconsciously, towards just intonation (pg 227), which is more closely based on the harmonic series (Section 3.3). When this happens, enharmonically spelled notes, scales, intervals, and chords, may not only be theoretically different. They may also actually be slightly different pitches. The differences between, say, a D sharp and an E flat, when this happens, are very small, but may be large enough to be noticeable. Many Non-western music traditions (Section 2.8) also do not use equal temperament. *Sharps and flats used to notate music in these traditions should not be assumed to mean a change in pitch equal to an equal-temperament half-step.* For definitions and discussions of equal temperament, just intonation, and other tuning systems, please see Tuning Systems (Section 6.2).

1.2 Time

1.2.1 Duration: Note Lengths in Written Music [11]

1.2.1.1 The Shape of a Note

In standard notation, a single musical sound is written as a **note**. The two most important things a written piece of music needs to tell you about a note are its pitch - how high or low it is - and its **duration** - how long it lasts.

To find out the pitch (Section 1.1.3) of a written note, you look at the clef (Section 1.1.2) and the key signature (Section 1.1.4), then see what line or space the note is on. The higher a note sits on the staff (Section 1.1.1), the higher it sounds. To find out the duration of the written note, you look at the tempo (Section 1.2.8) and the time signature (Section 1.2.3) and then see what the note looks like.

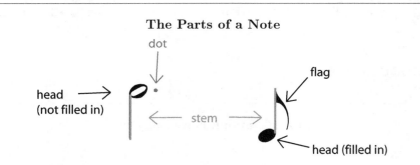

The Parts of a Note

Figure 1.36: All of the parts of a written note affect how long it lasts.

The pitch of the note depends only on what line or space the **head** of the note is on. (Please see pitch (Section 1.1.3) , clef (Section 1.1.2) and key signature (Section 1.1.4) for more information.)

---

[11]This content is available online at <http://cnx.org/content/m10945/2.9/>.

If the note does not have a head (see Figure 1.37), that means that it does not have one definite pitch.

Notes Without Heads

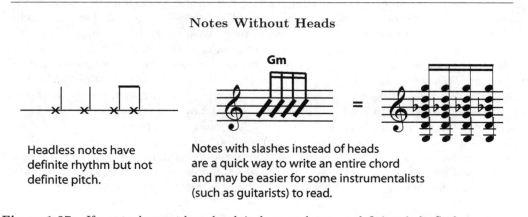

Headless notes have definite rhythm but not definite pitch.

Notes with slashes instead of heads are a quick way to write an entire chord and may be easier for some instrumentalists (such as guitarists) to read.

Figure 1.37: If a note does not have head, it does not have one definite pitch. Such a note may be a pitchless sound, like a drum beat or a hand clap, or it may be an entire chord rather than a single note.

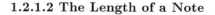

The head of the note may be filled in (black), or not. The note may also have (or not) a stem, one or more flags, beams connecting it to other notes, or one or more dots following the head of the note. All of these things affect how much time the note is given in the music.

NOTE: A dot that is someplace other than next to the head of the note *does not affect the rhythm*. Other dots are articulation (Section 1.3.2) marks. They may affect the actual length of the note (the amount of time it sounds), but do not affect the amount of time it must be given. (The extra time when the note could be sounding, but isn't, becomes an unwritten rest (Section 1.2.2).) If this is confusing, please see the explanation in articulation (Section 1.3.2).

1.2.1.2 The Length of a Note

Most Common Note Lengths

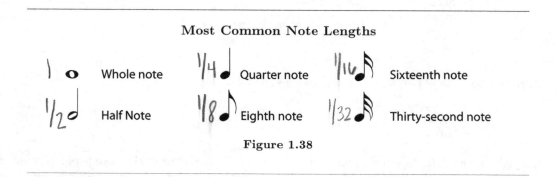

Figure 1.38

The simplest-looking note, with no stems or flags, is a **whole note**. All other note lengths are defined by how long they last compared to a whole note. A note that lasts half as long as a whole note is a **half note**. A note that lasts a quarter as long as a whole note is a **quarter note**. The pattern continues with **eighth notes, sixteenth notes, thirty-second notes, sixty-fourth notes**, and so on, each type of note being half the length of the previous type. (There are no such thing as third notes, sixth notes, tenth notes, etc.; see Dots, Ties, and Borrowed Divisions (Section 1.2.6) to find out how notes of unusual lengths are written.)

Figure 1.39: Note lengths work just like fractions in arithmetic: two half notes or four quarter notes last the same amount of time as one whole note. Flags are often replaced by beams that connect the notes into easy-to-read groups.

You may have noticed that some of the eighth notes in Figure 1.39 don't have flags; instead they have a **beam** connecting them to another eighth note. If flagged notes are next to each other, their flags can be replaced by beams that connect the notes into easy-to-read groups. The beams may connect notes that are all in the same beat, or, in some vocal music, they may connect notes that are sung on the same text syllable. Each note will have the same number of beams as it would have flags.

Notes with Beams

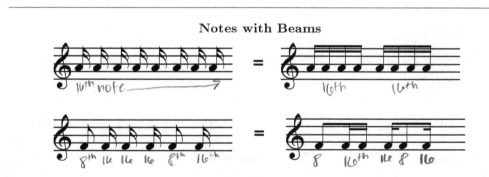

Figure 1.40: The notes connected with beams are easier to read quickly than the flagged notes. Notice that each note has the same number of beams as it would have flags, even if it is connected to a different type of note. The notes are often (but not always) connected so that each beamed group gets one beat. This makes the notes easier to read quickly.

You may have also noticed that the note lengths sound like fractions in arithmetic. In fact they work very much like fractions: two half notes will be equal to (last as long as) one whole note; four eighth notes will be the same length as one half note; and so on. (For classroom activities relating music to fractions, see Fractions, Multiples, Beats, and Measures[12].)

Example 1.2:

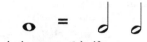

Figure 1.41

Exercise 1.8:

Draw the missing notes and fill in the blanks to make each side the same duration (length of time).

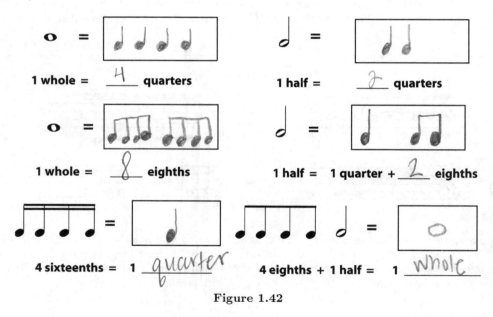

Figure 1.42

(Solution to Exercise 1.8 on p. 68.)

[12]"Fractions, Multiples, Beats, and Measures" <http://cnx.org/content/m11807/latest/>

So how long does each of these notes actually last? That depends on a couple of things. A written note lasts for a certain amount of time measured in beats (Section 1.2.3.1). To find out exactly how many beats it takes, you must know the time signature (Section 1.2.3). And to find out how long a beat is, you need to know the tempo (Section 1.2.8).

Example 1.3:

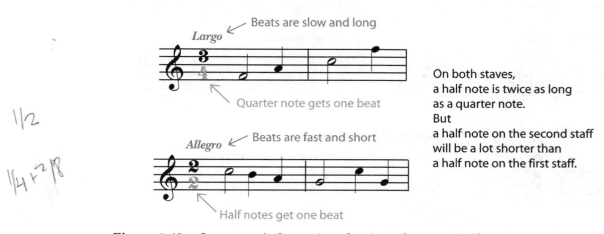

On both staves,
a half note is twice as long
as a quarter note.
But
a half note on the second staff
will be a lot shorter than
a half note on the first staff.

Figure 1.43: In any particular section of a piece of music, a half note is always twice as long as a quarter note. But how long each note actually lasts depends on the time signature and the tempo.

1.2.1.3 More about Stems

Whether a stem points up or down does not affect the note length at all. There are two basic ideas that lead to the rules for stem direction. One is that the music should be as easy as possible to read and understand. The other is that the notes should tend to be "in the staff" as much as reasonably possible.

Basic Stem Direction Rules

1. *Single Notes* - Notes below the middle line of the staff should be stem up. Notes on or above the middle line should be stem down.

2. *Notes sharing a stem (block chords)* - Generally, the stem direction will be the direction for the note that is furthest away from the middle line of the staff

3. *Notes sharing a beam* - Again, generally you will want to use the stem direction of the note farthest from the center of the staff, to keep the beam near the staff.

4. *Different rhythms being played at the same time by the same player* - Clarity requires that you write one rhythm with stems up and the other stems down.

5. *Two parts for different performers written on the same staff* - If the parts have the same rhythm, they may be written as block chords. If they do not, the stems for one part (the "high" part or "first" part) will point up and the stems for the other part will point down. This rule is especially important when the two parts cross; otherwise there is no way for the performers to know that the "low" part should be reading the high note at that spot.

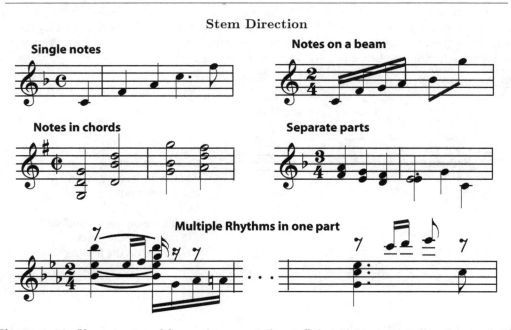

Figure 1.44: Keep stems and beams in or near the staff, but also use stem direction to clarify rhythms and parts when necessary.

1.2.2 Duration: Rest Length[13]

A **rest** stands for a silence in music. For each kind of note (Section 1.2.1), there is a written rest of the same length.

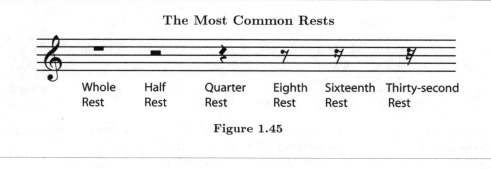

Figure 1.45

Exercise 1.9:

For each note on the first line, write a rest of the same length on the second line. The first measure (Section 1.2.3.1) is done for you.

[13]This content is available online at <http://cnx.org/content/m11887/1.4/>.

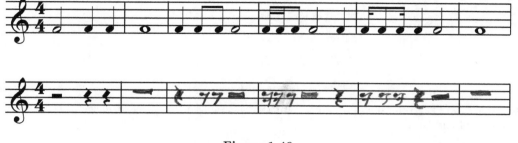

Figure 1.46

(Solution to Exercise 1.9 on p. 69.)

Rests don't necessarily mean that there is silence in the music at that point; only that that part is silent. Often, on a staff (Section 1.1.1) with multiple parts, a rest must be used as a placeholder for one of the parts, even if a single person is playing both parts. When the rhythms are complex, this is necessary to make the rhythm in each part clear.

Figure 1.47: When multiple simultaneous rhythms are written on the same staff, rests may be used to clarify individual rhythms, even if another rhythm contains notes at that point.

1.2.3 Time Signature[14]

The **time signature** appears at the beginning of a piece of music, right after the key signature (Section 1.1.4). Unlike the key signature, which is on every staff (Section 1.1.1), the time signature will not appear again in the music unless the meter changes. The meter (Section 1.2.4) of a piece of music is its basic rhythm; the time signature is the symbol that tells you the meter of the piece and how (with what type of note (Section 1.2.1)) it is written.

---

[14]This content is available online at <http://cnx.org/content/m10956/2.9/>.

Figure 1.48: The time signature appears at the beginning of the piece of music, right after the clef symbol and key signature.

1.2.3.1 Beats and Measures

Because music is heard over a period of time, one of the main ways music is organized is by dividing that time up into short periods called **beats**. In most music, things tend to happen right at the beginning of each beat. This makes the beat easy to hear and feel. When you clap your hands, tap your toes, or dance, you are "moving to the beat". Your claps are sounding at the beginning of the beat, too. This is also called being "on the downbeat", because it is the time when the conductor's baton[15] hits the bottom of its path and starts moving up again.

Example 1.4:

Listen to excerpts A, B, C and D. Can you clap your hands, tap your feet, or otherwise move "to the beat"? Can you feel the 1-2-1-2 or 1-2-3-1-2-3 of the meter? Is there a piece in which it is easier or harder to feel the beat?

- A[16]
- B[17]
- C[18]
- D[19]

The downbeat is the strongest part of the beat, but some downbeats are stronger than others. Usually a pattern can be heard in the beats: strong-weak-weak-strong-weak-weak, or strong-weak-strong-weak. So beats are organized even further by grouping them into **bars**, or **measures**. (The two words mean the same thing.) For example, for music with a beat pattern of strong-weak-weak-strong-weak-weak, or 1-2-3-1-2-3, a measure would have three beats in it. The **time signature** tells you two things: how many beats there are in each measure, and what type of note (Section 1.2.1) gets a beat.

---

[15]"Conducting" <http://cnx.org/content/m12404/latest/>
[16]http://cnx.org/content/m10956/latest/Tanz.mp3
[17]http://cnx.org/content/m10956/latest/EasyWinners.MID
[18]http://cnx.org/content/m10956/latest/Jetztkommt.MID
[19]http://cnx.org/content/m10956/latest/Greensleeves.mp3

Reading the Time Signature

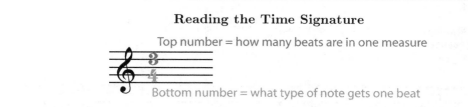

Figure 1.49: This time signature means that there are three quarter notes (or any combination of notes that equals three quarter notes) in every measure. A piece with this time signature would be "in three four time" or just "in three four".

Exercise 1.10:

Listen again to the music in Example 1.4. Instead of clapping, count each beat. Decide whether the music has 2, 3, or 4 beats per measure. In other words, does it feel more natural to count 1-2-1-2, 1-2-3-1-2-3, or 1-2-3-4-1-2-3-4? *(Solution to Exercise 1.10 on p. 69.)*

1.2.3.2 Meter: Reading Time Signatures

Most time signatures contain two numbers. The top number tells you how many beats there are in a measure. The bottom number tells you what kind of note gets a beat.

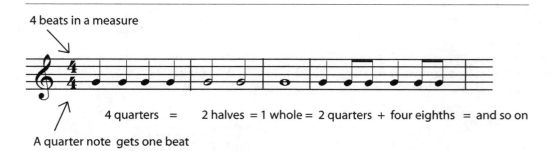

Figure 1.50: In "four four" time, there are four beats in a measure and a quarter note gets a beat. Any combination of notes that equals four quarters can be used to fill up a measure.

You may have noticed that the time signature looks a little like a fraction in arithmetic. Filling up measures feels a little like finding equivalent fractions[20], too. In "four four time", for example, there are four beats in a measure and a quarter note gets one beat. So four quarter notes would fill up one measure. But so would any other combination of notes that equals four quarters: one whole, two halves, one half plus two quarters, and so on.

---

[20]"Fractions, Multiples, Beats, and Measures" <http://cnx.org/content/m11807/latest/>

Example 1.5:

If the time signature is three eight, any combination of notes that adds up to three eighths will fill a measure. Remember that a dot (Section 1.2.6) is worth an extra half of the note it follows. Listen[21] to the rhythms in Figure 1.51.

Figure 1.51: If the time signature is three eight, a measure may be filled with any combination of notes and rests that adds up to three eight.

Exercise 1.11:

Write each of the time signatures below (with a clef symbol) at the beginning of a staff. Write at least four measures of music in each time signature. Fill each measure with a different combination of note lengths. Use at least one dotted note on each staff. If you need some staff paper, you can download this PDF file[22].

1. Two four time

2. Three eight time

3. Six four time

(Solution to Exercise 1.11 on p. 69.)

A few time signatures don't have to be written as numbers. Four four time is used so much that it is often called **common time**, written as a bold "C". When both fours are "cut" in half to twos, you have **cut time**, written as a "C" cut by a vertical slash.

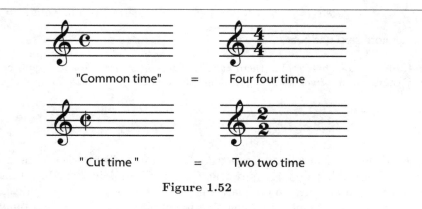

Figure 1.52

---

[21] http://cnx.org/content/m10956/latest/timesig1.MID
[22] http://cnx.org/content/m10956/latest/staffpaper1.pdf

1.2.3.3 Counting and Conducting

You may have already noticed that a measure in four four time looks the same as a measure in two two. After all, in arithmetic, four quarters adds up to the same thing as two halves. For that matter, why not call the time signature "one one" or "eight eight"?

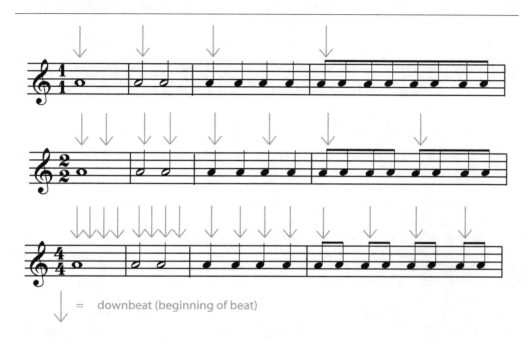

Figure 1.53: Measures in all of these meters look the same, but feel different. The difference is how many downbeats there are in a measure.

Or why not write two two as two four, giving quarter notes the beat instead of half notes? The music would look very different, but it would sound the same, as long as you made the beats the same speed. The music in each of the staves in Figure 1.54 would sound like this[23].

---

[23]http://cnx.org/content/m10956/latest/14k.mid

Figure 1.54: The music in each of these staves should sound exactly alike.

So why is one time signature chosen rather than another? The composer will normally choose a time signature that makes the music easy to read and also easy to count and conduct. Does the music feel like it has four beats in every measure, or does it go by so quickly that you only have time to tap your foot twice in a measure?

A common exception to this is six eight time, and the other time signatures (for example nine eight and twelve eight) commonly used to write compound meters (Section 1.2.4). A piece in six eight might have six beats in every measure, with an eighth note getting a beat. But it is more likely that the conductor will give only two beats per measure, with a dotted quarter (or three eighth notes) getting one beat. Since beats normally get divided into halves and quarters, this is the easiest way for composers to write beats that are divided into thirds. In the same way, three eight may only have one beat per measure; nine eight, three beats per measure; and twelve eight, four beats per measure.

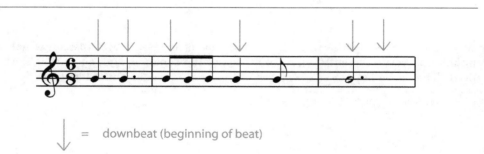

Figure 1.55: In six eight time, a dotted quarter usually gets one beat. This is the easiest way to write beats that are evenly divided into three rather than two.

1.2.4 Meter[24]

1.2.4.1 What is Meter?

The **meter** of a piece of music is the arrangment of its rhythms in a repetitive pattern of strong and weak beats. This does not necessarily mean that the rhythms themselves are repetitive, but they do strongly suggest a repeated pattern of pulses. It is on these pulses, the beat (Section 1.2.3.1) of the music, that you tap your foot, clap your hands, dance, etc.

Some music does not have a meter. Ancient music, such as Gregorian chants; new music, such as some experimental twentieth-century art music; and Non-Western music, such as some native American flute music, may not have a strong, repetitive pattern of beats. Other types of music, such as traditional Western African drumming, may have very complex meters that can be difficult for the beginner to identify.

But most Western (Section 2.8) music has simple, repetitive patterns of beats. This makes **meter** a very useful way to organize the music. Common notation (Section 1.1.1), for example, divides the written music into small groups of beats called measures, or bars (Section 1.2.3.1). The lines dividing each measure from the next help the musician reading the music to keep track of the rhythms (Section 2.1). A piece (or section of the piece) is assigned a time signature (Section 1.2.3) that tells the performer how many beats to expect in each measure, and what type of note (Section 1.2.1) should get one beat. (For more on reading time signatures, please see Time Signature (Section 1.2.3).)

Conducting[25] also depends on the meter of the piece; conductors use different conducting patterns for the different meters. These patterns emphasize the differences between the stronger and weaker beats to help the performers keep track of where they are in the music.

But the conducting patterns depend only on the pattern of strong and weak beats. In other words, they only depend on "how many beats there are in a measure", not "what type of note gets a beat". So even though the time signature is often called the "meter" of a piece, one can talk about meter without worrying about the time signature or even being able to read music. (Teachers, note that this means that children can be introduced to the concept of meter long before they are reading music. See Meter Activities[26] for some suggestions.)

1.2.4.2 Classifying Meters

Meters can be classified by counting the number of beats from one strong beat to the next. For example, if the meter of the music feels like "strong-weak-strong-weak", it is in **duple** meter. "strong-weak-weak-strong-weak-weak" is **triple** meter, and "strong-weak-weak-weak" is **quadruple**. (Most people don't bother classifying the more unusual meters, such as those with five beats in a measure.)

Meters can also be classified as either simple or compound. In a **simple** meter, each beat is basically divided into halves. In **compound** meters, each beat is divided into thirds.

A **borrowed division** occurs whenever the basic meter of a piece is interrupted by some beats that sound like they are "borrowed" from a different meter. One of the most common examples of this is the use of triplets (pg 44) to add some compound meter to a piece that is mostly in a simple meter. (See Dots, Ties, and Borrowed Divisions (Section 1.2.6) to see what borrowed divisions look like in common notation.)

1.2.4.3 Recognizing Meters

To learn to recognize meter, remember that (in most Western (Section 2.8) music) the beats and the subdivisions of beats are all equal and even. So you are basically listening for a running, even pulse underlying the rhythms of the music. For example, if it makes sense to count along with the

---

[24]This content is available online at <http://cnx.org/content/m12405/1.7/>.

[25]"Conducting" <http://cnx.org/content/m12404/latest/>

[26]"Musical Meter Activities" <http://cnx.org/content/m13616/latest/>

music "ONE-and-Two-and-ONE-and-Two-and" (with all the syllables very evenly spaced) then you probably have a simple duple meter. But if it's more comfortable to count "ONE-and-a-Two-and-a-ONE-and-a-Two-and-a", it's probably compound duple meter. (Make sure numbers always come on a pulse, and "one" always on the strongest pulse.)

This may take some practice if you're not used to it, but it can be useful practice for anyone who is learning about music. To help you get started, the figure below sums up the most-used meters. To help give you an idea of what each meter should feel like, here are some animations (with sound) of duple simple[27], duple compound[28], triple simple[29], triple compound[30], quadruple simple[31], and quadruple compound[32] meters. You may also want to listen to some examples of music that is in simple duple[33], simple triple[34], simple quadruple[35], compound duple[36], and compound triple[37] meters.

Meters

Meter	Count												Example Time Signature
Duple Simple	1	&	2	&									$\frac{2}{4}$
Triple Simple	1	&	2	&	3	&							$\frac{3}{4}$
Quadruple Simple	1	&	2	&	3	&	4	&					$\frac{4}{4}$
Duple Compound	1	&	a	2	&	a							$\frac{6}{8}$
Triple Compound	1	&	a	2	&	a	3	&	a				$\frac{9}{8}$
Quadruple Compound	1	&	a	2	&	a	3	&	a	4	&	a	$\frac{12}{8}$

Figure 1.56: Remember that meter is not the same as time signature; the time signatures given here are just examples. For example, 2/2 and 2/8 are also simple duple meters.

1.2.5 Pickup Notes and Measures[38]

1.2.5.1 Pickup Measures

Normally, all the measures (Section 1.1.1.1) of a piece of music must have exactly the number of beats (Section 1.2.3.1) indicated in the time signature (Section 1.2.3). The beats may be filled with

---

[27] http://cnx.org/content/m12405/latest/duplesimple.swf
[28] http://cnx.org/content/m12405/latest/duplecompound.swf
[29] http://cnx.org/content/m12405/latest/triplesimple.swf
[30] http://cnx.org/content/m12405/latest/triplecompound.swf
[31] http://cnx.org/content/m12405/latest/quadsimple.swf
[32] http://cnx.org/content/m12405/latest/quadcompound.swf
[33] http://cnx.org/content/m12405/latest/metdup.mp3
[34] http://cnx.org/content/m12405/latest/mettrip.mp3
[35] http://cnx.org/content/m12405/latest/metquad.mp3
[36] http://cnx.org/content/m12405/latest/metcompdup.mp3
[37] http://cnx.org/content/m12405/latest/metcomptrip.mp3
[38] This content is available online at <http://cnx.org/content/m12717/1.4/>.

any combination of notes or rests (with duration (Section 1.2.1) values also dictated by the time signature), but they must combine to make exactly the right number of beats. If a measure or group of measures has more or fewer beats, the time signature must change.

Figure 1.57: Normally, a composer who wants to put more or fewer beats in a measure must change the time signature, as in this example from Mussorgsky's *Boris Godunov*.

There is one common exception to this rule. (There are also some less common exceptions not discussed here.) Often, a piece of music does not begin on the strongest downbeat (pg 34). Instead, the strong beat that people like to count as "one" (the beginning of a measure), happens on the second or third note, or even later. In this case, the first measure may be a full measure that begins with some rests. But often the first measure is simply not a full measure. This shortened first measure is called a **pickup measure**.

If there is a pickup measure, the final measure of the piece should be shortened by the length of the pickup measure (although this rule is sometimes ignored in less formal written music). For example, if the meter (Section 1.2.4) of the piece has four beats, and the pickup measure has one beat, then the final measure should have only three beats. (Of course, any combination of notes and rests can be used, as long as the total in the first and final measures equals one full measure.

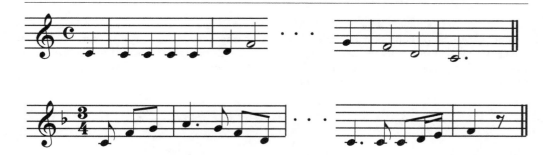

Figure 1.58: If a piece begins with a pickup measure, the final measure of the piece is shortened by the length of the pickup measure.

1.2.5.2 Pickup Notes

Any phrase (Section 2.3.4) of music (not just the first one) may begin someplace other than on a strong downbeat. All the notes before the first strong downbeat of any phrase are the **pickup notes** to that phrase.

Figure 1.59: Any phrase may begin with pickup notes. Each of these four phrases begins with one or two pickup notes. (You may listen to the tune here[39]; can you hear that the pickup notes lead to the stronger downbeat?)

A piece that is using pickup measures or pickup notes may also sometimes place a double bar (pg 3) (with or without repeat signs) inside a measure, in order to make it clear which phrase and which section of the music the pickup notes belong to. If this happens (which is a bit rare, because it can be confusing to read), there is still a single bar line where it should be, at the end of the measure.

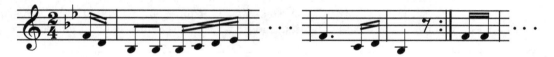

Figure 1.60: At the ends of sections of the music, a measure may be interrupted by a double bar that places the pickup notes in the correct section and assures that repeats have the correct number of beats. When this happens, the bar line will still appear at the end of the completed measure. This notation can be confusing, though, and in some music the pickups and repeats are written in a way that avoids these broken-up measures.

1.2.6 Dots, Ties, and Borrowed Divisions[40]

A half note is half the length of a whole note; a quarter note is half the length of a half note; an eighth note is half the length of a quarter note, and so on. (See Duration:Note Length (Section 1.2.1).) The same goes for rests. (See Duration: Rest Length (Section 1.2.2).) But what if you want a note (or rest) length that isn't half of another note (or rest) length?

1.2.6.1 Dotted Notes

One way to get a different length is by dotting the note or rest. A **dotted note** is one-and-a-half times the length of the same note without the dot. In other words, the note keeps its original length

---

[39]http://cnx.org/content/m12717/latest/GirlILeftBehind.MID
[40]This content is available online at <http://cnx.org/content/m11888/1.6/>.

and adds another half of that original length because of the dot. So a dotted half note, for example, would last as long as a half note plus a quarter note, or three quarters of a whole note.

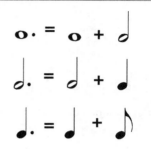

Figure 1.61: The dot acts as if it is adding another note half the length of the original note. A dotted quarter note, for example, would be the length of a quarter plus an eighth, because an eighth note is half the length of a quarter note.

Exercise 1.12:

Make groups of equal length on each side, by putting a dotted note or rest in the box.

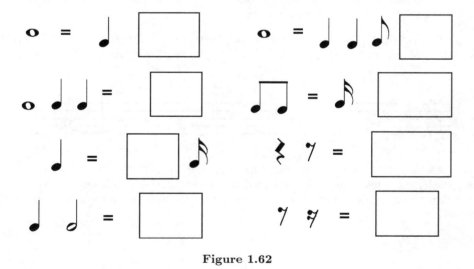

Figure 1.62

(Solution to Exercise 1.12 on p. 70.)

A note may have more than one dot. Each dot adds half the length that the dot before it added. For example, the first dot after a half note adds a quarter note length; the second dot would add an eighth note length.

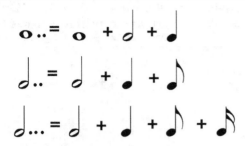

Figure 1.63: When a note has more than one dot, each dot is worth half of the dot before it.

1.2.6.2 Tied Notes

A dotted half lasts as long as a half note plus a quarter note. The same length may be written as a half note and a quarter note tied together. **Tied notes** are written with a curved line connecting two notes that are on the same line or the same space in the staff. Notes of any length may be tied together, and more than two notes may be tied together. *The sound they stand for will be a single note that is the length of all the tied notes added together.* This is another way to make a great variety of note lengths. Tied notes are also the only way to write a sound that starts in one measure (Section 1.2.3.1) and ends in a different measure.

NOTE: Ties may look like slurs (pg 60), but they are not the same; a slur connects to notes with different pitches (Section 1.1.3) and is a type of articulation (Section 1.3.2).

Figure 1.64: When these eight notes are played as written, only five distinct notes are heard: one note the length of two whole notes; then a dotted half note; then another note the same length as the dotted half note; then a quarter note; then a note the same length as a whole note plus a quarter note.

1.2.6.3 Borrowed Divisions

Dots and ties give you much freedom to write notes of varying lengths, but so far you must build your notes from halves of other notes. If you want to divide a note length into anything other than halves or halves of halves - if you want to divide a beat into thirds or fifths, for example - you must write the number of the division over the notes. These unusual subdivisions are called **borrowed divisions** because they sound as if they have been borrowed from a completely different meter (Section 1.2.4). They can be difficult to perform correctly and are avoided in music for beginners. The only one that is commonly used is **triplets**, which divide a note length into equal thirds.

Some Borrowed Divisions

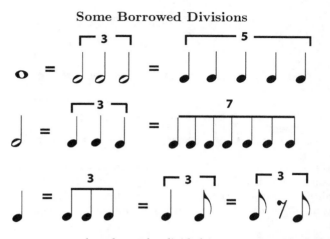

Figure 1.65: Any common note length can be divided into an unusual number of equal-length notes and rests, for example by dividing a whole note into three instead of two "half" notes. The notes are labeled with the appropriate number. If there might be any question as to which notes are involved in the borrowed division, a bracket is placed above them. Triplets are by far the most common borrowed division.

Borrowed Duplets

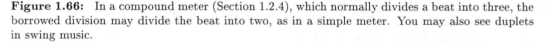

Figure 1.66: In a compound meter (Section 1.2.4), which normally divides a beat into three, the borrowed division may divide the beat into two, as in a simple meter. You may also see duplets in swing music.

Notes in jazzy-sounding music that has a "swing" beat are often assumed to be triplet rhythms, even when they look like regular divisions; for example, two written eighth notes (or a dotted quarter-sixteenth) might sound like a triplet quarter-eighth rhythm. In jazz and other popular music styles, a tempo (Section 1.2.8) notation that says **swing** usually means that all rhythms should be played as triplets. **Straight** means to play the rhythms as written.

NOTE: Some jazz musicians prefer to think of a swing rhythm as more of a heavy accent on the second eighth, rather than as a triplet rhythm, particularly when the tempo (Section 1.2.8) is fast. This distinction is not important for students of music theory, but jazz students will want to work hard on using both rhythm (Section 2.1) and articulation (Section 1.3.2) to produce a convincing "swing".

Swing Rhythms

Figure 1.67: Jazz or blues with a **"swing" rhythm** often assumes that all divisions are triplets. The swung triplets may be written as triplets, or they may simply be written as "straight" eighth notes or dotted eighth-sixteenths. If rhythms are not written as triplets, the tempo marking usually includes an indication to "swing", or it may simply be implied by the style and genre of the music.

1.2.7 Syncopation[41]

A **syncopation** or **syncopated rhythm** is any rhythm (Section 2.1) that puts an emphasis on a beat (Section 1.2.3.1), or a subdivision of a beat, that is not usually emphasized. One of the most obvious features of Western (Section 2.8) music, to be heard in most everything from Bach to blues, is a strong, steady beat that can easily be grouped evenly into measures (Section 1.2.3.1). (In other words, each measure has the same number of beats, and you can hear the measures in the music because the first beat of the measure is the strongest. See Time Signature (Section 1.2.3) and Meter (Section 1.2.4) for more on this.) This makes it easy for you to dance or clap your hands to the music. But music that follows the same rhythmic pattern all the time can get pretty boring. Syncopation is one way to liven things up. The music can suddenly emphasize the weaker beats of the measure, or it can even emphasize notes that are not on the beat at all. For example, listen[42] to the melody in Figure 1.68.

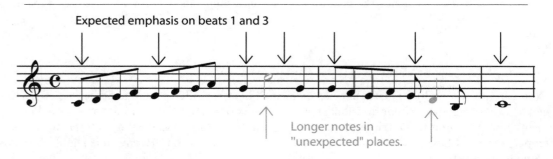

Figure 1.68: A syncopation may involve putting an "important" note on a weak beat, or off the beat altogether.

---

[41] This content is available online at <http://cnx.org/content/m11644/1.4/>.
[42] http://cnx.org/content/m11644/latest/Syncopation.MID

The first measure clearly establishes a simple quadruple meter (Section 1.2.4) ("ONE and two and THREE and four and"), in which important things, like changes in the melody, happen on beat one or three. But then, in the second measure, a syncopation happens; the longest and highest note is on beat two, normally a weak beat. In the syncopation in the third measure, the longest note doesn't even begin on a beat; it begins half-way through the third beat. (Some musicians would say "on the **up-beat**" or "on the 'and' of three".) Now listen to another example from a Boccherini minuet[43]. Again, some of the long notes begin half-way between the beats, or "on the up-beat". Notice, however, that in other places in the music, the melody establishes the meter very strongly, so that the syncopations are easily heard to be syncopations.

Figure 1.69: Syncopation is one of the most important elements in ragtime[44] music, as illustrated in this example from Scott Joplin's *Peacherine Rag*. Notice that the syncopated notes in the melody come on the second and fourth quarters of the beat, essentially alternating with the strong eighth-note pattern laid down in the accompaniment.

Another way to strongly establish the meter is to have the syncopated rhythm playing in one part of the music while another part plays a more regular rhythm, as in this passage[45] from Scott Joplin (see Figure 1.69). Syncopations can happen anywhere: in the melody (Section 2.3), the bass line (Accompaniment), the rhythm section, the chordal accompaniment (Accompaniment). Any spot in the rhythm that is normally weak (a weak beat, an upbeat, a sixteenth of a beat, a part of a triplet) can be given emphasis by a syncopation. It can suddenly be made important by a long or high note in the melody, a change in direction of the melody, a chord change, or a written accent (pg 57). Depending on the tempo (Section 1.2.8) of the music and the type of syncopation, a syncopated rhythm can make the music sound jaunty, jazzy, unsteady, surprising, uncertain, exciting, or just more interesting.

Figure 1.70: Syncopation can be added just by putting accents (pg 57) in unexpected places.

---

[43] http://cnx.org/content/m11644/latest/metsync.mp3
[44] "Ragtime" <http://cnx.org/ content/m10878/latest/>
[45] http://cnx.org/content/m11644/latest/sync2.mid

Other musical traditions tend to be more rhythmically complex than Western music, and much of the syncopation in modern American music is due to the influence of Non-Western (Section 2.8) traditions, particularly the African roots of the African-American tradition. Syncopation is such an important aspect of much American music, in fact, that the type of syncopation used in a piece is one of the most important clues to the style and genre of the music. Ragtime[46], for example, would hardly be ragtime without the jaunty syncopations in the melody set against the steady unsyncopated bass. The "swing" rhythm in big-band jazz and the "back-beat" of many types of rock are also specific types of syncopation. If you want practice hearing syncopations, listen to some ragtime or jazz. Tap your foot to find the beat, and then notice how often important musical "events" are happening "in between" your foot-taps.

1.2.8 Tempo[47]

The **tempo** of a piece of music is its speed. There are two ways to specify a tempo. Metronome markings are absolute and specific. Other tempo markings are verbal descriptions which are more relative and subjective. Both types of markings usually appear above the staff, at the beginning of the piece, and then at any spot where the tempo changes. Markings that ask the player to deviate slightly from the main tempo, such as ritardando (Gradual Tempo Changes) may appear either above or below the staff.

1.2.8.1 Metronome Markings

Metronome markings are given in beats per minute. They can be estimated using a clock with a second hand, but the easiest way to find them is with a **metronome**, which is a tool that can give a beat-per-minute tempo as a clicking sound or a pulse of light. Figure 1.71 shows some examples of metronome markings.

---

[46]"Ragtime" <http://cnx.org/content/m10878/latest/>
[47]This content is available online at <http://cnx.org/content/m11648/1.6/>.

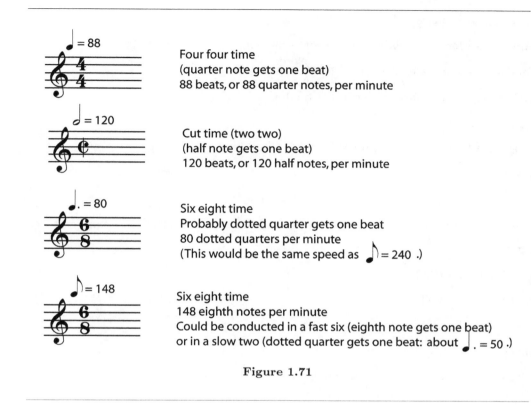

Figure 1.71

Metronomes often come with other tempo indications written on them, but this is misleading. For example, a metronome may have *allegro* marked at 120 beats per minute and *andante* marked at 80 beats per minute. *Allegro* should certainly be quite a bit faster than *andante*, but it may not be exactly 120 beats per minute.

1.2.8.2 Tempo Terms

A tempo marking that is a word or phrase gives you the composer's idea of *how fast the music should feel*. How fast a piece of music feels depends on several different things, including the texture and complexity of the music, how often the beat gets divided into faster notes, and how fast the beats themselves are (the metronome marking). Also, the same tempo marking can mean quite different things to different composers; if a metronome marking is not available, the performer should use a knowledge of the music's style and genre, and musical common sense, to decide on the proper tempo. When possible, listening to a professional play the piece can help with tempo decisions, but it is also reasonable for different performers to prefer slightly different tempos for the same piece.

Traditionally, tempo instructions are given in Italian.

Some Common Tempo Markings

- *Grave* - very slow and solemn (pronounced "GRAH-vay")

- *Largo* - slow and broad ("LAR-go")

- *Larghetto* - not quite as slow as largo ("lar-GET-oh")

- *Adagio* - slow ("uh-DAH-jee-oh")

- *Lento* - slow ("LEN-toe")

- *Andante* - literally "walking", a medium slow tempo ("on-DON-tay")

- *Moderato* - moderate, or medium ("MOD-er-AH-toe")

- *Allegretto* - Not as fast as allegro ("AL-luh-GRET-oh")

- *Allegro* - fast ("uh-LAY-grow")

- *Vivo, or Vivace* - lively and brisk ("VEE-voh")

- *Presto* - very fast ("PRESS-toe")

- *Prestissimo* - very, very fast ("press-TEE-see-moe")

These terms, along with a little more Italian, will help you decipher most tempo instructions.

More useful Italian

- *(un) poco* - a little ("oon POH-koe")

- *molto* - a lot ("MOLE-toe")

- *piu* - more ("pew")

- *meno* - less ("MAY-no")

- *mosso* - literally "moved"; motion or movement ("MOE-so")

Exercise 1.13:

Check to see how comfortable you are with Italian tempo markings by translating the following.

1.un poco allegro

2.molto meno mosso

3.piu vivo

4.molto adagio

5.poco piu mosso

(Solution to Exercise 1.13 on p. 70.)

Of course, tempo instructions don't have to be given in Italian. Much folk, popular, and modern music, gives instructions in English or in the composer's language. Tempo indications such as "Not too fast", "With energy", "Calmly", or "March tempo" give a good idea of how fast the music should feel.

1.2.8.3 Gradual Tempo Changes

If the tempo of a piece of music suddenly changes into a completely different tempo, there will be a new tempo given, usually marked in the same way (metronome tempo, Italian term, etc.) as the original tempo. Gradual changes in the basic tempo are also common in music, though, and these have their own set of terms. These terms often appear below the staff, although writing them above the staff is also allowed. These terms can also appear with modifiers (More useful Italian) like *molto* or *un poco*. You may notice that there are quite a few terms for slowing down. Again, the use of these terms will vary from one composer to the next; unless beginning and ending tempo markings are included, the performer must simply use good musical judgement to decide how much to slow down in a particular *ritardando* or *rallentando*.

Gradual Tempo Changes

- *accelerando* - (abbreviated *accel.*) accelerating; getting faster

- *ritardando* - (abbrev. *rit.*) slowing down

- *ritenuto* - (abbrev. *riten.*) slower

- *rallentando* - (abbrev. *rall.*) gradually slower

- *rubato* - don't be too strict with the rhythm; while keeping the basic tempo, allow the music to gently speed up and relax in ways that emphasize the phrasing

- *poco a poco* - little by little; gradually

- *Tempo I* - ("tempo one" or "tempo primo") back to the original tempo (this instruction usually appears above the staff)

1.2.9 Repeats and Other Musical Road Map Signs[48]

Repetition, either exact or with small or large variations, is one of the basic organizing principles of music. Repeated notes (Section 1.2.1), motifs (Section 2.3.5), phrases (Section 2.3.4), melodies (Section 2.3), rhythms (Section 2.1), chord progressions (Chords), and even entire repeated sections in the overall form (Section 5.7), are all very crucial in helping the listener make sense of the music. So good music is surprisingly repetitive!

So, in order to save time, ink, and page turns, common notation has many ways to show that a part of the music should be repeated exactly.

If the repeated part is very small - only one or two measures, for example - the repeat sign will probably look something like those in Figure 1.72. If you have very many such repeated measures in a row, you may want to number them (in pencil) to help you keep track of where you are in the music.

---

[48]This content is available online at <http://cnx.org/content/m12805/1.4/>.

Repeated Measures

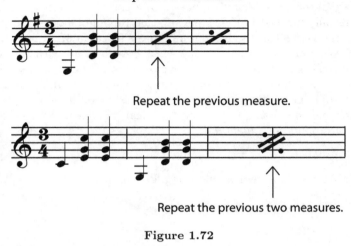

Repeat the previous measure.

Repeat the previous two measures.

Figure 1.72

For repeated sections of medium length - usually four to thirty-two measures - **repeat dots** with or without endings are the most common markings. Dots to the right of a double bar line (Section 1.1.1.1) begin the repeated section; dots to the left of a double bar line end it. If there are no beginning repeat dots, you should go all the way back to the beginning of the music and repeat from there.

Repeat Dots

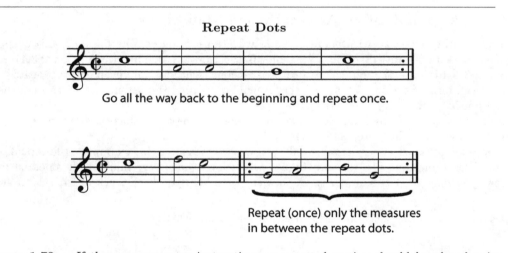

Go all the way back to the beginning and repeat once.

Repeat (once) only the measures
in between the repeat dots.

Figure 1.73: If there are no extra instructions, a repeated section should be played twice. Occasionally you will see extra instructions over the repeat dots, for example to play the section "3x" (three times).

It is very common for longer repeated sections of music to be repeated exactly until the last few measures. When this happens, the repeat dots will be put in an **ending**. The bracket over the music shows you which measures to play each time you arrive at that point in the music. For example, the second time you reach a set of endings, you will *skip the music in all the other endings; play only the measures in the second ending, and then do whatever the second ending directs you to do* (repeat, go on, skip to somewhere else, etc.).

Repeat Endings

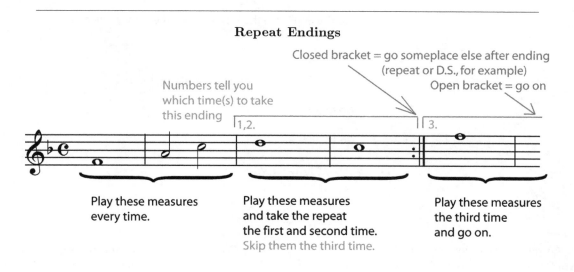

Figure 1.74: Some "endings" of a section of music may include a repeat, while others do not. Play only one ending each time (skipping over other, previously played endings when necessary), and then follow the "instructions" at the end of the ending (to repeat, go on, go someplace else, etc.).

When you are repeating large sections in more informally written music, you may simply find instructions in the music such as "to refrain", "to bridge", "to verses", etc. Or you may find extra instructions to play certain parts "only on the repeat". Usually these instructions are reasonably clear, although you may need to study the music for a minute to get the "road map" clear in your mind. Pencilled-in markings can be a big help if it's difficult to spot the place you need to skip to. In order to help clarify things, repeat dots and other repeat instructions are almost always marked by a double bar line (Section 1.1.1.1).

In Western classical music (Section 2.8), the most common instructions for repeating large sections are traditionally written (or abbreviated) in Italian. The most common instructions from that tradition are in Figure 1.75.

Other Common "Road Map" Signs

D.C.	or *da capo*	"To the head" - Go back to the very beginning
D.S.	or *dal segno*	"To the sign" - Go back to the sign
	al fine	"To the end" - On the repeat, stop when it says "*fine*"
	𝄋	Sign
	fine	"End" - On the last time through, stop here
to	⊕	Go to the coda section
	⊕	Coda section

Figure 1.75

Again, instructions can easily get quite complicated, and these large-section markings may require you to study your part for a minute to see how it is laid out, and even to mark (in pencil) circles and arrows that help you find the way quickly while you are playing. Figure 1.76 contains a few very simplistic examples of how these "road map signs" will work.

Example 1:
Play to the D.C., then go back to the beginning and play until you reach "*fine*", then stop.

Example 2: Play to the D.S., then go back to the sign and play until you find the "to coda". Go directly to the coda and play to the end.

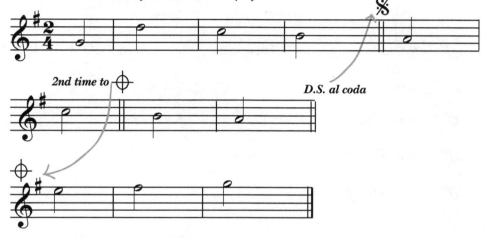

Figure 1.76: Here are some (shortened) examples of how these types of repeat instructions may be arranged. These types of signs usually mark longer repeated sections. In many styles of music, a short repeated section (usually marked with repeat dots) is often *not* repeated after a *da capo* or *dal segno*.

1.3 Style

1.3.1 Dynamics and Accents[49]

1.3.1.1 Dynamics

Sounds, including music, can be barely audible, or loud enough to hurt your ears, or anywhere in between. When they want to talk about the loudness of a sound, scientists and engineers talk about amplitude (Section 3.1.3). Musicians talk about **dynamics**. The amplitude of a sound is a particular number, usually measured in decibels, but dynamics are relative; an orchestra playing *fortissimo* is going to be much louder than a single violin playing *fortissimo*. The exact interpretation of each dynamic marking in a piece of music depends on:

- comparison with other dynamics in that piece
- the typical dynamic range for that instrument or ensemble

---

[49]This content is available online at <http://cnx.org/content/m11649/1.7/>.

- the abilities of the performer(s)

- the traditions of the musical genre being performed

- the acoustics of the performance space

Traditionally, dynamic markings are based on Italian words, although there is nothing wrong with simply writing things like "quietly" or "louder" in the music. *Forte* means loud and *piano* means soft. The instrument commonly called the "piano" by the way, was originally called a "pianoforte" because it could play dynamics, unlike earlier popular keyboard instruments like the harpsichord.

Typical Dynamic Markings

mf	**mezzo forte**	= medium loud	(pronounced "MET-soh FOR-tay")
f	**forte**	= loud	("FOR-tay")
ff	**fortissimo**	= very loud	("for-TISS-im-oh")
fff	**fortississimo**	= very, very loud	(FOR-tiss-SISS-im-oh)
ffff	and so on		
mp	**mezzo piano**	= medium soft	("MET-soh PYAN-oh")
p	**piano**	= soft	(PYAN-oh)
pp	**pianissimo**	= very soft	("PEE-an-ISS-im-oh")
ppp	**pianississimo**	= very, very soft	("PEE-an-iss-SISS-im-oh")
pppp	and so on		

Figure 1.77

When a composer writes a *forte* into a part, followed by a *piano*, the intent is for the music to be quite loud, and then suddenly quite soft. If the composer wants the change from one dynamic level to another to be gradual, different markings are added. A *crescendo* (pronounced "cresh-EN-doe") means "gradually get louder"; a *decrescendo* or *diminuendo* means "gradually get softer".

Gradual Dynamic Markings

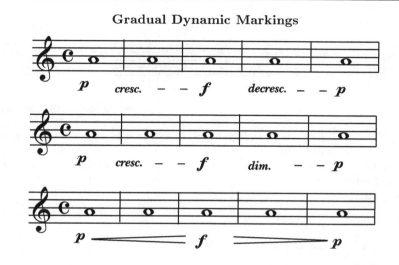

Figure 1.78: Here are three different ways to write the same thing: start softly (piano), gradually get louder (crescendo) until the music is loud (forte), then gradually get softer (decrescendo or diminuendo) until it is soft (piano) again.

1.3.1.2 Accents

A composer may want a particular note to be louder than all the rest, or may want the very beginning of a note to be loudest. **Accents** are markings that are used to indicate these especially-strong-sounding notes. There are a few different types of written accents (see Figure 1.79), but, like dynamics, the proper way to perform a given accent also depends on the instrument playing it, as well as the style and period of the music. Some accents may even be played by making the note longer or shorter than the other notes, in addition to, or even instead of being, louder. (See articulation (Section 1.3.2) for more about accents.)

Figure 1.79: The exact performance of each type of accent depends on the instrument and the style and period of the music, but the *sforzando* and *fortepiano*-type accents are usually louder and longer, and more likely to be used in a long note that starts loudly and then suddenly gets much softer. *Caret*-type accents are more likely to be used to mark shorter notes that should be stronger than unmarked notes.

1.3.2 Articulation[50]

1.3.2.1 What is Articulation?

The word **articulation** generally refers to how the pieces of something are joined together; for example, how bones are connected to make a skeleton or syllables are connected to make a word. Articulation depends on what is happening at the beginning and end of each segment, as well as in between the segments.

In music, the segments are the individual notes of a **line** in the music. This could be the melodic (Section 2.3) line, the bass (Accompaniment) line, or a part of the harmony (Section 2.5). The line might be performed by any musician or group of musicians: a singer, for example, or a bassoonist, a violin section, or a trumpet and saxophone together. In any case, it is a string of notes that follow one after the other and that belong together in the music.The **articulation** is what happens in between the notes. The **attack** - the beginning of a note - and the amount of **space** in between the notes are particularly important.

1.3.2.2 Performing Articulations

Descriptions of how each articulation is done cannot be given here, because they depend too much on the particular instrument that is making the music. In other words, the technique that a violin[51] player uses to slur notes will be completely different from the technique used by a trumpet[52] player, and a pianist and a vocalist will do different things to make a melody sound legato. In fact, the violinist will have some articulations available (such as **pizzicato**, or "plucked") that a trumpet player will never see.

So if you are wondering how to play slurs on your guitar or staccato on your clarinet, ask your music teacher or director. What you will find here is a short list of the most common articulations: their names, what they look like when notated, and a vague description of how they sound. The descriptions have to be vague, because articulation, besides depending on the instrument, also depends on the style of the music. Exactly how much space there should be between staccato eighth notes, for example, depends on tempo (Section 1.2.8) as well as on whether you're playing Rossini or Sousa. To give you some idea of the difference that articulation makes, though, here are

---

[50]This content is available online at <http://cnx.org/content/m11884/1.5/>.
[51]"Introduction to the Violin and FAQ" <http://cnx.org/content/m13437/latest/>
[52]"Trumpets and Cornets" <http://cnx.org/content/m12606/latest/>

audio examples of a violin playing a legato[53] and a staccato[54] passage. (For more audio examples of violin articulations, please see Common Violin Terminology[55].)

1.3.2.3 Common Articulations

Staccato notes are short, with plenty of space between them. Please note that this doesn't mean that the tempo (Section 1.2.8) or rhythm (Section 2.1) goes any faster. The tempo and rhythm are not affected by articulations; the staccato notes sound shorter than written only because of the extra space between them.

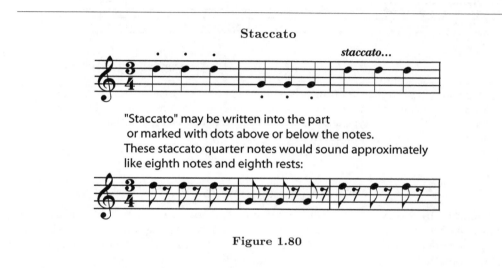

Figure 1.80

Legato is the opposite of staccato. The notes are very connected; there is no space between the notes at all. There is, however, still some sort of articulation that causes a slight but definite break between the notes (for example, the violin player's bow changes direction, the guitar player plucks the string again, or the wind player uses the tongue to interrupt the stream of air).

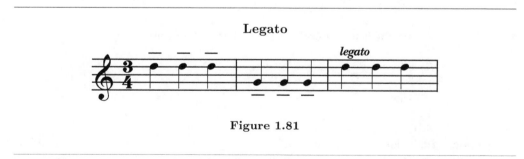

Figure 1.81

Accents - An accent (pg 57) requires that a note stand out more than the unaccented notes around it. Accents are usually performed by making the accented note, or the beginning of the

---

[53] http://cnx.org/content/m11884/latest/artleg.mp3
[54] http://cnx.org/content/m11884/latest/artstacc.mp3
[55] "Common Violin Terminology" <http://cnx.org/content/m13316/latest/>

accented note, louder than the rest of the music. Although this is mostly a quick change in dynamics (Section 1.3.1), it usually affects the articulation of the note, too. The extra loudness of the note often requires a stronger, more definite attack at the beginning of the accented note, and it is emphasized by putting some space before and after the accented notes. The effect of a lot of accented notes in a row may sound marcato (pg 62).

Figure 1.82: The performance of an accent depends on the style of music, but in general, sforzando and fortepiano accents involve a loud beginning to a longer note. They are usually heavier and longer than caret-type accents, which often rely more on a powerful attack (pg 58) to make a short note louder than the notes around it.

A **slur** is marked by a curved line joining any number of notes. When notes are slurred, only the first note under each slur marking has a definite articulation at the beginning. The rest of the notes are so seamlessly connected that there is no break between the notes. A good example of slurring occurs when a vocalist sings more than one note on the same syllable of text.

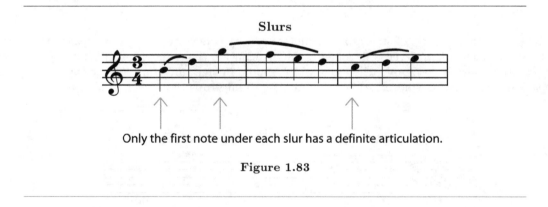

Figure 1.83

A tie (Section 1.2.6.3) looks like a slur, but it is between two notes that are the same pitch. *A tie is not really an articulation marking.* It is included here because it looks like one, which can cause confusion for beginners. When notes are tied together, they are played as if they are one single note that is the length of all the notes that are tied together. (Please see Dots, Ties, and Borrowed Divisions (Section 1.2.6).)

61

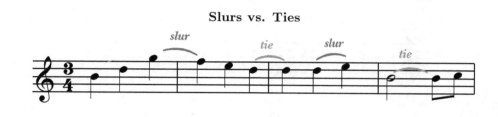

Slurs vs. Ties

Figure 1.84: A slur marking indicates no articulation - no break in the sound - between notes of different pitches. A tie is used between two notes of the same pitch. Since there is no articulation between them, they sound like a single note. The tied quarters here would sound exactly like a half note crossing the bar line. Like a note that crosses bar lines, the two-and-a-half-beat "note" in the fourth bar would be difficult to write without using a tie.

A **portamento** is a smooth glide between the two notes, including all the pitches (Section 1.1.3) in between. For some instruments, like violin[56] and trombone[57], this includes even the pitches in between the written notes. For other instruments, such as guitar[58], it means sliding through all of the possible notes between the two written pitches.

Portamento

Figure 1.85

Although unusual in traditional common notation (Section 1.1.1), a type of portamento that includes only one written pitch can be found in some styles of music, notably jazz, blues, and rock. As the notation (Figure 1.86) suggests, the proper performance of **scoops** and **fall-offs** requires that the portamento begins (in scoops) or ends (in fall-offs) with the slide itself, rather than with a specific note.

[56]"Introduction to the Violin and FAQ" <http://cnx.org/content/m13437/latest/>
[57]"Trombones" <http://cnx.org/content/m12602/latest/>
[58]"Guitars" <http://cnx.org/content/m12745/latest/>

Scoops and Fall-offs

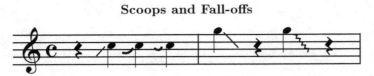

Figure 1.86: The notation for scoops and fall-offs has not been standardized, but either one will look something like a portamento or slur with a note on one end only.

Some articulations may be some combination of staccato, legato, and accent. **Marcato**, for example means "marked" in the sense of "stressed" or "noticeable". Notes marked *marcato* have enough of an accent and/or enough space between them to make each note seem stressed or set apart. They are usually longer than staccato but shorter than legato. Other notes may be marked with a combination of articulation symbols, for example legato with accents. As always, the best way to perform such notes depends on the instrument and the style of the music.

Some Possible Combination Markings

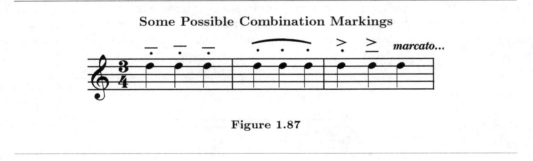

Figure 1.87

Plenty of music has no articulation marks at all, or marks on only a few notes. Often, such music calls for notes that are a little more separate or defined than legato, but still nowhere as short as staccato. Mostly, though, it is up to the performer to know what is considered proper for a particular piece. For example, most ballads are sung legato, and most marches are played fairly staccato or marcato, whether they are marked that way or not. Furthermore, singing or playing a phrase (Section 2.3.4) with musicianship often requires knowing which notes of the phrase should be legato, which should be more separate, where to add a little *portamento*, and so on. This does not mean the best players consciously decide how to play each note. Good articulation comes naturally to the musician who has mastered the instrument and the style of the music.

Solutions to Exercises in Chapter 1

Solution to Exercise 1.1 (p. 12):

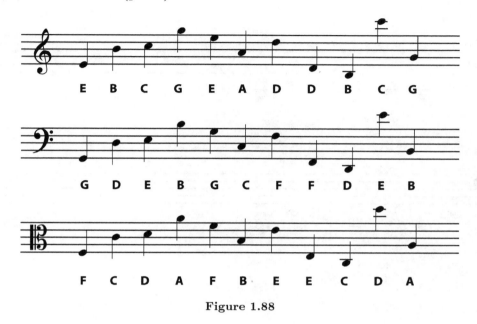

Figure 1.88

Solution to Exercise 1.2 (p. 12):

Figure 1.89 shows the answers for treble and bass clef. If you have done another clef, have your teacher check your answers.

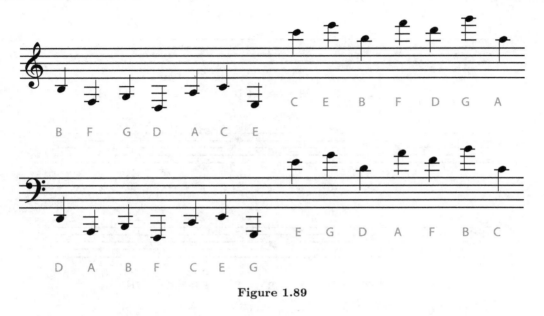

Figure 1.89

Solution to Exercise 1.3 (p. 13):

Figure 1.90 shows the answers for treble clef, and Figure 1.91 the answers for bass clef. If you are working in a more unusual clef, have your teacher check your answers.

Clef Practice

Practice writing your clef symbol on this staff. Write at least eight clef symbols

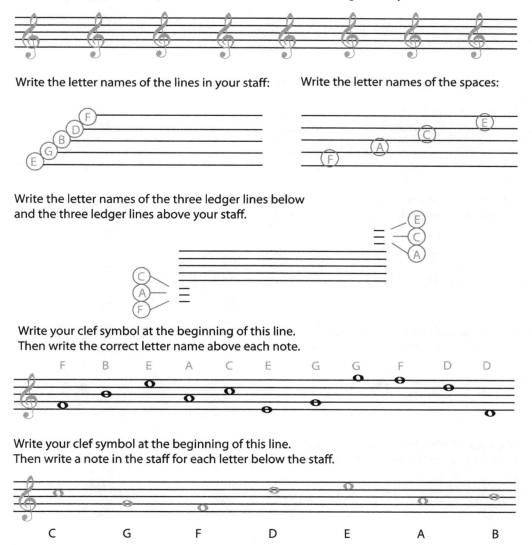

Write the letter names of the lines in your staff: Write the letter names of the spaces:

Write the letter names of the three ledger lines below
and the three ledger lines above your staff.

Write your clef symbol at the beginning of this line.
Then write the correct letter name above each note.

Write your clef symbol at the beginning of this line.
Then write a note in the staff for each letter below the staff.

C   G   F   D   E   A   B

Figure 1.90

Clef Practice

Practice writing your clef symbol on this staff. Write at least eight clef symbols

Write the letter names of the lines in your staff: Write the letter names of the spaces:

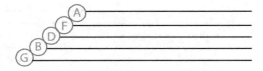   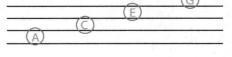

Write the letter names of the three ledger lines below
and the three ledger lines above your staff.

Write your clef symbol at the beginning of this line.
Then write the correct letter name above each note.

Write your clef symbol at the beginning of this line.
Then write a note in the staff for each letter below the staff.

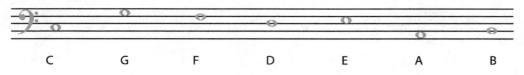

Figure 1.91

Solution to Exercise 1.4 (p. 21):

E flat major E major D flat major B major C sharp major

Figure 1.92

Solution to Exercise 1.5 (p. 23):

- C sharp and D flat
- F sharp and G flat
- G sharp and A flat
- A sharp and B flat

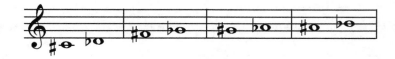

Figure 1.93

Solution to Exercise 1.6 (p. 23):

1. F flat; D double sharp
2. C flat; A double sharp
3. B sharp; D double flat
4. F double sharp; A double flat
5. G double sharp; B double flat

Solution to Exercise 1.7 (p. 25):

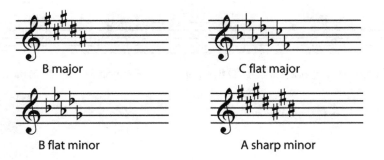

Figure 1.94

Solution to Exercise 1.8 (p. 30):

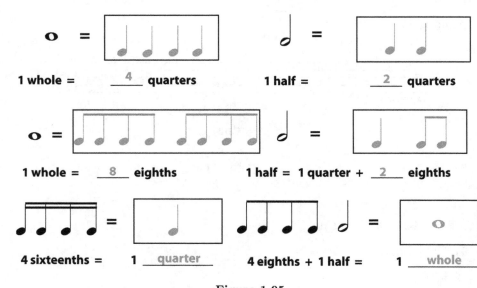

Figure 1.95

Solution to Exercise 1.9 (p. 32):

Figure 1.96

Solution to Exercise 1.10 (p. 35):

- A has a very strong, quick 1-2-3 beat.

- B is in a slow (easy) 2. You may feel it in a fast 4.

- C is in a stately 4.

- D is in 3, but the beat may be harder to feel than in A because the rhythms are more complex and the performer is taking some liberties with the tempo (Section 1.2.8).

Solution to Exercise 1.11 (p. 36):

There are an enormous number of possible note combinations for any time signature. That's one of the things that makes music interesting. Here are some possibilities. If you are not sure that yours are correct, check with your music instructor.

Figure 1.97: These are only a few of the many, many possible note combinations that could be used in these time signatures.

Solution to Exercise 1.12 (p. 43):

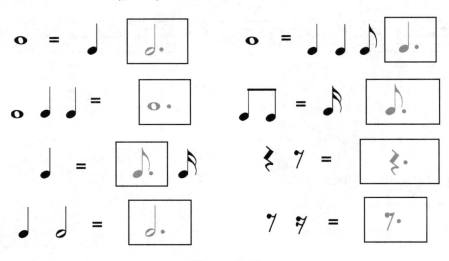

Figure 1.98

Solution to Exercise 1.13 (p. 50):

1. a little fast

2. much less motion = much slower

3. more lively = faster

4. very slow

5. a little more motion = a little faster

Chapter 2

Definitions

2.1 Rhythm[1]

Rhythm, melody (Section 2.3), harmony (Section 2.5), timbre (Section 2.2), and texture (Section 2.4) are the essential aspects of a musical performance. They are often called the basic elements of music. The main purpose of music theory is to describe various pieces of music in terms of their similarities and differences in these elements, and music is usually grouped into genres based on similarities in all or most elements. It's useful, therefore, to be familiar with the terms commonly used to describe each element. Because harmony is the most highly developed aspect of Western music (Section 2.8), music theory tends to focus almost exclusively on melody and harmony. Music does not have to have harmony, however, and some music doesn't even have melody. So perhaps the other three elements can be considered the most basic components of music.

Music cannot happen without time. The placement of the sounds in time is the rhythm of a piece of music. Because music must be heard over a period of time, rhythm is one of the most basic elements of music. In some pieces of music, the rhythm is simply a "placement in time" that cannot be assigned a beat (Section 1.2.3.1) or meter (Section 1.2.4), but most rhythm terms concern more familiar types of music with a steady beat. See Meter (Section 1.2.4) for more on how such music is organized, and Duration (Section 1.2.1) and Time Signature (Section 1.2.3) for more on how to read and write rhythms. See Simple Rhythm Activities[2] for easy ways to encourage children to explore rhythm.

Rhythm Terms

- **Rhythm** - The term "rhythm" has more than one meaning. It can mean the basic, repetitive pulse of the music, or a rhythmic pattern that is repeated throughout the music (as in "feel the rhythm"). It can also refer to the pattern in time of a single small group of notes (as in "play this rhythm for me").

- **Beat** - Beat also has more than one meaning, but always refers to music with a steady pulse. It may refer to the pulse itself (as in "play this note on beat two of the measure (Section 1.2.3.1)"). **On the beat** or **on the downbeat** refer to the moment when the pulse is strongest. **Off the beat** is in between pulses, and the **upbeat** is exactly halfway between pulses. **Beat** may also refer to a specific repetitive rhythmic pattern that maintains the pulse (as in "it has a Latin beat"). Note that once a strong feeling of having a beat is established, it is not necessary for something to happen on every beat; a beat can still be "felt" even if it is not specifically heard.

---

[1] This content is available online at <http://cnx.org/content/m11646/1.4/>.
[2] "Simple Rhythm Activities" <http://cnx.org/content/m14258/latest/>

- **Measure or bar** - Beats are grouped into measures or bars. The first beat is usually the strongest, and in most music, most of the bars have the same number of beats. This sets up an underlying pattern in the pulse of the music: for example, strong-weak-strong-weak-strong-weak, or strong-weak-weak-strong-weak-weak. (See Meter (Section 1.2.4).)

- **Rhythm Section** - The rhythm section of a band is the group of instruments that usually provide the background rhythm and chords. The rhythm section almost always includes a percussionist (usually on a drum set) and a bass player (usually playing a plucked string bass of some kind). It may also include a piano and/or other keyboard players, more percussionists, and one or more guitar players or other strummed or plucked strings. Vocalists, wind instruments, and bowed strings are usually not part of the rhythm section.

- **Syncopation** - Syncopation occurs when a strong note happens either on a weak beat or off the beat. See Syncopation (Section 1.2.7).

2.2 Timbre[3]

One of the basic elements of music is called **color**, or **timbre** (pronounced "TAM-ber"). Timbre describes all of the aspects of a musical sound that do not have anything to do with the sound's pitch (Section 1.1.3), loudness (Section 1.3.1), or length (Section 1.2.1). In other words, if a flute[4] plays a note, and then an oboe[5] plays the same note, for the same length of time, at the same loudness, you can still easily tell the two notes apart, because a flute sounds different from an oboe. This difference is in the timbre of the sounds.

Timbre is caused by the fact that each note from a musical instrument is a complex wave containing more than one frequency. For instruments that produce notes with a clear and specific pitch (Section 1.1.3), the frequencies involved are part of a harmonic series (Section 3.3). For other instruments (such as drums), the sound wave may have an even greater variety of frequencies. We hear each mixture of frequencies not as separate sounds, but as the color of the sound. Small differences in the balance of the frequencies - how many you can hear, their relationship to the fundamental pitch, and how loud they are compared to each other - create the many different musical colors.

The harmonics at the beginning of each note - the **attack** - are especially important for timbre, so it is actually easier to identify instruments that are playing short notes with strong articulations (Section 1.3.2) than it is to identify instruments playing long, smooth notes.

The human ear and brain are capable of hearing and appreciating very small variations in timbre. A listener can hear not only the difference between an oboe and a flute, but also the difference between two different oboes. The general sound that one would expect of a type of instrument - a trombone[6] for example - is usually called its **timbre** or **color**. Variations in timbre between specific instruments - two different trombones, for example, or two different trombone players, or the same trombone player using different types of sound in different pieces - may be called differences in timbre or color, or may be called differences in **tone** or in **tone quality**. Tone quality may refer specifically to "quality", as when a young trombonist is encouraged to have a "fuller" or "more focussed" tone quality, or it can refer neutrally to differences in sound, as when an orchestral trombonist is asked to play with a "brassy" tone quality in one passage and a "mellow" tone quality in another.

Many words are used to describe timbre. Some are somewhat interchangeable, and some may have slightly different meanings for different musicians, so no attempt will be made to provide definitions. Here are a few words commonly used to describe either timbre or tone quality.

---

[3]This content is available online at <http://cnx.org/content/m11059/2.7/>.
[4]"Flutes" <http://cnx.org/content/m12603/latest/>
[5]"The Oboe and its Relatives" <http://cnx.org/content/m12615/latest/>
[6]"Trombones" <http://cnx.org/content/m12602/latest/>

- Reedy

- Brassy

- Clear

- Focussed or unfocussed

- Breathy (pronounced "BRETH-ee")

- Rounded

- Piercing

- Strident

- Harsh

- Warm

- Mellow

- Resonant

- Dark or Bright

- Heavy or Light

- Flat

- Having much, little, or no vibrato (a controlled wavering in the sound); or narrow or wide, or slow or fast, vibrato

For more information on what causes timbre, please see Harmonic Series I (Section 3.3), Standing Waves and Musical Instruments (Section 3.2), and Standing Waves and Wind Instruments[7].) For activities that introduce children to the concept of timbre, please see Timbre Activities[8]

2.3 Melody[9]

2.3.1 Introduction

Melody is one of the most basic elements of music. A note is a sound with a particular pitch (Section 1.1.3) and duration (Section 1.2.1). String a series of notes together, one after the other, and you have a **melody**. But the melody of a piece of music isn't just any string of notes. It's the notes that catch your ear as you listen; the line that sounds most important is the melody. There are some common terms used in discussions of melody that you may find it useful to know. First of all, the **melodic line** of a piece of music is the string of notes that make up the melody. Extra notes, such as trills and slides, that are not part of the main melodic line but are added to the melody either by the composer or the performer to make the melody more complex and interesting are called **ornaments** or **embellishments**. Below are some more concepts that are associated with melody.

---

[7]"Standing Waves and Wind Instruments" <http://cnx.org/content/m12589/latest/>

[8]"Timbre Activities" <http://cnx.org/content/m14259/latest/>

[9]This content is available online at <http://cnx.org/content/m11647/1.7/>.

2.3.2 The Shape or Contour of a Melody

A melody that stays on the same pitch (Section 1.1.3) gets boring pretty quickly. As the melody progresses, the pitches may go up or down slowly or quickly. One can picture a line that goes up steeply when the melody suddenly jumps to a much higher note, or that goes down slowly when the melody gently falls. Such a line gives the **contour** or **shape** of the melodic line. You can often get a good idea of the shape of this line by looking at the melody as it is written on the staff, but you can also hear it as you listen to the music.

Figure 2.1: Arch shapes (in which the melody rises and then falls) are easy to find in many melodies.

You can also describe the shape of a melody verbally. For example, you can speak of a "rising melody" or of an "arch-shaped" phrase (Section 2.3.4). Please see The Shape of a Melody[10] for children's activities covering melodic contour.

2.3.3 Melodic Motion

Another set of useful terms describe how quickly a melody goes up and down. A melody that rises and falls slowly, with only small pitch changes between one note and the next, is **conjunct**. One may also speak of such a melody in terms of **step-wise** or **scalar** motion, since most of the intervals (Section 4.5) in the melody are half or whole steps (Section 4.2) or are part of a scale (Section 4.3).

A melody that rises and falls quickly, with large intervals (Section 4.5) between one note and the next, is a **disjunct** melody. One may also speak of "leaps" in the melody. Many melodies are a mixture of conjunct and disjunct motion.

---

[10]"The Shape of a Melody" <http://cnx.org/content/m11832/latest/>

Figure 2.2: A melody may show conjuct motion, with small changes in pitch from one note to the next, or disjunct motion, with large leaps. Many melodies are an interesting, fairly balanced mixture of conjunct and disjunct motion.

2.3.4 Melodic Phrases

Melodies are often described as being made up of phrases. A musical **phrase** is actually a lot like a grammatical phrase. A phrase in a sentence (for example, "into the deep, dark forest" or "under that heavy book") is a group of words that make sense together and express a definite idea, but the phrase is not a complete sentence by itself. A melodic phrase is a group of notes that make sense together and express a definite melodic "idea", but it takes more than one phrase to make a complete melody.

How do you spot a phrase in a melody? Just as you often pause between the different sections in a sentence (for example, when you say, "wherever you go, there you are"), the melody usually pauses slightly at the end of each phrase. In vocal music, the musical phrases tend to follow the phrases and sentences of the text. For example, listen[11] to the phrases in the melody of "The Riddle Song" and see how they line up with the four sentences in the song.

---

[11] http://cnx.org/content/m11647/latest/phrases1.mid

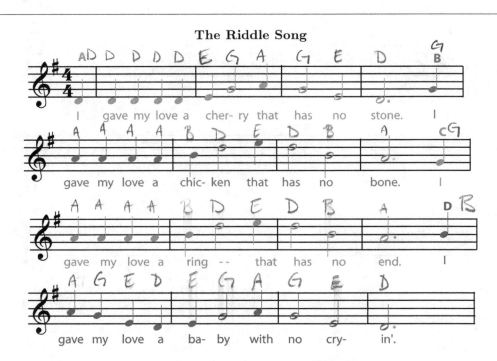

Figure 2.3:   This melody has four phrases, one for each sentence of the text.

But even without text, the phrases in a melody can be very clear. Even without words, the notes are still grouped into melodic "ideas". Listen[12] to the first strain of Scott Joplin's[13] "The Easy Winners" to see if you can hear four phrases in the melody.

One way that a composer keeps a piece of music interesting is by varying how strongly the end of each phrase sounds like "the end". Usually, full-stop ends come only at the end of the main sections of the music. (See form (Section 5.7) and cadence (Section 5.6) for more on this.) By varying aspects of the melody, the rhythm (Section 2.1), and the harmony (Section 2.5), the composer gives the ends of the other phrases stronger or weaker "ending" feelings. Often, phrases come in definite pairs, with the first phrase feeling very unfinished until it is completed by the second phrase, as if the second phrase were answering a question asked by the first phrase. When phrases come in pairs like this, the first phrase is called the **antecedent** phrase, and the second is called the **consequent** phrase. Listen to antecedent[14] and consequent[15] phrases in the tune "Auld Lang Syne".

---

[12] http://cnx.org/content/m11647/latest/phrases2.MID
[13] "Scott Joplin" <http://cnx.org/content/m10879/latest/>
[14] http://cnx.org/content/m11647/latest/antecedent.MID
[15] http://cnx.org/content/m11647/latest/consequent.MID

Antecedent and Consequent Phrases

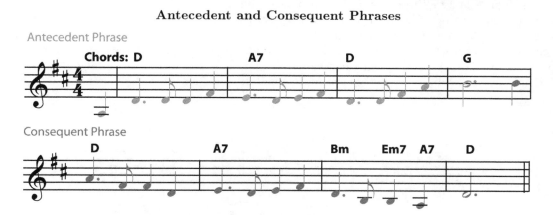

Figure 2.4: The rhythm of the first two phrases of "Auld Lang Syne" is the same, but both the melody and the harmony lead the first phrase to feel unfinished until it is answered by the second phrase. Note that both the melody and harmony of the second phrase end on the tonic (pg 127), the "home" note and chord of the key.

Of course, melodies don't always divide into clear, separated phrases. Often the phrases in a melody will run into each other, cut each other short, or overlap. This is one of the things that keeps a melody interesting.

2.3.5 Motif

Another term that usually refers to a piece of melody (although it can also refer to a rhythm (Section 2.1) or a chord progression (Chords)) is "motif". **A motif** is a short musical idea - shorter than a phrase - that occurs often in a piece of music. A short melodic idea may also be called a **motiv**, a **motive**, a **cell**, or a **figure**. These small pieces of melody will appear again and again in a piece of music, sometimes exactly the same and sometimes changed. When a motif returns, it can be slower or faster, or in a different key. It may return "upside down" (with the notes going up instead of down, for example), or with the pitches or rhythms altered.

Figure 2.5: The "fate motif"[16] from the first movement of Beethoven's Symphony No. 5. This is a good example of a short melodic idea (a **cell**, **motive**, or **figure**) that is used in many different ways throughout the movement.

---

[16]http://cnx.org/content/m11647/latest/motif1.mid

Most figures and motifs are shorter than phrases, but some of the *leitmotifs* of Wagner's operas are long enough to be considered phrases. **A leitmotif** (whether it is a very short cell or a long phrase) is associated with a particular character, place, thing, or idea in the opera and may be heard whenever that character is on stage or that idea is an important part of the plot. As with other motifs, leitmotifs may be changed when they return. For example, the same melody may sound quite different depending on whether the character is in love, being heroic, or dying.

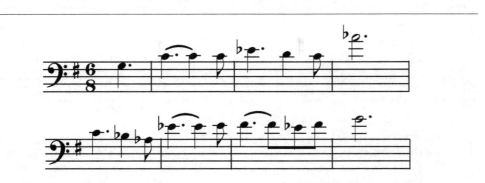

Figure 2.6: A melodic phrase based on the Siegfried leitmotif[17], from Wagner's opera *The Valkyrie.*

2.3.6 Melodies in Counterpoint

Counterpoint (Section 2.6) has more than one melody at the same time. This tends to change the rules for using and developing melodies, so the terms used to talk about contrapuntal melodies are different, too. For example, the melodic idea that is most important in a fugue (Section 2.6.2) is called its **subject**. Like a motif, a subject has often changed when it reappears, sounding higher or lower, for example, or faster or slower. For more on the subject (pun intended), please see Counterpoint (Section 2.6).

2.3.7 Themes

A longer section of melody that keeps reappearing in the music - for example, in a "theme and variations" - is often called a **theme**. Themes generally are at least one phrase long and often have several phrases. Many longer works of music, such as symphony movements, have more than one melodic theme.

---

[17]http://cnx.org/content/m11647/latest/motif2.mid

Theme from Beethoven's Symphony No. 9

Figure 2.7: The tune[18] of this theme will be very familiar to most people, but you may want to listen to the entire last movement of the symphony to hear the different ways that Beethoven uses the melody again and again.

The musical scores for movies and television can also contain melodic **themes**, which can be developed as they might be in a symphony or may be used very much like operatic leitmotifs (pg 77). For example, in the music John Williams composed for the *Star Wars* movies, there are melodic themes that are associated with the main characters. These themes are often complete melodies with many phrases, but a single phrase can be taken from the melody and used as a motif. A single phrase of Ben Kenobi's Theme[19], for example, can remind you of all the good things he stands for, even if he is not on the movie screen at the time.

2.3.8 Suggestions for Presenting these Concepts to Children

Melody is a particularly easy concept to convey to children, since attention to a piece of music is naturally drawn to the melody. If you would like to introduce some of these concepts and terms to children, please see A Melody Activity[20], The Shape of a Melody[21], Melodic Phrases[22], and Theme and Motif in Music[23].

[18]http://cnx.org/content/m11647/latest/Bninth.mid
[19]http://cnx.org/content/m11647/latest/motif3.mid
[20]"A Melody Activity" <http://cnx.org/content/m11833/latest/>
[21]"The Shape of a Melody" <http://cnx.org/content/m11832/latest/>
[22]"Melodic Phrases" <http://cnx.org/content/m11879/latest/>
[23]"Theme and Motif in Music" <http://cnx.org/content/m11880/latest/>

2.4 Texture[24]

2.4.1 Introduction

Texture is one of the basic elements of music. When you describe the **texture** of a piece of music, you are describing how much is going on in the music at any given moment. For example, the texture of the music might be thick or thin, or it may have many or few layers. It might be made up of rhythm only, or of a melody line with chordal accompaniment, or many interweaving melodies. Below you will find some of the formal terms musicians use to describe texture. Suggestions for activities to introduce the concept of texture to young students can be found in Musical Textures Activities[25].

2.4.2 Terms that Describe Texture

There are many informal terms that can describe the texture of a piece of music (thick, thin, bass-heavy, rhythmically complex, and so on), but the formal terms that are used to describe texture all describe the relationships of melodies (Section 2.3) and harmonies (Section 2.5). Here are definitions and examples of the four main types of texture. For specific pieces of music that are good examples of each type of texture, please see below (Section 2.4.3).

2.4.2.1 Monophonic

Monophonic music has only one melodic (Section 2.3) line, with no harmony (Section 2.5) or counterpoint (Section 2.6). There may be rhythmic (Section 2.1) accompaniment, but only one line that has specific pitches (Section 1.1.3). Monophonic music can also be called **monophony**. It is sometimes called **monody**, although the term "monody" can also refer to a particular type of solo song (with instrumental accompaniment) that was very popular in the 1600's.

Examples of Monophony

- One person whistling a tune

- A single bugle sounding "Taps"

- A group of people all singing a song together, without harmonies or instruments

- A fife and drum corp, with all the fifes playing the same melody

2.4.2.2 Homophonic

Homophonic music can also be called **homophony**. More informally, people who are describing homophonic music may mention chords (Chords), accompaniment (Accompaniment), harmony or harmonies (Section 2.5). Homophony has one clearly melodic (Section 2.3) line; it's the line that naturally draws your attention. All other parts provide accompaniment or fill in the chords. In most well-written homophony, the parts that are not melody may still have a lot of melodic interest. They may follow many of the rules of well-written counterpoint (Section 2.6), and they can sound quite different from the melody and be interesting to listen to by themselves. But when they are sung or played with the melody, it is clear that they are not independent melodic parts, either because they have the same rhythm as the melody (i.e. are not independent) or because their main purpose is to fill in the chords or harmony (i.e. they are not really melodies).

---

[24]This content is available online at <http://cnx.org/content/m11645/1.6/>.

[25]"Musical Textures Activities" <http://cnx.org/content/m14260/latest/>

Examples of Homophony

- Choral music in which the parts have mostly the same rhythms at the same time is homophonic. Most traditional Protestant hymns and most "barbershop quartet" music is in this category.

- A singer accompanied by a guitar picking or strumming chords.

- A small jazz combo with a bass, a piano, and a drum set providing the "rhythm" background for a trumpet improvising a solo.

- A single bagpipes or accordion player playing a melody with drones or chords.

2.4.2.3 Polyphonic

Polyphonic music can also be called **polyphony**, **counterpoint**, or **contrapuntal** music. If more than one independent melody (Section 2.3) is occurring at the same time, the music is polyphonic. (See counterpoint (Section 2.6).)

Examples of Polyphony

- Rounds, canons, and fugues (Section 2.6.2) are all polyphonic. (Even if there is only one melody, if different people are singing or playing it at different times, the parts sound independent.)

- Much Baroque music is contrapuntal, particularly the works of J.S. Bach.

- Most music for large instrumental groups such as bands or orchestras is contrapuntal at least some of the time.

- Music that is mostly homophonic can become temporarily polyphonic if an independent countermelody is added. Think of a favorite pop or gospel tune that, near the end, has the soloist "ad libbing" while the back-up singers repeat the refrain.

2.4.2.4 Heterophonic

A **heterophonic** texture is rare in Western (Section 2.8) music. In **heterophony**, there is only one melody, but different variations of it are being sung or played at the same time.

- Heterophony can be heard in the Bluegrass, "mountain music", Cajun, and Zydeco traditions. Listen for the tune to be played by two instruments (say fiddle and banjo) at the same time, with each adding the embellishments, ornaments (Section 2.3), and flourishes that are characteristic of the instrument.

- Some Middle Eastern, South Asian, central Eurasian, and Native American music traditions include heterophony. Listen for traditional music (most modern-composed music, even from these cultures, has little or no heterophony) in which singers and/or instrumentalists perform the same melody at the same time, but give it different embellishments or ornaments.

2.4.3 Suggested Listening

Monophony

- Here is an excerpt[26] from James Romig's[27] Sonnet 2, played by John McMurtery.

- A Bach unaccompanied cello suite

- Gregorian chant

- Long sections of "The People that Walked in Darkness" aria in Handel's "Messiah" are monophonic (the instruments are playing the same line as the voice). Apparently Handel associates monophony with "walking in darkness"!

Homophony

- A classic Scott Joplin rag such as "Maple Leaf Rag" or "The Entertainer"

- The "graduation march" section of Edward Elgar's "Pomp and Circumstance No. 1"

- The "March of the Toreadors" from Bizet's *Carmen*

- No. 1 ("Granada") of Albeniz' Suite Espanola for guitar

- The latest hit tune by a major pop solo vocalist

- The opening section of the "Overture" Of Handel's "Messiah" (The second section of the overture is polyphonic)

Polyphony

- Pachelbel's Canon

- Anything titled "fugue" or "invention"

- The final "Amen" chorus of Handel's "Messiah"

- The trio strain of Sousa's "Stars and Stripes Forever", with the famous piccolo countermelody

- The "One Day More" chorus from the musical "Les Miserables"

- The first movement of Holst's 1st Suite for Military Band

Heterophony

- There is some heterophony (with some instruments playing more ornaments than others) in "Donulmez Aksamin" and in "Urfaliyim Ezelden" on the Turkish Music[28] page.

- The performance of "Lonesome Valley" by the Fairfield Four on the "O Brother, Where Art Thou" soundtrack is quite heterophonic. (Old-style blues owes more to African than to Western traditions.)

---

[26]http://cnx.org/content/m11645/latest/sonnet2exc.mp3
[27]http://www.jamesromig.com
[28]http://www.focusmm.com/turkey/tr_musmn.htm

2.5 Harmony[29]

When you have more than one pitch (Section 1.1.3) sounding at the same time in music, the result is **harmony**. Harmony is one of the basic elements of music, but it is not as basic as some other elements, such as rhythm (Section 2.1) and melody (Section 2.3). You can have music that is just rhythms, with no pitches at all. You can also have music that is just a single melody, or just a melody with rhythm accompaniment (Accompaniment).

But as soon as there is more than one pitch sounding at a time, you have harmony. Even if nobody is actually playing chords (Chords), or even if the notes are part of independent contrapuntal (Section 2.6) lines, you can hear the relationship of any notes that happen at the same time, and it is this relationship that makes the harmony.

> NOTE: Harmony does not have to be particularly "harmonious"; it may be quite dissonant (Section 5.3), in fact. For the purpose of definitions, the important fact is the notes sounding at the same time.

Harmony is the most emphasized and most highly developed element in Western music (Section 2.8), and can be the subject of an entire course on music theory. Many of the concepts underlying Western harmony are explained in greater detail elsewhere (see Triads (Section 5.1) and Beginning Harmonic Analysis (Section 5.5), for example), but here are some basic terms and short definitions that you may find useful in discussions of harmony:

Harmony Textures

- **implied harmony** - A melody all by itself (Monophony (Section 2.4.2)) can have an implied harmony, even if no other notes are sounding at the same time. In other words, the melody can be constructed so that it strongly suggests a harmony that could accompany it. For example, when you sing a melody by itself, you may be able to "hear" in your mind the chords that usually go with it. A Bach unaccompanied cello suite also has strongly implied harmonies; if someone really wanted to play an accompaniment (Accompaniment), the appropriate chords (Chords) could be found pretty easily. But some melodies don't imply any harmony; they are not meant to be played with harmony, and don't need it to be legitimate music. (Good examples of this include plainchant, some modern art music, and some Non-Western (Section 2.8) music, for example, Native American flute music.)

- **drones** - The simplest way to add harmony to a melody is to play it with drones. A drone is a note that changes rarely or not at all. Drones can be most easily found in bagpipes music, Indian Classical[30] music and other musics that use instruments that traditionally play drone notes. (See Harmony with Drones[31].)

- **parallel harmony** - Parallel harmony occurs when different lines in the music go up or down together (usually following the melody). (See Parallel Harmonies[32] for examples.)

- **homophony** - Homophony is a texture (Section 2.4) of music in which there is one line that is obviously the melody. The rest of the notes are harmony and accompaniment (Accompaniment). (See Homophonic (Section 2.4.2.2).)

- **polyphony** or **counterpoint** - Both of these terms refer to a texture of music in which there is more than one independent melodic line at the same time, and they are all fairly equal in importance. (See Polyphonic (Section 2.4.2.3) and Counterpoint (Section 2.6).)

[29]This content is available online at <http://cnx.org/content/m11654/1.6/>.
[30]"Listening to Indian Classical Music" <http://cnx.org/content/m12502/latest/>
[31]"Harmony with Drones" <http://cnx.org/content/m11844/latest/>
[32]"Parallel Harmonies" <http://cnx.org/content/m11878/latest/>

Chords

- **chords** - In Western (Section 2.8) music, most harmony is based on chords. **Chords** are groups of notes built on major (Section 4.3) or minor (Section 4.4) triads (Section 5.1). In traditional triadic chords, there are always at least three notes in a chord (there can be more than three), but some of the notes may be left out and only "implied" by the harmony. The notes of the chord may be played at the same time (**block chords**), or may overlap, or may be played separately but in a quick enough succession that they will be "heard" as a chord (**arpeggiated chords**).

- **chord progression** - A series of chords played one after another is a chord progression. Musicians may describe a specific chord progression (for example, "two measures of G major, then a half measure of A minor and a half measure of D seventh", or just "G, A minor, D seventh") or speak more generally of classes of chord progressions (for example a "blues chord progression"). Please see Beginning Harmonic Analysis (Section 5.5) for more information.

Harmonic Analysis

- **harmonic rhythm** - The harmonic rhythm of a piece refers to how often the chords change. Music in which the chords change rarely has a slow harmonic rhythm; music in which the chords change often has a fast harmonic rhythm. Harmonic rhythm can be completely separate from other rhythms and tempos. For example, a section of music with many short, quick notes but only one chord has fast rhythms but a slow harmonic rhythm.

- **cadence** - A cadence is a point where the music feels as if it has come to a temporary or permanent stopping point. In most Western (Section 2.8) music, cadence is tied very strongly to the harmony. For example, most listeners will feel that the strongest, most satisfying ending to a piece of music involves a dominant chord (Section 5.5.4) followed by a tonic chord (Section 5.5.4). In fact, a song that does not end on the tonic chord will sound quite unsettled and even unfinished to most listeners. (See Cadence (Section 5.6).)

- **diatonic** - Diatonic (pg 91) harmony stays in a particular major (Section 4.3) or minor (Section 4.4) key.

- **chromatic** - Chromatic (pg 91) harmony includes many notes and chords that are not in the key and so contains many accidentals (pg 17).

- **dissonance** - A dissonance is a note, chord, or interval (Section 4.5) that does not fit into the triadic (Section 5.1) harmonies that we have learned to expect from music. A dissonance may sound surprising, jarring, even unpleasant.

Accompaniment

- **accompaniment** - All the parts of the music that are not melody are part of the accompaniment. This includes rhythmic parts, harmonies, the bass line, and chords.

- **melodic line** - This is just another term for the string of notes that make up the melody (Section 2.3).

- **bass line** - The bass line is the string of notes that are the lowest notes being sung or played. Because of basic laws of physics, the bass line sets up the harmonics (Section 3.3) that all the other parts - including the melody - must fit into. This makes it a very important line both for tuning (Section 6.2) and for the harmony. The bass line also often outlines the chord progression (Chords), and it is often the most noticeable line of the accompaniment.

- **inner parts** or **inner voices** - Accompaniment parts that fill in the music in between the melody (which is often the highest part) and the bass line.

- **descant** - The melody is not always the highest line in the music. Attention is naturally drawn to high notes, so a part that is higher than the melody is sometimes given a special name such as "descant". This term is an old one going all the way back to when harmonies first began to be added to medieval chant. (See Counterpoint (pg 86) for more about descants.)

Suggestions for activities that introduce young students to harmony may be found in Harmony with Drones[33], Simple Chordal Harmony[34], Parallel Harmonies[35], and Independent Harmonies[36].

2.6 Counterpoint[37]

2.6.1 Introduction

Counterpoint is an important element of music, but it is not one of the basic elements. Many pieces of music have rhythm (Section 2.1), melody (Section 2.3), harmony (Section 2.5), color (Section 2.2), and texture (Section 2.4), but no real counterpoint. In fact, when describing the texture of a piece of music, two of the most important questions that need to be addressed are: is there counterpoint, and how important is it?

When there is *more than one independent melodic line happening at the same time* in a piece of music, we say that the music is **contrapuntal**. The independent melodic lines are called **counterpoint**. The music that is made up of counterpoint can also be called **polyphony**, or one can say that the music is **polyphonic** or speak of the **polyphonic texture** of the music. Traditionally, vocal music is more likely to be described as **polyphony** and instrumental music is more likely to be described as **counterpoint**. But all of these terms refer to two or more independent, simultaneous melodies. "Simultaneous" means the melodies are happening at the same time. "Independent" means that at any given moment what is happening in one melody (both in the rhythms (Section 2.1) and in the pitches (Section 1.1.3)) is probably not the same thing that is happening in the other melody.

First, some examples of music that is *not* counterpoint. Obviously, there is no counterpoint if there is no melody at all. If there is one melodic line accompanied only by rhythm, or drones, or only by chords, there is no counterpoint.

Even if different people are singing or playing different parts, it is not necessarily considered counterpoint if the parts are not independent enough, or if one of the parts is very clearly a dominating melody. Many traditional choral pieces are a good example of this. There are four very different singing parts (soprano, alto, tenor, and bass), and each part, sung alone, can seem like its own melody, a melody that does not sound at all like the melody of the piece. But the parts have basically the same rhythms, so that the effect, when sung together, is of chords being sung. "Barbershop"-style music is another good example of this homophonic (Section 2.4.2.2), or chordal, kind of texture, which is not considered counterpoint.

Now for some familiar examples of counterpoint. One of the simplest and most familiar types of counterpoint is the round. In a **round**, everyone sings the same melody, but they start singing it at different times. Although everyone is singing exactly the same tune, at any particular time different people will be singing different parts of it, so the final effect is of independent parts. You may also have heard some Bach fugues or inventions; there are no better examples of counterpoint than these. Another example that may be familiar is the soloist in a pop or gospel song who, after

[33]"Harmony with Drones" <http://cnx.org/content/m11844/latest/>
[34]"Simple Chordal Harmony" <http://cnx.org/content/m11875/latest/>
[35]"Parallel Harmonies" <http://cnx.org/content/m11878/latest/>
[36]"Independent Harmonies" <http://cnx.org/content/m11874/latest/>
[37]This content is available online at <http://cnx.org/content/m11634/1.5/>.

the refrain has been repeated a few times, takes off on a countermelody or descant (pg 86) part while everyone else continues to sing the refrain. The melody instruments in a dixieland band are also generally playing independent parts, giving this genre its "busy" sound. In fact, when music sounds very "busy" or "complex" or when there is so much going on that it gets difficult to decide where the melody is or what part to sing along with, it is likely that you are hearing counterpoint.

Although there is plenty of music that has no counterpoint, independent parts are one of the most basic ways to make music sound rich and interesting. Even if a piece of music cannot really be called "counterpoint" or "polyphony", because it clearly has one melody, the accompaniment (Accompaniment) lines may still be quite contrapuntal. Even music that most people would describe as homophonic (Section 2.4.2.2) or chordal (Chords), because all the lines have exactly the same rhythm, is often written following the voice-leading rules of counterpoint. This gives the music a much richer, more interesting texture (Section 2.4). Next time you are listening to your favorite song or your favorite piece of music, don't hum along with the melody. Instead, listen to the bass line. Listen to the harmonies (Section 2.5), the inner voices (Accompaniment) and the instrumental accompaniment parts. Chances are that you will hear some interesting lines, even little pieces of melody, that are completely different from the part you normally hear.

2.6.2 Some Useful Terms

- *Canon* - In a canon, different voices (or instruments) sing (or play) the same melody, with no changes, but at different times. The melody is usually sung at the same pitch or an octave (Section 4.1) higher or lower, but there are also canons in which the second part sings or plays the melody a perfect fourth or fifth (pg 140) higher or lower than the first part.

- *Round* - In a canon, obviously every section of the canon must "fit" with the section that comes after it. (In other words, they must sound good when sung or played at the same time). A round is a special type of canon in which the last section also fits with the first section, so that the canon can be repeated over and over without stopping. Rounds are usually pretty short and always start at the same note, or the octave.

- *Fugue* - A fugue usually has at least three independent parts, or **voices**. The different voices enter at different times on the same melodic theme (called the **subject**), so that the beginning may sound like a canon. But then the different voices develop the theme in different directions. A second melodic theme (called the **countersubject**) is usually introduced, and the middle of the fugue gets quite intricate, with the subject and countersubject popping in and out of various voices, sometimes in surprising ways (upside-down, for example).

- *Countermelody or descant* - Sometimes a piece of music that is basically melody-with-accompaniment (homophonic) will include a single part that is truly independent of the melody. For example, a choral piece might be chordal for a few verses and then, to keep the music interesting and fresh, add an independent part for a flute or for the highest sopranos on the third verse. This is a countermelody, sometimes called a descant part. Gospel and pop singers often add countermelodies, sometimes imrovised, and classical music also contains many, many examples of countermelodies.

2.7 Range[38]

2.7.1 Introduction

The **range** of a voice or instrument is the set of pitches (Section 1.1.3), from lowest to highest, that it can sing or play. A range can be described using the appropriate octave identification (Section 4.1.2),

---

[38]This content is available online at <http://cnx.org/content/m12381/1.6/>.

for example, "from one-line c to two-line g". But it is often easiest to write the range on a staff, as the two notes at the high and low ends of the range.

A piece of music, or one performer's part in that piece, may also be described as having a range, from the lowest to highest note written for the performer in that piece. There is usually a difference (sometimes a large one) between the total range of the part and a smaller range that the part stays in most of the time (heading to the extreme highs and lows only occasionally). This smaller range is called the **tessitura** of the part. One can also speak of the tessitura of a performer's voice, which is the range in which it sounds the best (so that matching the tessitura of the part and of the performer is a very good idea). Notice the similarity between this second definition and the term power range (pg 89), sometimes used to describe the most powerful or useful part of an instrument's range.

A **register** is a distinctive part of a vocal or instrumental range. For example, singers may speak of the **head register**, in the upper part of their range, and the **chest register** in the lower part of their range. These two registers sound and feel very different, and the singer may have even have two distinct tessituras, one in each register. The large range of the clarinet[39] is also divided into distinctive registers with different capabilities and very different timbres (Section 2.2). Even when an instrument does not have a very large variation in timbre over its range, its players may speak of the difficulty of "playing in the high register" or a "dull timbre in the low register".

Describing a Range

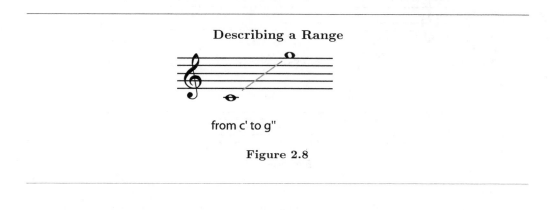

from c' to g"

Figure 2.8

2.7.2 Vocal Ranges

A typical choral arrangement divides women into higher and lower voices and men into higher or lower voices. Most voices can be assigned one of these four ranges, and this gives the composer four vocal lines to work with, which is usually enough. The four main vocal ranges are:

- **Soprano** – A high female (or boy's) voice

- **Alto** – A low female (or boy's) voice

- **Tenor** – A high (adult) male voice

- **Bass** – A low (adult) male voice

Arrangements for these four voices are labelled SATB (for Soprano Alto Tenor Bass). The ranges of the four voices overlap, but singers may find themselves straining or getting an unpleasant sound at the top or a weak sound at the bottom of their ranges. So although the full ranges of an alto and a soprano may look quite similar, the soprano gets a strong, clear sound on the higher notes, and the alto a strong, clear sound in the lower part of the range. But there are vocalists whose strong,

[39]"Clarinets" <http://cnx.org/content/m12604/latest/>

best-sounding range falls in a distinctly different place from any of these four voices. The names for some of these ranges are:

- **Coloratura Soprano** – This is not really a different range from the soprano, but a coloratura soprano has a voice that is unusually high, light, and agile, even for a soprano.

- **Mezzo-soprano** – In between soprano and alto

- **Contralto** – Contralto and alto originally referred to the same voice. But some people today use "contralto" to refer to a female voice that is even lower than a typical alto

- **Countertenor** – A male voice that is unusually high, light, and agile, even for a tenor

- **Baritone** – A male voice that falls in between tenor and bass

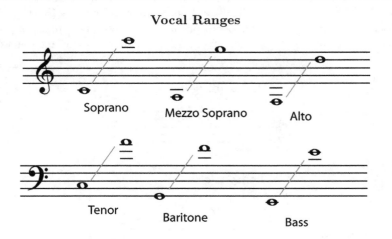

Figure 2.9: Voices are as individual as faces; some altos will have a narrower or wider range, or the sweetest and most powerful part of their range in a different place than other altos. These are approximate, average ranges for each voice category.

2.7.3 Instrumental Ranges

The same terms used to identify vocal ranges are also often used to identify particular instruments. For example a bass trombone[40] has a lower range than a tenor trombone, and an alto saxophone[41] sounds higher than a tenor saxophone. Some other terms that are used to describe instrument ranges are:

- **Contra** – Means lower: for example a contrabassoon sounds lower than a regular bassoon[42], and a contrabass clarinet is even lower than a bass clarinet.

- **Piccolo**- Means higher (literally "smaller"): for example, a piccolo trumpet is higher than a regular trumpet.

---

[40]"Trombones" <http://cnx.org/content/m12602/latest/>
[41]"Saxophones" <http://cnx.org/content/m12611/latest/>
[42]"Bassoons" <http://cnx.org/content/m12612/latest/>

- **A Note Name** – If an instrument comes in several different sizes (and ranges), the name of a particular size of the instrument may be a note name: for example, an F horn[43], a B flat clarinet[44], and a C trumpet[45]. The note name is the name of the fundamental harmonic[46] of the instrument. An instrument with a slightly higher fundamental will have a slightly higher range; an instrument with a much lower fundamental will have a much lower range. Some instruments that are identified this way are transposing instruments[47], but others are not.

The ranges of some instruments are definite and absolute. For example, even a beginning piano player can play the highest and lowest keys; and even the best player cannot play beyond these. But the ranges of many instruments are, like vocal ranges, not so definite. For example, an experienced horn or clarinet player can play much higher and lower notes than a beginner. An exceptional trumpet player may be able to play - with good sound and technique – high notes that the average high school trumpet player cannot play at all.

Other instruments may be a mix of absolute and indefinite ranges. For example, on any string instrument, nobody can play lower than the note that the lowest string is tuned to. But experienced players can easily play very high notes that inexperienced players have trouble playing well.

So it is sometimes useful to distinguish between a **possible range**, which includes the notes that a very experienced player can get, and a **practical range**, that includes all the notes that any competent player (including a good younger player) can get.

> NOTE: Outside of the instrument's practical range, it may be a strain for even a very good player to play long or tricky passages. So if you are composing or arranging, it's a very good idea to be able to distinguish between these two ranges for the voices or instruments you include.

Some sources even list the **power range** of an instrument or voice. This is the part of the range where the instrument or voice is particularly strong. It may be in the middle of the range, or at the top or bottom, but writing in the power range should guarantee that the part is easy to play (or sing), sounds clear and strong, and can be easily heard, even when many other instruments are playing.

2.8 Classifying Music[48]

One of the first things needed when you begin the study of any subject is a little introduction to the "lingo." Since music is such a huge subject, some of the words used to talk about it are the terms that divide it up into smaller subjects, the way science is divided into biology, physics, and so on. So here are a few terms that may be useful if you are wondering what kind of music you want to learn more about.

2.8.1 Western and Non-Western

Most of the music books you'll find on the shelf are about **Western** music. From the end of the Middle Ages to modern times, composers and performers in western Europe gradually developed widely accepted standards for tuning (Section 6.2), melody (Section 2.3), harmony (Section 2.5), meter (Section 1.2.4), notation (Section 1.1.1), form (Section 5.7), counterpoint (Section 2.6) and other music basics. These rules are a sort of grammar for the language of music. Just as the the basic

---

[43]"The French Horn" <http://cnx.org/content/m11617/latest/>
[44]"Clarinets" <http://cnx.org/content/m12604/latest/>
[45]"Trumpets and Cornets" <http://cnx.org/content/m12606/latest/>
[46]"Harmonic Series" <http://cnx.org/content/m11118/latest/#p1c>
[47]"Transposing Instruments" <http://cnx.org/content/m10672/latest/>
[48]This content is available online at <http://cnx.org/content/m11421/1.8/>.

rules for putting together sentences and paragraphs help people understand each other, knowing what to expect from a piece of music helps people understand and like it.

Of course, music, like language, changes through the centuries. A Bach invention, a Brahms symphony, and a Beatles song are different forms in different genres, and at first they may sound as if they have nothing in common. But they all use the same musical "language" and follow basically the same rules. They are all examples of Western music, and are all more like each other than they are like a Navajo lullaby, a Chinese opera, or a west African praise song.

Wherever Europeans went during the colonial era, they took their music with them. So, in places like Australia and the Americas, not only do most of the people speak European languages, much of their music also sounds Western. What are the rules of this European musical language? A complete answer to that question would be long and complex, since Western music, like any living language shared by many different communities, has many "local dialects". The short answer is: Western music is generally tonal (Section 2.8.3), based on major (Section 4.3) or minor (Section 4.4) scales, using an equal temperament tuning (Section 6.2.3.2), in an easy-to-recognize meter (Section 1.2.4), with straightforward rhythms (Section 2.1), fairly strict rules on harmony (Section 2.5) and counterpoint (Section 2.6), and not much improvisation. This is, of course, a huge generalization. Twentieth century art music, in particular, was very interested in breaking down or even rejecting these rules. But because they are flexible enough to allow plenty of interesting but easy-to-grasp music, the rules are still widely used, particularly in popular music. In fact, the use of these traditional rules for Western music is now so widespread that it is sometimes called **common practice**. They are what makes Western music sound familiar and easy to understand.

Non-Western music is any music that grew out of a different culture or musical tradition than the European. For someone who grew up listening to Western music, Non-Western music will have a recognizably exotic sound. This comes from the use of different tuning systems (Section 6.2), different scales (Section 4.8), different vocal styles and performance practices, and different approaches to melody and harmony.

> NOTE: You may find the terms "Western" and "Non-Western" to be too Eurocentric, but they are very well entrenched, so you'll need to know what they mean. If you want to avoid using the terms yourself, you can be more specific. You can speak, for example, of European classical or the European-American folk tradition, as opposed to Indian Classical[49], Japanese folk, or African-American musics.

2.8.2 Jazz, Blues, and World Music

Much of the music that is popular today cannot really be classified as completely Western or Non-Western. Since colonial times, when European cultures came into contact with many Non-Western cultures, musicians on all sides have been experimenting with music that is a blend of "the best of both worlds." Many musical styles have been invented that mix Western and Non-Western traditions. Perhaps the oldest and most widely popular of these styles are the ones that join European and African musical traditions. These include various **Latin** (from Central and South America, some of which also include Native American influences) and **Caribbean** traditions, and from North America, many different kinds of **jazz** and **blues**. Most American popular (Section 2.8.5) musics also grew out of this blending of traditions.

But the process of inventing new ways of fusing Western and Non-Western music continues today in countries all over the world. The term **World Music** is often used as a catch-all category referring to almost any music with widespread popularity that clearly does not sound like North American popular music. This includes older blended traditions such as rumba and samba, newer but well-established blended genres such as reggae and Afrobeat, and groups with unique experimental

---
[49]"Listening to Indian Classical Music" <http://cnx.org/content/m12502/latest/>

sounds borrowing from more than one tradition. Folk and traditional music from around the world is also sometimes included, but the most popular genres in this category tend to be those, such as Flamenco, Hungarian folk, and Celtic music, that are easy for Western-trained ears to understand. African-American traditions are so basic to popular music that they are generally not included in World music, but other North American traditions, such as Native American and Cajun traditions, sometimes are.

2.8.3 Tonal, Atonal, and Modal Music

As mentioned above, Western music has not remained static through the centuries, either. It has changed and evolved as composers experimented with new sounds, ideas, and even new or evolving instruments.

Medieval European music, like many Non-Western traditions, was modal (Section 6.3). This means that a piece of music was not in a particular key (Section 4.3) based on a major (Section 4.3) or minor (Section 4.4) scale. Instead, it was in a particular **mode**. A mode may look very much like a scale, since it lists the notes that are "allowed" in the piece of music and defines the tonic (pg 127) of the music. But a mode is usually also a collection of melodies, melodic phrases, or patterns that are found in that mode and not others (since the various modes are more different from each other than the various scales). Modes also may imply or suggest specific moods or they may be meant to have particular effects on the character of the listener.

Different keys may also evoke different moods, but the main purpose of a key is to define the chords (Chords) and harmonic progressions (Section 5.5) that will be expected from a piece of music. From the Renaissance to the present day, most Western music has tended to be tonal. **Tonal** music is music in which the progression of the melody and harmony gives the strong feeling that the piece has a note and chord that are its "home base", so to speak (the tonic (pg 127) of the key). Think of a very familiar tune, perhaps "Row, Row, Row your Boat" or "Happy Birthday to You". Imagine how frustrating it would be to end that tune without singing the last note or playing the final chord. If you did this, most people would be so dissatisfied that they might supply that last note for you. That note is the **tonal center** of the tune, and without it, there is a feeling that the song has not reached its proper resting place. In tonal music, just about any melody is allowed, as long as it fits into the harmonies as they wander away from and then head back to their home base. Most Western tonal music is based on major and minor scales, both of which easily give that strongly tonal feeling. Some other scales, such as blues scales (Section 4.8.5), also work well within a tonal framework, but others, such as whole-tone scales (pg 156), do not.

Most of the Western music that is popular today is tonal, but around the beginning of the twentieth century, composers of "Classical" or Art music (see below (Section 2.8.4)) began experimenting with methods of composing **atonal** music. "Atonal" literally means "not tonal". As the name implies, atonal music treats all notes and harmonies as equal and in fact tries to avoid melodies and harmonies that will make the piece sound tonal. One type of atonal music is **twelve-tone** music, which seeks to use each of the notes of the chromatic scale (pg 123) equally. Other pieces may even dispense with the idea that music has to consist of notes; compositions may be collections of sounds and silences. Since the music is not organized by the familiar rules of Western music, many people have trouble appreciating atonal music without some help or study.

Music can be more or less tonal without becoming completely atonal, however. Music that does not stray at all from its key is called **diatonic**. Many Western children's songs, folk songs, and pop songs are in this category. But composers often add some notes or even whole sections of music that are from a different key, to make the music a little more complex and interesting. Music that goes even further, and freely uses all the notes of the chromatic scale (pg 123), but still manages to have a tonal "home", is called **chromatic**. Music that has more than one tonal center at the same time (Ives was particularly fond of this composition technique) is called **polytonal**.

2.8.4 Classical and Art Music

Popular music is, by definition, music that appeals to many people. You don't have to know anything about music to like a pop tune - it's "catchy". **Art music** is a catch-all term for any music that is enjoyed by a smaller crowd. This can include the more challenging types of jazz and rock music, as well as Classical. Most people agree that the appreciation of art music requires some study, careful listening, or other extra effort. But it can be harder to agree on what exactly belongs in this category. This is at least partly because popular tastes do change. For example, most operas were written to be popular, middle-class entertainments, and artists such as Liszt and Paganini enjoyed rock-star-like fame and popularity in their day. Today, however, nineteenth century operas are no longer considered popular entertainment, and popular works that could technically be considered opera - except for the fact that they are written in popular musical styles - are instead grouped with musicals. As another example, ragtime[50] was wildly popular during Scott Joplin's[51] lifetime. It later fell out of favor and was known only to some jazz connoisseurs. Then in the 1970's it became popular again.

   Classical music is a confusing term with more than one meaning. In the visual arts, the term **classical** refers to ancient Greece and Rome. In the 1700's, Western Europeans became very interested in the ancient classical style, which was imitated by many artists, sculptors, and architects. Art historians call that period the **neoclassical** ("new classical"). Unfortunately, nobody really knows what the music of ancient times sounded like. So instead of being influenced by the sound of ancient Greek music, eighteenth-century composers were influenced by the ideals of classical art. The music of Mozart, Haydn, and the early works of Beethoven are in this style, which we call classical rather than neoclassical, because the original classical music of ancient Greece and Rome is lost. (And actually, it probably would sound very exotic and Non-Western to us if we could listen to it!)

   So the original classical music comes from one fairly short era. The other great composers of Western music lived during other periods: Bach and Handel were Baroque era composers, for example; Brahms and Wagner, Romantic[52]; and Ravel and Debussy, Impressionist. But most people do not know which music is from which period. So all of the music of the great Western composers of the past (as well as modern art music that is part of the same tradition) is lumped together and called **classical**. The art music of other cultures is also often called classical; for example, people speak of the classical music of India.

2.8.5 Folk and Popular music

The terms "folk music" and "pop music" also have more than one meaning. The **folk music** of a culture is the music that is passed down from one generation to the next, often without writing it down. It includes many different kinds of music: lullabies and children's singing games, tunes that everyone enjoys singing together or dancing to, songs for celebrations, ceremonies, and holidays. Folk music can gradually change as it gets passed along. Usually nobody remembers who originally wrote it, or who changed it, and there may be more than one version of any particular folk song. Since ancient times, folk music has been the music of ordinary people, not the ruling class or professional musicians. In every culture, children learned and remembered the music that everyone enjoyed the most, and the music that was important to their traditions.

   The modern recording industry has changed things, though. In many cultures, pop music has largely replaced folk music as the music that everyone knows. Unlike folk music, it has usually been written recently and belongs to professional musicians, and new popular tunes quickly replace old ones. Even the types of music that are considered popular can change quickly. The term **pop music**

---

[50]"Ragtime" <http://cnx.org/content/m10878/latest/>
[51]"Scott Joplin" <http://cnx.org/content/m10879/latest/>
[52]"The Music of the Romantic Era" <http://cnx.org/content/m11606/latest/>

can refer to a specific kind of popular music, as in "bubblegum pop". **Popular music** is also a general term for any type of music that is or has been a top seller. This includes most types of rock music and some kinds of jazz.

As the rise of recording pushed aside traditional music, some musicians made a point of recording traditional folk songs, so they would not be lost altogether. Some also wrote new songs in a "folk" style that enjoyed some popularity, particularly in the 1960's. Although these modern tunes do not fit the traditional definition, they are also called **folk music**.

2.8.6 Suggestions for Listening and Further Study

It can be difficult to follow a discussion of music without hearing some examples. If you would like to hear some music in the categories above, or you are planning to present this lesson to a class, here are some easy-to-find suggestions. Some categories also include suggestions for where to start if you want more information.

2.8.6.1 Tonal, Atonal, and Modal Music

- To hear tonal music, turn on the radio and listen to just about any station, unless your Classical station is playing twentieth century music.

- In the modal music category, medieval chant and the classical music of India are easiest to find.

- Even in the category of twentieth century music, the shelves tend to be stocked with the work of composers who stayed with some sort of tonality (Ralph Vaughan Williams, George Gershwin, and Aaron Copland, for example). For atonality look for John Cage, Arnold Schoenberg, Anton Webern, or Edgard Varese.

2.8.6.2 Western Classical

- From the actual classical period: listen to anything by Mozart or Haydn, or Beethoven's early works.

- From other periods: listen to Bach or Vivaldi (Baroque), Brahms, Schubert, Chopin, or Tchaikovsky, or Beethoven's later works (Romantic), Ravel or Debussy (Impressionist), Stravinsky, Hindemith, or Schoenberg (Modern).

- *A History of Western Music* by Donald Jay Grout is a scholarly source of information.

- *The Music Makers*, edited by Clive Unger-Hamilton, is an easy-to-read combination of history and reference book.

- Most standard music dictionaries and encyclopedias also focus almost exclusively on Western Classical music.

- For children, there are many appropriate picture books and even videos on the lives and music of the most famous composers. Also, look for picture books that summarize the plot of a famous opera or ballet.

- Any standard music theory book or course will introduce the basics of Western music.

2.8.6.3 Non-Western Classical

- The only easy-to-find items in this category are Indian Classical music, for example the performances of Ravi Shankar.

- A web search for classical music from a particular country may turn up some sound clips. At the time of this writing, for example, sound clips could be found of Chinese Opera[53] and Tunisian[54] classical music.

2.8.6.4 Western Folk

- For the sound of traditional Western folk music, look for collections of folk music from England or Australia, sea shanties, or American cowboy songs. For young students, Wee Sing's "Fun 'n' Folk" and "Sing-Alongs" book-and-tape sets are good sources.

- To hear modern folk-style music, listen to Joan Baez, John Denver, Bob Dylan's protest music, Simon and Garfunkel, or Peter, Paul and Mary.

- The Rough Guide series of books and recordings includes some that examine modern folk artists. This would be a good place to start learning more on the subject of modern folk music.

2.8.6.5 Non-Western Folk

- If you live in a Western culture, it can be difficult to find recordings of non-Western folk music, since most Western listeners do not have a taste for it. For children, Wee Sing publishes an "Around the World" book and tape with children's songs from all over.

- The Music for Little People catalogue also has some recordings that introduce children to music from other cultures.

- For adults, Ellipsis Arts publishes traditional music from non-Western cultures. Check your local library's recording section for music from Africa or Asia, or for the music of native Americans or Australians.

- Some of the Rough Guide series focus on specific folk or traditional musics.

2.8.6.6 Music that Combines Western and Non-Western Traditions

- For music that has been combining elements of both for long enough to have developed its own traditions, listen to any jazz, blues, gospel, Latin dance, or reggae. There are many books on these musics, particularly on jazz and reggae. For a comprehensive audiovisual overview of jazz, try Ken Burns' PBS documentary.

- Almost all popular music is heavily influenced by both African and European traditions. Turn on the radio.

- To hear what is going on in modern Non-Western cultures as their musicians are influenced by American and European pop, listen to "World" music. The Rough Guide series is a good place to start learning about this subject.

---

[53]http://www.chinapage.com/beijing-opera.html
[54]http://www.radiotunis.com/music.html

Chapter 3

The Physical Basis

3.1 Acoustics for Music Theory[1]

3.1.1 Music is Organized Sound Waves

Music is sound that's organized by people on purpose, to dance to, to tell a story, to make other people feel a certain way, or just to sound pretty or be entertaining. Music is organized on many different levels. Sounds can be arranged into melodies (Section 2.3), harmonies (Section 2.5), rhythms (Section 2.1), textures (Section 2.4) and phrases (Section 2.3.4). Beats (Section 1.2.3.1), measures (Section 1.1.1.1), cadences (Section 5.6), and form (Section 5.7) all help to keep the music organized and understandable. But the most basic way that music is organized is by arranging the actual sound waves themselves so that the sounds are interesting and pleasant and go well together.

A rhythmic, organized set of thuds and crashes is perfectly good music - think of your favorite drum solo - but many musical instruments are designed specifically to produce the regular, evenly spaced sound waves that we hear as particular pitches (Section 1.1.3). Crashes, thuds, and bangs are loud, short jumbles of lots of different wavelengths. These are the kinds of sound we often call "noise", when they're random and disorganized, but as soon as they are organized in time (rhythm (Section 2.1)), they begin to sound like music. (When used as a scientific term, **noise** refers to *continuous* sounds that are random mixtures of different wavelengths, not shorter crashes and thuds.)

However, to get the melodic kind of sounds more often associated with music, the sound waves must themselves be organized and regular, not random mixtures. Most of the sounds we hear are brought to our ears through the air. A movement of an object causes a disturbance of the normal motion of the air molecules near the object. Those molecules in turn disturb other nearby molecules out of their normal patterns of random motion, so that the disturbance itself becomes a thing that moves through the air - a sound wave. If the movement of the object is a fast, regular vibration, then the sound waves are also very regular. We hear such regular sound waves as **tones**, sounds with a particular pitch (Section 1.1.3). It is this kind of sound that we most often associate with music, and that many musical instruments are designed to make.

---

[1]This content is available online at <http://cnx.org/content/m13246/1.7/>.

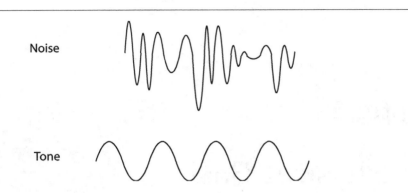

Figure 3.1: A random jumble of sound waves is heard as a noise. A regular, evenly-spaced sound wave is heard as a tone.

Musicians have terms that they use to describe tones. (Musicians also have other meanings for the word "tone", but this course will stick to the "a sound with pitch" meaning.) This kind of (regular, evenly spaced) wave is useful for things other than music, however, so scientists and engineers also have terms that describe pitched sound waves. As we talk about where music theory comes from, it will be very useful to know both the scientific and the musical terms and how they are related to each other.

For example, the closer together those evenly-spaced waves are, the higher the note sounds. Musicians talk about the pitch (Section 1.1.3) of the sound, or name specific notes (Section 1.1.2), or talk about tuning (Section 6.2). Scientists and engineers, on the other hand, talk about the frequency (pg 99) and the wavelength (pg 99) of the sound. They are all essentially talking about the same things, but talking about them in slightly different ways, and using the scientific ideas of wavelength and frequency can help clarify some of the main ideas underlying music theory.

3.1.2 Longitudinal and Transverse Waves

So what are we talking about when we speak of sound waves? Waves are disturbances; they are changes in something - the surface of the ocean, the air, electromagnetic fields. Normally, these changes are travelling (except for standing waves (Section 3.2)); the disturbance is moving away from whatever created it, in a kind of domino effect.

Most kinds of waves are **transverse** waves. In a transverse wave, as the wave is moving in one direction, it is creating a disturbance in a different direction. The most familiar example of this is waves on the surface of water. As the wave travels in one direction - say south - it is creating an up-and-down (not north-and-south) motion on the water's surface. This kind of wave is fairly easy to draw; a line going from left-to-right has up-and-down wiggles. (See Figure 3.2.)

Transverse and Longitudinal Waves

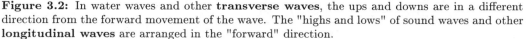

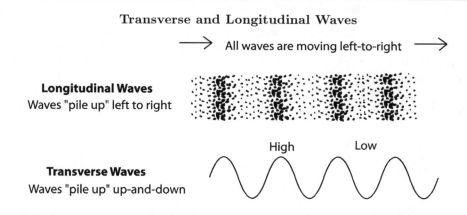

Figure 3.2: In water waves and other **transverse waves**, the ups and downs are in a different direction from the forward movement of the wave. The "highs and lows" of sound waves and other **longitudinal waves** are arranged in the "forward" direction.

But sound waves are not transverse. Sound waves are **longitudinal waves**. If sound waves are moving south, the disturbance that they are creating is giving the air molecules extra north-and-south (not east-and-west, or up-and-down) motion. If the disturbance is from a regular vibration, the result is that the molecules end up squeezed together into evenly-spaced waves. This is very difficult to show clearly in a diagram, so *most diagrams, even diagrams of sound waves, show transverse waves*.

Longitudinal waves may also be a little difficult to imagine, because there aren't any examples that we can see in everyday life (unless you like to play with toy slinkies). A mathematical description might be that in longitudinal waves, the waves (the disturbances) are along the same axis as the direction of motion of the wave; transverse waves are at right angles to the direction of motion of the wave. If this doesn't help, try imagining yourself as one of the particles that the wave is disturbing (a water drop on the surface of the ocean, or an air molecule). As it comes from behind you, a transverse waves lifts you up and then drops down; a longitudinal wave coming from behind pushes you forward and pulls you back. You can view here animations of longitudinal and transverse waves[2], single particles being disturbed by a transverse wave or by a longitudinal wave[3], and particles being disturbed by transverse and longitudinal waves[4]. (There were also some nice animations of longitudinal waves available as of this writing at Musemath[5].)

The result of these "forward and backward" waves is that the "high point" of a sound wave is where the air molecules are bunched together, and the "low point" is where there are fewer air molecules. In a pitched sound, these areas of bunched molecules are very evenly spaced. In fact, they are so even, that there are some very useful things we can measure and say about them. *In order to clearly show you what they are, most of the diagrams in this course will show sound waves as if they are transverse waves.*

---

[2]http://cnx.org/content/m13246/latest/Waves.swf
[3]http://cnx.org/content/m13246/latest/Pulses.swf
[4]http://cnx.org/content/m13246/latest/Translong.swf
[5]http://www.musemath.com

3.1.3 Wave Amplitude and Loudness

Both transverse and longitudinal waves cause a **displacement** of something: air molecules, for example, or the surface of the ocean. The amount of displacement at any particular spot changes as the wave passes. If there is no wave, or if the spot is in the same state it would be in if there was no wave, there is no displacement. Displacement is biggest (furthest from "normal") at the highest and lowest points of the wave. In a sound wave, then, there is no displacement wherever the air molecules are at a normal density. The most displacement occurs wherever the molecules are the most crowded or least crowded.

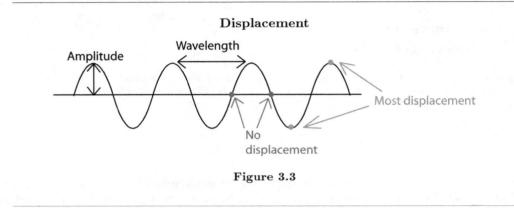

Figure 3.3

The **amplitude** of the wave is a measure of the displacement: how big is the change from no displacement to the peak of a wave? Are the waves on the lake two inches high or two feet? Are the air molecules bunched very tightly together, with very empty spaces between the waves, or are they barely more organized than they would be in their normal course of bouncing off of each other? Scientists measure the amplitude of sound waves in **decibels**. Leaves rustling in the wind are about 10 decibels; a jet engine is about 120 decibels.

Musicians call the loudness of a note its **dynamic level**. **Forte** (pronounced "FOR-tay") is a loud dynamic level; **piano** is soft. Dynamic levels don't correspond to a measured decibel level. An orchestra playing "fortissimo" (which basically means "even louder than forte") is going to be quite a bit louder than a string quartet playing "fortissimo". (See Dynamics (Section 1.3.1) for more of the terms that musicians use to talk about loudness.) Dynamics are more of a performance issue than a music theory issue, so amplitude doesn't need much discussion here.

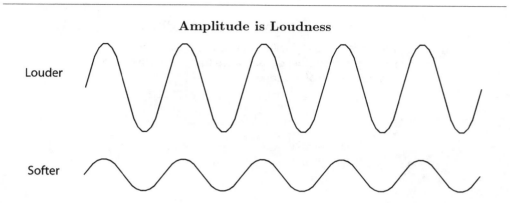

Figure 3.4: The size of a wave (how much it is "piled up" at the high points) is its **amplitude**. For sound waves, the bigger the amplitude, the louder the sound.

3.1.4 Wavelength, Frequency, and Pitch

The aspect of evenly-spaced sound waves that really affects music theory is the spacing between the waves, the distance between, for example, one high point and the next high point. This is the **wavelength**, and it affects the pitch (Section 1.1.3) of the sound; the closer together the waves are, the higher the tone sounds.

All sound waves are travelling at about the same speed - the speed of sound. So waves with a shorter wavelength arrive (at your ear, for example) more often (frequently) than longer waves. This aspect of a sound - how often a peak of a wave goes by, is called **frequency** by scientists and engineers. They measure it in **hertz**, which is how many peaks go by per second. People can hear sounds that range from about 20 to about 17,000 hertz.

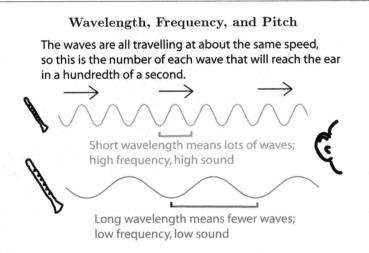

Wavelength, Frequency, and Pitch

The waves are all travelling at about the same speed, so this is the number of each wave that will reach the ear in a hundredth of a second.

Short wavelength means lots of waves; high frequency, high sound

Long wavelength means fewer waves; low frequency, low sound

Figure 3.5: Since the sounds are travelling at about the same speed, the one with the shorter wavelength "waves" more frequently; it has a higher frequency, or pitch. In other words, it sounds higher.

The word that musicians use for frequency is **pitch**. The shorter the wavelength, the higher the frequency, and the higher the pitch, of the sound. In other words, short waves sound high; long waves sound low. Instead of measuring frequencies, musicians name the pitches (Section 1.1.2) that they use most often. They might call a note "middle C" or "second line G" or "the F sharp in the bass clef". (See Octaves and Diatonic Music (Section 4.1) and Tuning Systems (Section 6.2) for more on naming specific frequencies.) These notes have frequencies (Have you heard of the "A 440" that is used as a tuning note?), but the actual frequency of a middle C can vary a little from one orchestra, piano, or performance, to another, so musicians usually find it more useful to talk about note names.

Most musicians cannot name the frequencies of any notes other than the tuning A (440 hertz). The human ear can easily distinguish two pitches that are only one hertz apart when it hears them both, but it is the very rare musician who can hear specifically that a note is 442 hertz rather than 440. So why should we bother talking about frequency, when musicians usually don't? As we will see, the physics of sound waves - and especially frequency - affects the most basic aspects of music, including pitch (Section 1.1.3), tuning (Section 6.2), consonance and dissonance (Section 5.3), harmony (Section 2.5), and timbre (Section 2.2).

3.2 Standing Waves and Musical Instruments[6]

3.2.1 What is a Standing Wave?

Musical tones (pg 101) are produced by musical instruments, or by the voice, which, from a physics perspective, is a very complex wind[7] instrument. So the physics of music is the physics of the kinds of sounds these instruments can make. What kinds of sounds are these? They are tones caused by

---

[6]This content is available online at <http://cnx.org/content/m12413/1.8/>.

[7]"Wind Instruments: Some Basics" <http://cnx.org/content/m12364/latest/>

standing waves produced in or on the instrument. So the properties of these standing waves, which are always produced in very specific groups, or series, have far-reaching effects on music theory.

Most sound waves, including the musical sounds that actually reach our ears, are not standing waves. Normally, when something makes a wave, the wave travels outward, gradually spreading out and losing strength, like the waves moving away from a pebble dropped into a pond.

But when the wave encounters something, it can bounce (reflection) or be bent (refraction). In fact, you can "trap" waves by making them bounce back and forth between two or more surfaces. Musical instruments take advantage of this; they produce pitches (Section 1.1.3) by trapping sound waves.

Why are trapped waves useful for music? Any bunch of sound waves will produce some sort of noise. But to be a **tone** - a sound with a particular pitch (Section 1.1.3) - a group of sound waves has to be very regular, all exactly the same distance apart. That's why we can talk about the frequency (pg 99) and wavelength (pg 99) of tones.

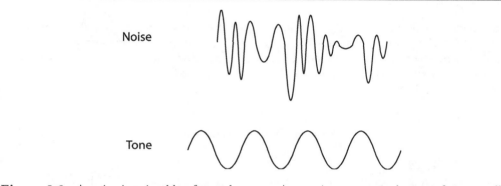

Figure 3.6: A noise is a jumble of sound waves. A tone is a very regular set of waves, all the same size and same distance apart.

So how can you produce a tone? Let's say you have a sound wave trap (for now, don't worry about what it looks like), and you keep sending more sound waves into it. Picture a lot of pebbles being dropped into a very small pool. As the waves start reflecting off the edges of the pond, they interfere with the new waves, making a jumble of waves that partly cancel each other out and mostly just roils the pond - noise.

But what if you could arrange the waves so that reflecting waves, instead of cancelling out the new waves, would reinforce them? The high parts of the reflected waves would meet the high parts of the oncoming waves and make them even higher. The low parts of the reflected waves would meet the low parts of the oncoming waves and make them even lower. Instead of a roiled mess of waves cancelling each other out, you would have a pond of perfectly ordered waves, with high points and low points appearing regularly at the same spots again and again. To help you imagine this, here are animations of a single wave reflecting back and forth[8] and standing waves[9].

This sort of orderliness is actually hard to get from water waves, but relatively easy to get in sound waves, so that several completely different types of sound wave "containers" have been developed into musical instruments. The two most common - strings and hollow tubes - will be discussed below, but first let's finish discussing what makes a good standing wave container, and how this affects music theory.

---

[8]http://cnx.org/content/m12413/latest/ReflectingWave.swf
[9]http://cnx.org/content/m12413/latest/WaterWaves.swf

In order to get the necessary constant reinforcement, the container has to be the perfect size (length) for a certain wavelength, so that waves bouncing back or being produced at each end reinforce each other, instead of interfering with each other and cancelling each other out. And it really helps to keep the container very narrow, so that you don't have to worry about waves bouncing off the sides and complicating things. So you have a bunch of regularly-spaced waves that are trapped, bouncing back and forth in a container that fits their wavelength perfectly. If you could watch these waves, it would not even look as if they are traveling back and forth. Instead, waves would seem to be appearing and disappearing regularly at exactly the same spots, so these trapped waves are called **standing waves**.

> NOTE: Although standing waves are harder to get in water, the phenomenon does apparently happen very rarely in lakes, resulting in freak disasters. You can sometimes get the same effect by pushing a tub of water back and forth, but this is a messy experiment; you'll know you are getting a standing wave when the water suddenly starts sloshing much higher - right out of the tub!

For any narrow "container" of a particular length, there are plenty of possible standing waves that don't fit. But there are also many standing waves that do fit. The longest wave that fits it is called the **fundamental**. It is also called the **first harmonic**. The next longest wave that fits is the **second harmonic**, or the **first overtone**. The next longest wave is the **third harmonic**, or **second overtone**, and so on.

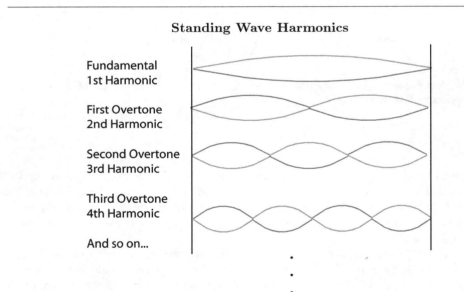

Standing Wave Harmonics

Fundamental
1st Harmonic

First Overtone
2nd Harmonic

Second Overtone
3rd Harmonic

Third Overtone
4th Harmonic

And so on...

Figure 3.7: There is a whole set of standing waves, called **harmonics**, that will fit into any "container" of a specific length. This set of waves is called a **harmonic series**.

Notice that it doesn't matter what the length of the fundamental is; the waves in the second harmonic must be half the length of the first harmonic; that's the only way they'll both "fit". The waves of the third harmonic must be a third the length of the first harmonic, and so on. This has a direct effect on the frequency and pitch of harmonics, and so it affects the basics of music tremendously. To find out more about these subjects, please see Frequency, Wavelength, and Pitch[10], Harmonic Series[11], or Musical Intervals, Frequency, and Ratio[12].

3.2.2 Standing Waves on Strings

You may have noticed an interesting thing in the animation (pg 101) of standing waves: there are spots where the "water" goes up and down a great deal, and other spots where the "water level" doesn't seem to move at all. All standing waves have places, called **nodes**, where there is no wave motion, and **antinodes**, where the wave is largest. It is the placement of the nodes that determines which wavelengths "fit" into a musical instrument "container".

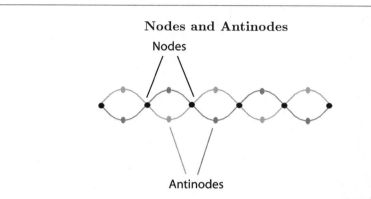

Nodes and Antinodes

Nodes

Antinodes

Figure 3.8: As a standing wave waves back and forth (from the red to the blue position), there are some spots called **nodes** that do not move at all; basically there is no change, no waving up-and-down (or back-and-forth), at these spots. The spots at the biggest part of the wave - where there is the most change during each wave - are called **antinodes**.

One "container" that works very well to produce standing waves is a thin, very taut string that is held tightly in place at both ends. (There were some nice animations of waves on strings available as of this writing at Musemath[13].) Since the string is taut, it vibrates quickly, producing sound waves, if you pluck it, or rub it with a bow. Since it is held tightly at both ends, that means there has to be a node (pg 103) at each end of the string. Instruments that produce sound using strings are called chordophones[14], or simply strings[15].

---

[10]"Frequency, Wavelength, and Pitch" <http://cnx.org/content/m11060/latest/>

[11]"Harmonic Series" <http://cnx.org/content/m11118/latest/>

[12]"Musical Intervals, Frequency, and Ratio" <http://cnx.org/content/m11808/latest/>

[13]http://www.musemath.com

[14]"Classifying Musical Instruments" <http://cnx.org/content/m11896/latest/#s21>

[15]"Orchestral Instruments" <http://cnx.org/content/m11897/latest/#s11>

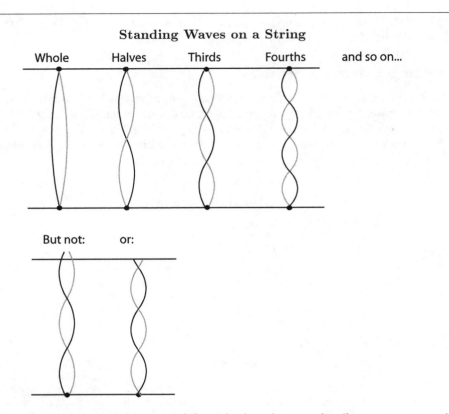

Figure 3.9: A string that's held very tightly at both ends can only vibrate at very particular wavelengths. The whole string can vibrate back and forth. It can vibrate in halves, with a node at the middle of the string as well as each end, or in thirds, fourths, and so on. But any wavelength that doesn't have a node at each end of the string, can't make a standing wave on the string. To get any of those other wavelengths, you need to change the length of the vibrating string. That is what happens when the player holds the string down with a finger, changing the vibrating length of the string and changing where the nodes are.

The fundamental (pg 102) wave is the one that gives a string its pitch (Section 1.1.3). But the string is making all those other possible vibrations, too, all at the same time, so that the actual vibration of the string is pretty complex. The other vibrations (the ones that basically divide the string into halves, thirds and so on) produce a whole series of **harmonics**. We don't hear the harmonics as separate notes, but we do hear them. They are what gives the string its rich, musical, string-like sound - its timbre (Section 2.2). (The sound of a single frequency alone is a much more mechanical, uninteresting, and unmusical sound.) To find out more about harmonics and how they affect a musical sound, see Harmonic Series[16].

Exercise 3.1:

When the string player puts a finger down tightly on the string,

    1.How has the part of the string that vibrates changed?

---

[16]"Harmonic Series" <http://cnx.org/content/m11118/latest/>

2.How does this change the sound waves that the string makes?

3.How does this change the sound that is heard?

(Solution to Exercise 3.1 on p. 114.)

3.2.3 Standing Waves in Wind Instruments

The string disturbs the air molecules around it as it vibrates, producing sound waves in the air. But another great container for standing waves actually holds standing waves of air inside a long, narrow tube. This type of instrument is called an aerophone[17], and the most well-known of this type of instrument are often called wind instruments[18] because, although the instrument itself does vibrate a little, most of the sound is produced by standing waves in the column of air inside the instrument.

If it is possible, have a reed player and a brass player demonstrate to you the sounds that their mouthpieces make without the instrument. This will be a much "noisier" sound, with lots of extra frequencies in it that don't sound very musical. But, when you put the mouthpiece on an instrument shaped like a tube, only some of the sounds the mouthpiece makes are the right length for the tube. Because of feedback from the instrument, the only sound waves that the mouthpiece can produce now are the ones that are just the right length to become **standing waves** in the instrument, and the "noise" is refined into a musical tone.

---

[17]"Classifying Musical Instruments" <http://cnx.org/content/m11896/latest/#s22>

[18]"Orchestral Instruments" <http://cnx.org/content/m11897/latest/#s1>

Standing Waves in Wind Instruments

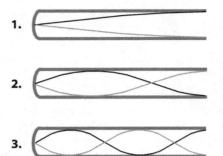

1. Transverse standing waves shown inside tubes actually represent movement back and forth between two extremes.

2. Usually, nodes are shown at closed ends and antinodes at open ends. This represents the air displacement waves; the air cannot move back and forth through the closed end,

3. but it is free to rush back and forth through the open tube end.

The three transverse waves above, for example, represent air movement that goes back and forth between the state on the left and the state on the right (the shorter the arrow, the less the air in that area is moving) :

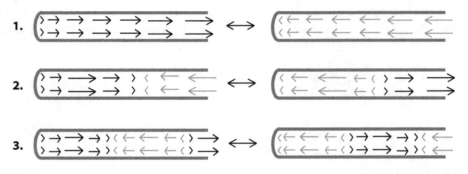

Figure 3.10: Standing Waves in a wind instrument are usually shown as displacement waves, with nodes at closed ends where the air cannot move back-and-forth.

The standing waves in a wind instrument are a little different from a vibrating string. The wave on a string is a **transverse wave**, moving the string back and forth, rather than moving up and down along the string. But the wave inside a tube, since it is a sound wave already, is a **longitudinal wave**; the waves do not go from side to side in the tube. Instead, they form along the length of the tube.

Longitudinal Waves in Pipes

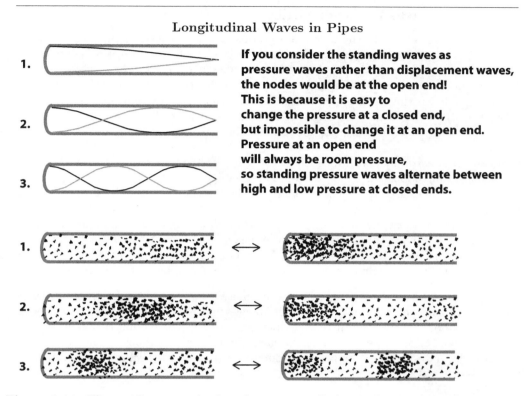

If you consider the standing waves as pressure waves rather than displacement waves, the nodes would be at the open end! This is because it is easy to change the pressure at a closed end, but impossible to change it at an open end. Pressure at an open end will always be room pressure, so standing pressure waves alternate between high and low pressure at closed ends.

Figure 3.11: The standing waves in the tubes are actually longitudinal sound waves. Here the displacement standing waves in Figure 3.10 are shown instead as longitudinal air pressure waves. Each wave would be oscillating back and forth between the state on the right and the one on the left. See Standing Waves in Wind Instruments[19] for more explanation.

The harmonics of wind instruments are also a little more complicated, since there are two basic shapes (cylindrical[20] and conical[21]) that are useful for wind instruments, and they have different properties. The standing-wave tube of a wind instrument also may be open at both ends, or it may be closed at one end (for a mouthpiece, for example), and this also affects the instrument. Please see Standing Waves in Wind Instruments[22] if you want more information on that subject. For the purposes of understanding music theory, however, the important thing about standing waves in winds is this: the harmonic series they produce is essentially the same as the harmonic series on a string. In other words, the second harmonic is still half the length of the fundamental, the third harmonic is one third the length, and so on. (Actually, for reasons explained in Standing Waves in Wind Instruments[23], some harmonics are "missing" in some wind instruments, but this mainly affects the timbre (Section 2.2) and some aspects of playing the instrument. It does not affect the basic relationships in the harmonic series.)

---

[19] "Standing Waves and Wind Instruments" <http://cnx.org/content/m12589/latest/>
[20] "Wind Instruments: Some Basics" <http://cnx.org/content/m12364/latest/#p1c>
[21] "Wind Instruments: Some Basics" <http://cnx.org/content/m12364/latest/#p1c>
[22] "Standing Waves and Wind Instruments" <http://cnx.org/content/m12589/latest/>
[23] "Standing Waves and Wind Instruments" <http://cnx.org/content/m12589/latest/>

3.2.4 Standing Waves in Other Objects

So far we have looked at two of the four main groups of musical instruments: chordophones and aerophones. That leaves membranophones[24] and idiophones[25]. **Membranophones** are instruments in which the sound is produced by making a membrane vibrate; drums are the most familiar example. Most drums do not produce tones; they produce rhythmic "noise" (bursts of irregular waves). Some drums do have pitch (Section 1.1.3), due to complex-patterned standing waves on the membrane that are reinforced in the space inside the drum. This works a little bit like the waves in tubes, above, but the waves produced on membranes, though very interesting, are too complex to be discussed here.

Idiophones are instruments in which the body of the instrument itself, or a part of it, produces the original vibration. Some of these instruments (cymbals, for example) produce simple noise-like sounds when struck. But in some, the shape of the instrument - usually a tube, block, circle, or bell shape - allows the instrument to ring with a standing-wave vibration when you strike it. The standing waves in these carefully-shaped-and-sized idiophones - for example, the blocks on a xylophone - produce pitched tones, but again, the patterns of standing waves in these instruments are a little too complicated for this discussion. If a percussion instrument does produce pitched sounds, however, the reason, again, is that it is mainly producing harmonic-series overtones[26].

> NOTE: Although percussion[27] specializes in "noise"-type sounds, even instruments like snare drums follow the basic physics rule of "bigger instrument makes longer wavelengths and lower sounds". If you can, listen to a percussion player or section that is using snare drums, cymbals, or other percussion of the same type but different sizes. Can you hear the difference that size makes, as opposed to differences in timbre (Section 2.2) produced by different types of drums?

Exercise 3.2:

Some idiophones, like gongs, ring at many different pitches when they are struck. Like most drums, they don't have a particular pitch, but make more of a "noise"-type sound. Other idiophones, though, like xylophones, are designed to ring at more particular frequencies. Can you think of some other percussion instruments that get particular pitches? (Some can get enough different pitches to play a tune.)   *(Solution to Exercise 3.2 on p. 114.)*

3.3 Harmonic Series I: Timbre and Octaves[28]

3.3.1 Introduction

Have you ever wondered how a trumpet[29] plays so many different notes with only three valves[30], or how a bugle plays different notes with no valves at all? Have you ever wondered why an oboe[31] and a flute[32] sound so different, even when they're playing the same note? What is a string player doing when she plays "harmonics"? Why do some notes sound good together while other notes seem to clash with each other? The answers to all of these questions have to do with the harmonic series.

---

[24]"Classifying Musical Instruments" <http://cnx.org/content/m11896/latest/#s23>
[25]"Classifying Musical Instruments" <http://cnx.org/content/m11896/latest/#s24>
[26]"Harmonic Series" <http://cnx.org/content/m11118/latest/>
[27]"Orchestral Instruments" <http://cnx.org/content/m11897/latest/#s14>
[28]This content is available online at <http://cnx.org/content/m13682/1.5/>.
[29]"Trumpets and Cornets" <http://cnx.org/content/m12606/latest/>
[30]"Wind Instruments: Some Basics" <http://cnx.org/content/m12364/latest/#p2f>
[31]"The Oboe and its Relatives" <http://cnx.org/content/m12615/latest/>
[32]"Flutes" <http://cnx.org/content/m12603/latest/>

3.3.2 Physics, Harmonics and Color

Most musical notes are sounds that have a particular pitch (Section 1.1.3). The pitch depends on the main frequency (Section 3.1.4) of the sound; the higher the frequency, and shorter the wavelength (Section 3.1.4), of the sound waves, the higher the pitch is. But musical sounds don't have just one frequency. Sounds that have only one frequency are not very interesting or pretty. They have no more musical color (Section 2.2) than the beeping of a watch alarm. On the other hand, sounds that have too many frequencies, like the sound of glass breaking or of ocean waves crashing on a beach, may be interesting and even pleasant. But they don't have a particular pitch, so they usually aren't considered musical notes.

Frequency and Pitch

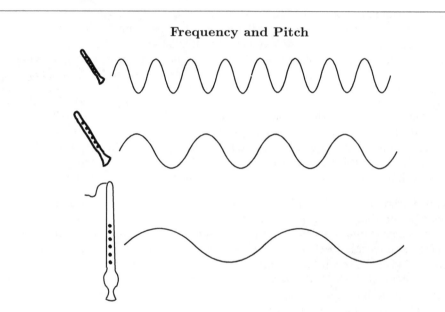

Figure 3.12: The shorter the wavelength, and higher the frequency, the higher the note sounds.

When someone plays or sings a musical tone (pg 101), only a very particular set of frequencies is heard. Each note that comes out of the instrument is actually a smooth mixture of many different pitches. These different pitches are called **harmonics**, and they are blended together so well that you do not hear them as separate notes at all. Instead, the harmonics give the note its color.

What is the color (Section 2.2) of a sound? Say an oboe plays a middle C (pg 120). Then a flute plays the same note at the same dynamic (Section 1.3.1) level as the oboe. It is still easy to tell the two notes apart, because an oboe sounds different from a flute. This difference in the sounds is the **color**, or **timbre** (pronounced "TAM-ber") of the notes. Like a color you see, the color of a sound can be bright and bold or deep and rich. It can be heavy, light, dark, thin, smooth, murky, or clear. Some other words that musicians use to describe the timbre of a sound are: reedy, brassy, piercing, mellow, hollow, focussed, transparent, breathy (pronounced BRETH-ee) or full. Listen to recordings of a violin[33] and a viola[34]. Although these instruments are quite similar, the viola has a noticeably "deeper" and the violin a noticeably "brighter" sound that is not simply a matter of

---

[33]http://cnx.org/content/m13682/latest/timvl.mp3
[34]http://cnx.org/content/m13682/latest/timvla.mp3

the violin playing higher notes. Now listen to the same phrase played by an electric guitar[35], an acoustic guitar with twelve steel strings[36] and an acoustic guitar with six nylon strings[37]. The words musicians use to describe timbre are somewhat subjective, but most musicians would agree with the statement that, compared with each other, the first sound is mellow, the second bright, and the third rich.

Exercise 3.3:

Listen to recordings of different instruments playing alone or playing very prominently above a group. Some suggestions: an unaccompanied violin or cello sonata, a flute, oboe, trumpet, or horn concerto, Asaian or native American flute music, classical guitar, bagpipes, steel pan drums, panpipes, or organ. For each instrument, what "color" words would you use to describe the timbre of each instrument? Use as many words as you can that seem appropriate, and try to think of some that aren't listed above. Do any of the instruments actually make you think of specific shades of color, like fire-engine red or sky blue?

(Solution to Exercise 3.3 on p. 114.)

Where do the harmonics, and the timbre, come from? When a string vibrates, the main pitch you hear is from the vibration of the whole string back and forth. That is the **fundamental**, or first harmonic. But the string also vibrates in halves, in thirds, fourths, and so on. (Please see Standing Waves and Musical Instruments (Section 3.2) for more on the physics of how harmonics are produced.) Each of these fractions also produces a harmonic. The string vibrating in halves produces the second harmonic; vibrating in thirds produces the third harmonic, and so on.

NOTE: This method of naming and numbering harmonics is the most straightforward and least confusing, but there are other ways of naming and numbering harmonics, and this can cause confusion. Some musicians do not consider the fundamental to be a harmonic; it is just the fundamental. In that case, the string halves will give the first harmonic, the string thirds will give the second harmonic and so on. When the fundamental is included in calculations, it is called the first **partial**, and the rest of the harmonics are the second, third, fourth partials and so on. Also, some musicians use the term **overtones** as a synonym for harmonics. For others, however, an overtone is any frequency (not necessarily a harmonic) that can be heard resonating with the fundamental. The sound of a gong or cymbals will include overtones that aren't harmonics; that's why the gong's sound doesn't seem to have as definite a pitch as the vibrating string does. If you are uncertain what someone means when they refer to "the second harmonic" or "overtones", ask for clarification.

---

[35] http://cnx.org/content/m13682/latest/electricGUITARS.wav
[36] http://cnx.org/content/m13682/latest/12stringGUITARS.wav
[37] http://cnx.org/content/m13682/latest/nylonGUITARS.wav

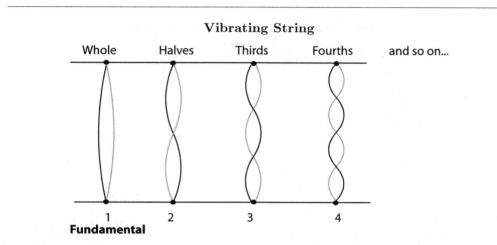

Figure 3.13: The fundamental pitch is produced by the whole string vibrating back and forth. But the string is also vibrating in halves, thirds, quarters, fifths, and so on, producing **harmonics**. All of these vibrations happen at the same time, producing a rich, complex, interesting sound.

A column of air vibrating inside a tube is different from a vibrating string, but the column of air can also vibrate in halves, thirds, fourths, and so on, of the fundamental, so the harmonic series will be the same. So why do different instruments have different timbres? The difference is the relative loudness of all the different harmonics compared to each other. When a clarinet[38] plays a note, perhaps the odd-numbered harmonics are strongest; when a French horn[39] plays the same note, perhaps the fifth and tenth harmonics are the strongest. This is what you hear that allows you to recognize that it is a clarinet or horn that is playing. The relative strength of the harmonics changes from note to note on the same instrument, too; this is the difference you hear between the sound of a clarinet playing low notes and the same clarinet playing high notes.

NOTE: You will find some more extensive information on instruments and harmonics in Standing Waves and Musical Instruments (Section 3.2) and Standing Waves and Wind Instruments[40].

3.3.3 The Harmonic Series

A harmonic series can have any note as its fundamental, so there are many different harmonic series. But the relationship between the frequencies of a harmonic series is always the same. The second harmonic always has exactly half the wavelength (and twice the frequency) of the fundamental; the third harmonic always has exactly a third of the wavelength (and so three times the frequency) of the fundamental, and so on. For more discussion of wavelengths and frequencies, see Acoustics for Music Theory (Section 3.1).

[38]"Clarinets" <http://cnx.org/content/m12604/latest/>
[39]"The French Horn" <http://cnx.org/content/m11617/latest/>
[40]"Standing Waves and Wind Instruments" <http://cnx.org/content/m12589/latest/>

Harmonic Series Wavelengths and Frequencies

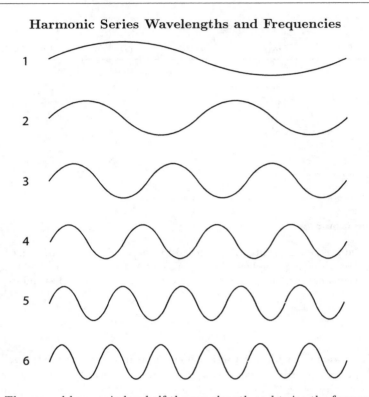

Figure 3.14: The second harmonic has half the wavelength and twice the frequency of the first. The third harmonic has a third the wavelength and three times the frequency of the first. The fourth harmonic has a quarter the wavelength and four times the frequency of the first, and so on. Notice that the fourth harmonic is also twice the frequency of the second harmonic, and the sixth harmonic is also twice the frequency of the third harmonic.

Say someone plays a note, a middle C (pg 120). Now someone else plays the note that is twice the frequency of the middle C. Since this second note was already a harmonic of the first note, the sound waves of the two notes reinforce each other and sound good together. If the second person played instead the note that was just a litle bit more than twice the frequency of the first note, the harmonic series of the two notes would not fit together at all, and the two notes would not sound as good together. There are many combinations of notes that share some harmonics and make a pleasant sound together. They are considered consonant (Section 5.3). Other combinations share fewer or no harmonics and are considered dissonant (Section 5.3) or, when they really clash, simply "out of tune" with each other. The scales (Section 4.8) and harmonies (Section 2.5) of most of the world's musics are based on these physical facts.

> NOTE: In real music, consonance and dissonance also depend on the standard practices of a musical tradition, especially its harmony and tuning (Section 6.2) practices, but these are also often related to the harmonic series.

For example, a note that is twice the frequency of another note is one octave (Section 4.1) higher than the first note. So in the figure above, the second harmonic is one octave higher than the first; the fourth harmonic is one octave higher than the second; and the sixth harmonic is one octave higher than the third.

Exercise 3.4:

1. Which harmonic will be one octave higher than the fourth harmonic?

2. Predict the next four sets of octaves in a harmonic series.

3. What is the pattern that predicts which notes of a harmonic series will be one octave apart?

4. Notes one octave apart are given the same name. So if the first harmonic is a "A", the second and fourth will also be A's. Name three other harmonics that will also be A's.

(Solution to Exercise 3.4 on p. 114.)

A mathematical way to say this is "if two notes are an octave apart, the ratio[41] of their frequencies is two to one (2:1)". Although the notes themselves can be any frequency, the 2:1 ratio is the same for all octaves. Other frequency ratios between two notes also lead to particular pitch relationships between the notes, so we will return to the harmonic series later, after learning to name those pitch relationships, or intervals (Section 4.5).

---

[41]"Musical Intervals, Frequency, and Ratio" <http://cnx.org/content/m11808/latest/>

Solutions to Exercises in Chapter 3

Solution to Exercise 3.1 (p. 104):

1. The part of the string that can vibrate is shorter. The finger becomes the new "end" of the string.

2. The new sound wave is shorter, so its frequency is higher.

3. It sounds higher; it has a higher pitch.

Figure 3.15: When a finger holds the string down tightly, the finger becomes the new end of the vibrating part of the string. The vibrating part of the string is shorter, and the whole set of sound waves it makes is shorter.

Solution to Exercise 3.2 (p. 108):

There are many, but here are some of the most familiar:

- Chimes

- All xylophone-type instruments, such as marimba, vibraphone, and glockenspiel

- Handbells and other tuned bells

- Steel pan drums

Solution to Exercise 3.3 (p. 110):
  Although trained musicians will generally agree that a particular sound is reedy, thin, or full, there are no hard-and-fast, right-or-wrong answers to this exercise.

Solution to Exercise 3.4 (p. 113):

1. The eighth harmonic

2. The fifth and tenth harmonics; the sixth and twelfth harmonics; the seventh and fourteenth harmonics; and the eighth and sixteenth harmonics

3. The note that is one octave higher than a harmonic is also a harmonic, and its number in the harmonic series is twice (2 X) the number of the first note.

4. The eighth, sixteenth, and thirty-second harmonics will also be A's.

Chapter 4

Notes and Scales

4.1 Octaves and the Major-Minor Tonal System[1]

4.1.1 Where Octaves Come From

Musical notes, like all sounds, are made of sound waves. The sound waves that make musical notes are very evenly-spaced waves, and the qualities of these regular waves - for example how big they are or how far apart they are - affect the sound of the note. A note can be high or low, depending on how often (how frequently) one of its waves arrives at your ear. When scientists and engineers talk about how high or low a sound is, they talk about its frequency[2]. The higher the **frequency** of a note, the higher it sounds. They can measure the frequency of notes, and like most measurements, these will be numbers, like "440 vibrations per second."

---

[1]This content is available online at <http://cnx.org/content/m10862/2.18/>.

[2]"Frequency, Wavelength, and Pitch" <http://cnx.org/content/m11060/latest/#p1e>

High and Low Frequencies

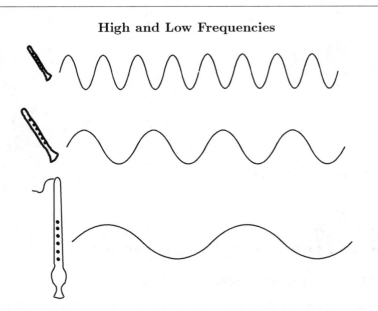

Figure 4.1: A sound that has a shorter wavelength has a higher frequency and a higher pitch.

But people have been making music and talking about music since long before we knew that sounds were waves with frequencies. So when musicians talk about how high or low a note sounds, they usually don't talk about frequency; they talk about the note's pitch (Section 1.1.3). And instead of numbers, they give the notes names, like "C". (For example, musicians call the note with frequency "440 vibrations per second" an "A".)

But to see where octaves come from, let's talk about frequencies a little more. Imagine a few men are singing a song together. Nobody is singing harmony; they are all singing the same pitch - the same frequency - for each note.

Now some women join in the song. They can't sing where the men are singing; that's too low for their voices. Instead they sing notes that are exactly double the frequency that the men are singing. That means their note has exactly two waves for each one wave that the men's note has. These two frequencies fit so well together that it sounds like the women are singing the same notes as the men, in the same key (Section 4.3). They are just singing them one octave higher. *Any note that is twice the frequency of another note is one **octave** higher.*

Notes that are one octave apart are so closely related to each other that musicians give them the same name. A note that is an octave higher or lower than a note named "C natural" will also be named "C natural". A note that is one (or more) octaves higher or lower than an "F sharp" will also be an "F sharp". (For more discussion of how notes are related because of their frequencies, see The Harmonic Series[3], Standing Waves and Musical Instruments (Section 3.2), and Standing Waves and Wind Instruments[4].)

---

[3]"Harmonic Series" <http://cnx.org/content/m11118/latest/>
[4]"Standing Waves and Wind Instruments" <http://cnx.org/content/m12589/latest/>

Octave Frequencies

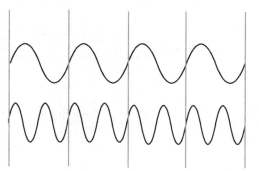

Figure 4.2: When two notes are one octave apart, one has a frequency exactly two times higher than the other - it has twice as many waves. These waves fit together so well, in the instrument, and in the air, and in your ears, that they sound almost like different versions of the same note.

4.1.2 Naming Octaves

The notes in different octaves are so closely related that when musicians talk about a note, a "G" for example, it often doesn't matter which G they are talking about. We can talk about the "F sharp" in a G major scale (Section 4.3) without mentioning which octave the scale or the F sharp are in, because the scale is the same in every octave. Because of this, many discussions of music theory don't bother naming octaves. Informally, musicians often speak of "the B on the staff" or the "A above the staff", if it's clear which staff (Section 1.1.1) they're talking about.

But there are also two formal systems for naming the notes in a particular octave. Many musicians use **Helmholtz** notation. Others prefer **scientific pitch notation**, which simply labels the octaves with numbers, starting with C1 for the lowest C on a full-sized keyboard. Figure 3 shows the names of the octaves most commonly used in music.

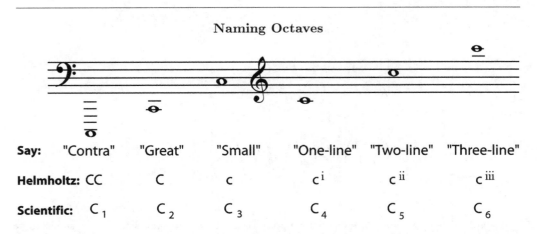

Figure 4.3: The octaves are named from one C to the next higher C. For example, all the notes in between "one line c" and "two line c" are "one line" notes.

The octave below contra can be labelled CCC or Co; higher octaves can be labelled with higher numbers or more lines. Octaves are named from one C to the next higher C. For example, all the notes between "great C" and "small C" are "great". *One-line c is also often called "middle C". No other notes are called "middle", only the C.*

Example 4.1:

Naming Notes within a Particular Octave

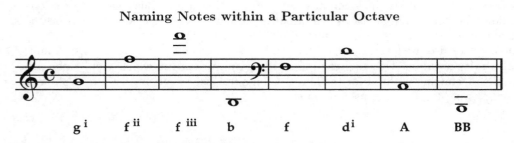

Figure 4.4: Each note is considered to be in the same octave as the C below it.

Exercise 4.1:

Give the correct octave name for each note.

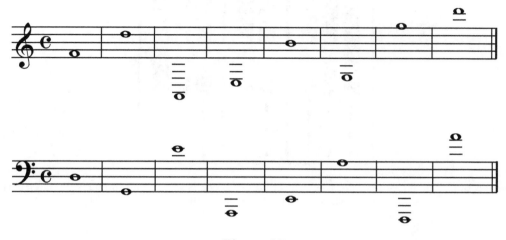

Figure 4.5

(Solution to Exercise 4.1 on p. 162.)

4.1.3 Dividing the Octave into Scales

The word "octave" comes from a Latin root meaning "eight". It seems an odd name for a frequency that is two times, not eight times, higher. The octave was named by musicians who were more interested in how octaves are divided into scales, than in how their frequencies are related. Octaves aren't the only notes that sound good together. The people in different musical traditions have different ideas about what notes they think sound best together. In the Western (Section 2.8) musical tradition - which includes most familiar music from Europe and the Americas - the octave is divided up into twelve equally spaced notes. If you play all twelve of these notes within one octave you are playing a chromatic scale (pg 123). Other musical traditions - traditional Chinese music for example - have divided the octave differently and so they use different scales. (Please see Major Keys and Scales (Section 4.3), Minor Keys and Scales (Section 4.4), and Scales that aren't Major or Minor (Section 4.8) for more about this.)

You may be thinking "OK, that's twelve notes; that still has nothing to do with the number eight", but out of those twelve notes, only seven are used in any particular major (Section 4.3) or minor (Section 4.4) scale. Add the first note of the next octave, so that you have that a "complete"-sounding scale ("do-re-mi-fa-so-la-ti" and then "do" again), and you have the eight notes of the **octave**. These are the **diatonic** scales, and they are the basis of most Western (Section 2.8) music.

Now take a look at the piano keyboard. Only seven letter names are used to name notes: A, B, C, D, E, F, and G. The eighth note would, of course, be the next A, beginning the next octave. To name the other notes, the notes on the black piano keys, you have to use a sharp or flat (Section 1.1.3) sign.

Keyboard

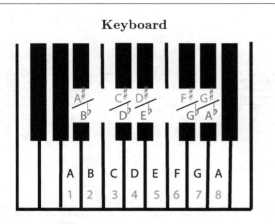

Figure 4.6: The white keys are the natural notes. Black keys can only be named using sharps or flats. The pattern repeats at the eighth tone of a scale, the octave.

Whether it is a popular song, a classical symphony, or an old folk tune, most of the music that feels comfortable and familiar (to Western listeners) is based on either a major or minor scale. It is **tonal** music that mostly uses only seven of the notes within an octave: only one of the possible A's (A sharp, A natural, or A flat), one of the possible B's (B sharp, B natural, or B flat), and so on. The other notes in the chromatic scale are (usually) used sparingly to add interest or to (temporarily) change the key in the middle of the music. For more on the keys and scales that are the basis of tonal music, see Major Keys and Scales (Section 4.3) and Minor Keys and Scales (Section 4.4).

4.2 Half Steps and Whole Steps[5]

The **pitch** of a note is how high or low it sounds. Musicians often find it useful to talk about how much higher or lower one note is than another. This distance between two pitches is called the **interval** between them. In Western music (Section 2.8), the small interval from one note to the next closest note higher or lower is called a **half step** or **semi-tone**.

---

[5]This content is available online at <http://cnx.org/content/m10866/2.17/>.

Half Steps

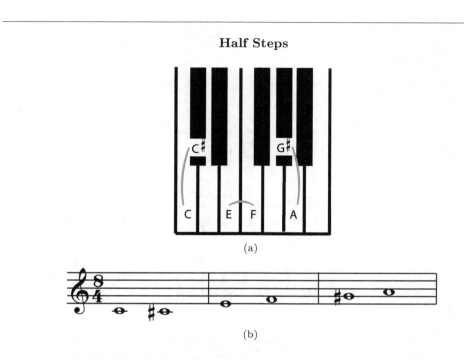

(a)

(b)

Figure 4.7: Three half-step intervals: between C and C sharp (or D flat); between E and F; and between G sharp (or A flat) and A.

Listen[6] to the half steps in Figure 4.7.

The intervals in Figure 4.7 look different on a staff (Section 1.1.1); sometimes they are on the same line, sometimes not. But it is clear at the keyboard that in each case there is no note in between them.

So a scale (Section 4.3) that goes up or down by half steps, a **chromatic scale**, plays all the notes on both the white and black keys of a piano. It also plays all the notes easily available on most Western (Section 2.8) instruments. (A few instruments, like trombone[7] and violin[8], can easily play pitches that aren't in the chromatic scale, but even they usually don't.)

One Octave Chromatic Scale

Figure 4.8: All intervals in a *chromatic scale* are half steps. The result is a scale that plays all the notes easily available on most instruments.

---

[6]http://cnx.org/content/m10866/latest/6f.mid
[7]"Trombones" <http://cnx.org/content/m12602/latest/>
[8]"Introduction to the Violin and FAQ" <http://cnx.org/content/m13437/latest/>

Listen[9] to a chromatic scale.

If you go up or down two half steps from one note to another, then those notes are a **whole step**, or **whole tone** apart.

Whole Steps

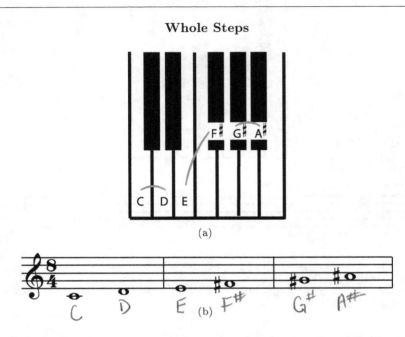

(a)

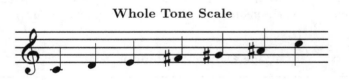

Figure 4.9: Three whole step intervals: between C and D; between E and F sharp; and between G sharp and A sharp (or A flat and B flat).

A **whole tone scale**, a scale made only of whole steps, sounds very different from a chromatic scale.

Whole Tone Scale

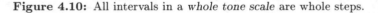

Figure 4.10: All intervals in a *whole tone scale* are whole steps.

Listen[10] to a whole tone scale.

You can count any number of whole steps or half steps between notes; just remember to count all sharp or flat notes (the black keys on a keyboard) as well as all the natural notes (the white keys) that are in between.

[9]http://cnx.org/content/m10866/latest/6a.mid
[10]http://cnx.org/content/m10866/latest/6b.mid

Example 4.2:

The interval between C and the F above it is 5 half steps, or two and a half steps.

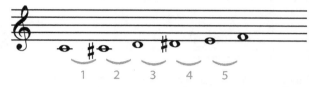

Figure 4.11: Going from C up to F takes five half steps.

Exercise 4.2:

Identify the intervals below in terms of half steps and whole steps. If you have trouble keeping track of the notes, use a piano keyboard, a written chromatic scale, or the chromatic fingerings for your instrument to count half steps.

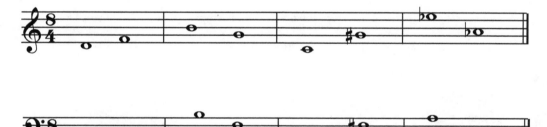

Figure 4.12

(Solution to Exercise 4.2 on p. 162.)

Exercise 4.3:

Fill in the second note of the interval indicated in each measure. If you need staff paper for this exercise, you can print out this staff paper[11] PDF file.

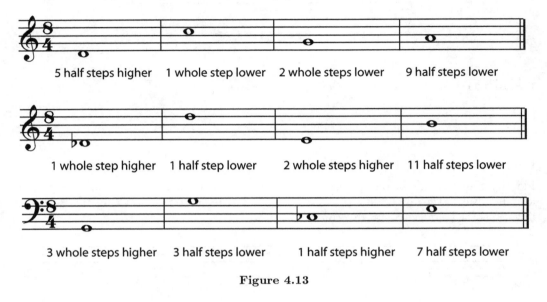

Figure 4.13

(Solution to Exercise 4.3 on p. 163.)

4.3 Major Keys and Scales[12]

The simple, sing-along, nursery rhymes and folk songs we learn as children, the cheerful, toe-tapping pop and rock we dance to, the uplifting sounds of a symphony: most music in a major key has a bright sound that people often describe as cheerful, inspiring, exciting, or just plain fun.

Music in a particular **key** tends to use only some of the many possible notes available; these notes are listed in the **scale** associated with that key. The notes that a major key uses tend to build "bright"-sounding major chords. They also give a strong feeling of having a tonal center (pg 127), a note or chord that feels like "home" in that key. The "bright"-sounding major chords and the strong feeling of tonality are what give major keys their pleasant moods.

Exercise 4.4:

Listen to these excerpts. Three are in a major key and two in a minor key. Can you tell which is which simply by listening?

- 1.[13]
- 2.[14]
- 3.[15]

---

[11] http://cnx.org/content/m10866/latest/staffpaper1.pdf

[12] This content is available online at <http://cnx.org/content/m10851/2.18/>.

[13] http://cnx.org/content/m10851/latest/Guitar1.mp3

[14] http://cnx.org/content/m10851/latest/Guitar2.mp3

[15] http://cnx.org/content/m10851/latest/Guitar3.mp3

- 4.[16]
- 5.[17]

(Solution to Exercise 4.4 on p. 163.)

4.3.1 Tonal Center

A scale starts with the note that names the key. This note is the **tonal center** of that key, the note where music in that key feels "at rest". It is also called the **tonic**, and it's the "do" in "do-re-mi". For example, music in the key of A major almost always ends on an A major chord, the chord (Chords) built on the note A. It often also begins on that chord, returns to that chord often, and features a melody and a bass line that also return to the note A often enough that listeners will know where the tonal center of the music is, even if they don't realize that they know it. (For more information about the tonic chord and its relationship to other chords in a key, please see Beginning Harmonic Analysis (Section 5.5).)

> **Example 4.3:**
>
> Listen to these examples. Can you hear that they do not feel "done" until the final tonic is played?
>
> - Example A[18]
> - Example B[19]

4.3.2 Major Scales

To find the rest of the notes in a major key, start at the tonic and go up following this pattern: *whole step, whole step, half step, whole step, whole step, whole step, half step*. This will take you to the tonic one octave higher than where you began, and includes all the notes in the key in that octave.

---

[16]http://cnx.org/content/m10851/latest/Tanz.mp3
[17]http://cnx.org/content/m10851/latest/Greensleeves.mp3
[18]http://cnx.org/content/m10851/latest/Tonal1.MID
[19]http://cnx.org/content/m10851/latest/tonic2.MID

Example 4.4:

These major scales all follow the same pattern of whole steps and half steps. They have different sets of notes because the pattern starts on different notes.

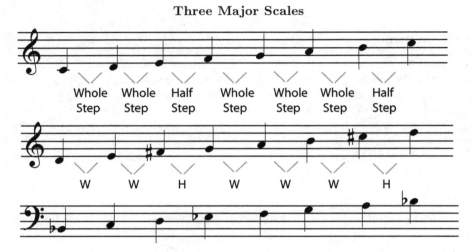

Three Major Scales

Figure 4.14: All major scales have the same pattern of half steps and whole steps, beginning on the note that names the scale - the tonic (pg 127).

Listen to the difference between the C major[20], D major[21], and B flat major[22] scales.

Exercise 4.5:

For each note below, write a major scale, one octave, ascending (going up), beginning on that note. If you're not sure whether a note should be written as a flat, sharp, or natural, remember that you won't ever skip a line or space, or write two notes of the scale on the same line or space. If you need help keeping track of half steps, use a keyboard, a picture of a keyboard (Figure 4.6), a written chromatic scale (pg 123), or the chromatic scale fingerings for your instrument. If you need more information about half steps and whole steps, see Half Steps and Whole Steps (Section 4.2).

If you need staff paper for this exercise, you can print out this staff paper[23] PDF file.

---

[20]http://cnx.org/content/m10851/latest/tonmjC.mp3
[21]http://cnx.org/content/m10851/latest/tonmjD.mp3
[22]http://cnx.org/content/m10851/latest/tonmjBflat.mp3
[23]http://cnx.org/content/m10851/latest/staffpaper1.pdf

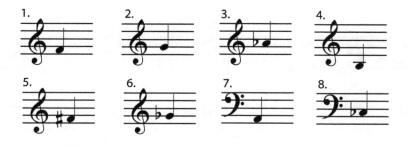

Figure 4.15

(Solution to Exercise 4.5 on p. 164.)

In the examples above, the sharps and flats are written next to the notes. In common notation, the sharps and flats *that belong in the key* will be written at the beginning of each staff, in the **key signature**. For more practice identifying keys and writing key signatures, please see Key Signature (Section 1.1.4). For more information about how keys are related to each other, please see The Circle of Fifths (Section 4.7).

4.3.3 Music in Different Keys

What difference does key make? Since the major scales all follow the same pattern, they all sound very much alike. Here is a folk tune ("The Saucy Sailor") written in D major and in F major.

(a)

(b)

Figure 4.16: The same tune looks very different written in two different major keys.

Listen to this tune in D major[24] and in F major[25]. The music may look quite different, but the only difference when you listen is that one sounds higher than the other. So why bother with different keys at all? Before equal temperament (Section 6.2.3.2) became the standard tuning system, major keys sounded more different from each other than they do now. Even now, there are subtle differences between the sound of a piece in one key or another, mostly because of differences in the timbre (Section 2.2) of various notes on the instruments or voices involved. But today the most common reason to choose a particular key is simply that the music is easiest to sing or play in that key. (Please see Transposition (Section 6.4) for more about choosing keys.)

4.4 Minor Keys and Scales[26]

4.4.1 Music in a Minor Key

Each major key (Section 4.3) uses a different set of notes (Section 1.2.1) (its major scale (Section 4.3.2)). In each major scale, however, the notes are arranged in the same major scale pattern and build the same types of chords that have the same relationships with each other. (See Beginning Harmonic Analysis (Section 5.5) for more on this.) So music that is in, for example, C major, will not sound significantly different from music that is in, say, D major. But music that is in D minor will have a different quality, because the notes in the minor scale follow a different pattern and so have different relationships with each other. Music in minor keys has a different sound and emotional feel, and develops differently harmonically. So you can't, for example, transpose (Section 6.4)

---

[24]http://cnx.org/content/m10851/latest/SaucySailorD.MID
[25]http://cnx.org/content/m10851/latest/SaucySailorF.MID
[26]This content is available online at <http://cnx.org/content/m10856/2.18/>.

a piece from C major to D minor (or even to C minor) without changing it a great deal. Music that is in a minor key is sometimes described as sounding more solemn, sad, mysterious, or ominous than music that is in a major key. To hear some simple examples in both major and minor keys, see Major Keys and Scales (Exercise 4.4).

4.4.2 Minor Scales

Minor scales sound different from major scales because they are based on a different pattern of intervals (Section 4.5). Just as it did in major scales, starting the minor scale pattern on a different note will give you a different key signature (Section 1.1.4), a different set of sharps or flats. The scale that is created by playing all the notes in a minor key signature is a **natural minor scale**. To create a natural minor scale, start on the tonic note (pg 127) and go up the scale using the interval pattern: *whole step, half step, whole step, whole step, half step, whole step, whole step.*

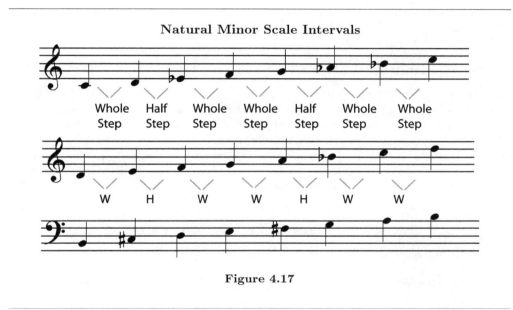

Figure 4.17

Listen[27] to these minor scales.

Exercise 4.6:

For each note below, write a natural minor scale, one octave, ascending (going up) beginning on that note. If you need staff paper, you may print the staff paper[28] PDF file.

[27]http://cnx.org/content/m10856/latest/3a.mid
[28]http://cnx.org/content/m10856/latest/staffpaper1.pdf

Figure 4.18

(*Solution to Exercise 4.6 on p. 165.*)

4.4.3 Relative Minor and Major Keys

Each minor key shares a key signature (Section 1.1.4) with a major key. A minor key is called the **relative minor** of the major key that has the same key signature. Even though they have the same key signature, a minor key and its **relative major** sound very different. They have different tonal centers (pg 127), and each will feature melodies, harmonies, and chord progressions (Chords) built around their (different) tonal centers. In fact, certain strategic accidentals (pg 17) are very useful in helping establish a strong tonal center in a minor key. These useful accidentals are featured in the melodic minor (Section 4.4.3) and harmonic minor (Section 4.4.3) scales.

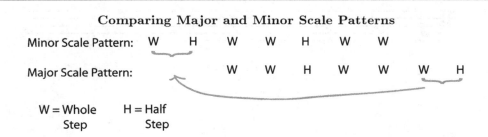

Figure 4.19: The interval patterns for major and natural minor scales are basically the same pattern starting at different points.

It is easy to predict where the relative minor of a major key can be found. Notice that the pattern for minor scales overlaps the pattern for major scales. In other words, they are the same pattern starting in a different place. (If the patterns were very different, minor key signatures would not be the same as major key signatures.) The pattern for the minor scale starts a half step plus a whole step lower than the major scale pattern, so *a relative minor is always three half steps lower than its relative major.* For example, C minor has the same key signature as E flat major, since E flat is a minor third higher than C.

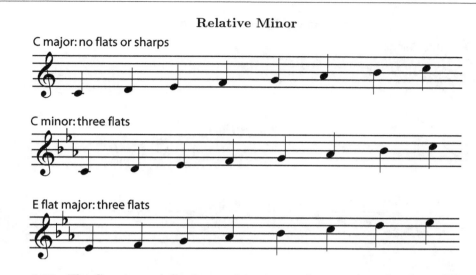

Figure 4.20: The C major and C minor scales start on the same note, but have different key signatures. C minor and E flat major start on different notes, but have the same key signature. C minor is the **relative minor** of E flat major.

Exercise 4.7:

What are the relative majors of the minor keys in Figure 4.18? *(Solution to Exercise 4.7 on p. 166.)*

4.4.4 Harmonic and Melodic Minor Scales

All of the scales above are **natural minor scales**. They contain only the notes in the minor key signature. There are two other kinds of minor scales that are commonly used, both of which include notes that are not in the key signature. The **harmonic minor scale** *raises the seventh note of the scale by one half step, whether you are going up or down the scale.* Harmonies in minor keys often use this raised seventh tone in order to make the music feel more strongly centered on the tonic (pg 127). (Please see Beginning Harmonic Analysis (Section 5.5.5) for more about this.) In the **melodic minor scale**, *the sixth and seventh notes of the scale are each raised by one half step when going up the scale, but return to the natural minor when going down the scale.* Melodies in minor keys often use this particular pattern of accidentals (pg 17), so instrumentalists find it useful to practice melodic minor scales.

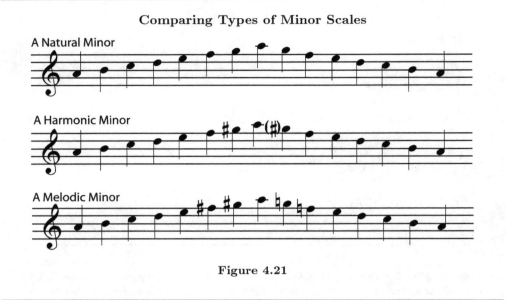

Figure 4.21

Listen to the differences between the natural minor[29], harmonic minor[30], and melodic minor[31] scales.

Exercise 4.8:

Rewrite each scale from Figure 4.18 as an ascending harmonic minor scale.   *(Solution to Exercise 4.8 on p. 166.)*

Exercise 4.9:

Rewrite each scale from Figure 4.18 as an ascending and descending melodic minor scale. *(Solution to Exercise 4.9 on p. 167.)*

4.4.5 Jazz and "Dorian Minor"

Major and minor scales are traditionally the basis for Western Music (Section 2.8), but jazz theory also recognizes other scales, based on the medieval church modes (pg 236), which are very useful for improvisation. One of the most useful of these is the scale based on the dorian mode, which is often called the **dorian minor**, since it has a basically minor sound. Like any minor scale, dorian minor may start on any note, but like dorian mode, it is often illustrated as natural notes beginning on d.

---

[29]http://cnx.org/content/m10856/latest/tonminnatural.mp3
[30]http://cnx.org/content/m10856/latest/tonminharmonic.mp3
[31]http://cnx.org/content/m10856/latest/tonminmelodic.mp3

Dorian Minor

W   H   W   W   W   H   W

Figure 4.22: The "dorian minor" can be written as a scale of natural notes starting on d. Any scale with this interval pattern can be called a "dorian minor scale".

Comparing this scale to the natural minor scale makes it easy to see why the dorian mode sounds minor; only one note is different.

Comparing Dorian and Natural Minors

Natural

Dorian

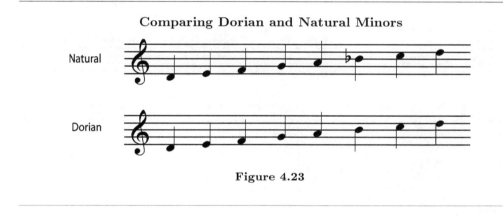

Figure 4.23

You may find it helpful to notice that the "relative major" of the Dorian begins one whole step lower. (So, for example, D Dorian has the same key signature as C major.) In fact, the reason that Dorian is so useful in jazz is that it is the scale used for improvising while a ii chord (Section 5.5.2) is being played (for example, while a d minor chord is played in the key of C major), a chord which is very common in jazz. (See Beginning Harmonic Analysis (Section 5.5) for more about how chords are classified within a key.) The student who is interested in modal jazz will eventually become acquainted with all of the **modal scales**. Each of these is named for the medieval church mode (pg 236) which has the same interval pattern, and each can be used with a different chord within the key. Dorian is included here only to explain the common jazz reference to the "dorian minor" and to give notice to students that the jazz approach to scales can be quite different from the traditional classical approach.

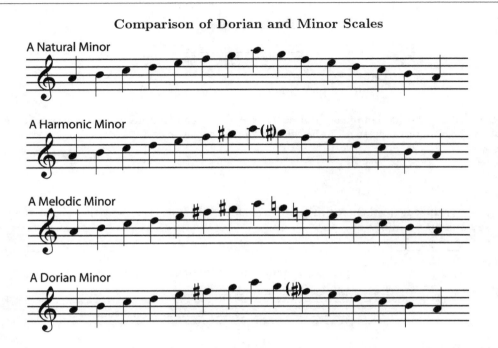

Figure 4.24: You may also find it useful to compare the dorian with the minor scales from Figure 4.21. Notice in particular the relationship of the altered notes in the harmonic, melodic, and dorian minors.

4.5 Interval[32]

4.5.1 The Distance Between Pitches

The **interval** between two notes is the distance between the two pitches (Section 1.1.3) - in other words, how much higher or lower one note is than the other. This concept is so important that it is almost impossible to talk about scales (Section 4.3), chords (Chords), harmonic progression (Chords), cadence (Section 5.6), or dissonance (Section 5.3) without referring to intervals. So if you want to learn music theory, it would be a good idea to spend some time getting comfortable with the concepts below and practicing identifying intervals.

Scientists usually describe the distance between two pitches in terms of the difference between their frequencies[33]. Musicians find it more useful to talk about interval. Intervals can be described using half steps and whole steps (Section 4.2). For example, you can say "B natural is a half step below C natural", or "E flat is a step and a half above C natural". But when we talk about larger intervals in the major/minor system (Section 4.1), there is a more convenient and descriptive way to name them.

---

[32]This content is available online at <http://cnx.org/content/m10867/2.21/>.

[33]"Frequency, Wavelength, and Pitch" <http://cnx.org/content/m11060/latest/>

4.5.2 Naming Intervals

The first step in naming the interval is to find the distance between the notes *as they are written on the staff*. Count every line and every space in between the notes, as well as the lines or spaces that the notes are on. This gives you the number for the interval.

Example 4.5:

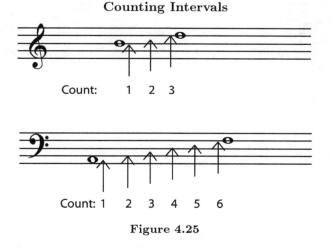

Figure 4.25

To find the interval, count the lines or spaces that the two notes are on as well as all the lines or spaces in between. The interval between B and D is a third. The interval between A and F is a sixth. Note that, at this stage, key signature (Section 1.1.4), clef (Section 1.1.2), and accidentals (pg 17) do not matter at all.

The **simple intervals** are one octave or smaller.

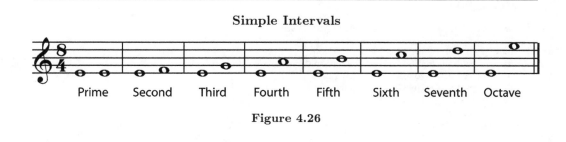

Figure 4.26

If you like you can listen to each interval as written in Figure 4.26: prime[34], second[35], third[36], fourth[37], fifth[38], sixth[39], seventh[40], octave[41].

Compound intervals are larger than an octave.

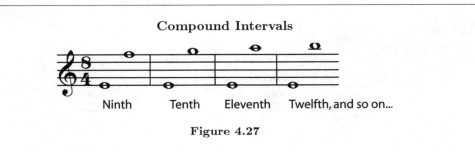

Compound Intervals

Ninth   Tenth   Eleventh   Twelfth, and so on...

Figure 4.27

Listen to the compound intervals in Figure 4.27: ninth[42], tenth[43], eleventh[44].

Exercise 4.10:

Name the intervals.

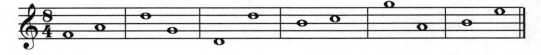

Figure 4.28

(Solution to Exercise 4.10 on p. 167.)

Exercise 4.11:

Write a note that will give the named interval.

---

[34]http://cnx.org/content/m10867/latest/prime.mid
[35]http://cnx.org/content/m10867/latest/second.mid
[36]http://cnx.org/content/m10867/latest/third.mid
[37]http://cnx.org/content/m10867/latest/fourht.mid
[38]http://cnx.org/content/m10867/latest/fifth.mid
[39]http://cnx.org/content/m10867/latest/sixth.mid
[40]http://cnx.org/content/m10867/latest/seventh.mid
[41]http://cnx.org/content/m10867/latest/octave.mid
[42]http://cnx.org/content/m10867/latest/ninth.mid
[43]http://cnx.org/content/m10867/latest/tenth.mid
[44]http://cnx.org/content/m10867/latest/eleventh.mid

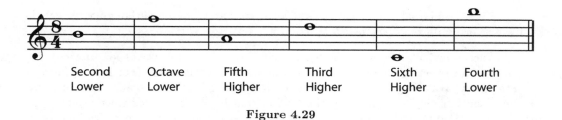

Second Lower   Octave Lower   Fifth Higher   Third Higher   Sixth Higher   Fourth Lower

Figure 4.29

(Solution to Exercise 4.11 on p. 168.)

4.5.3 Classifying Intervals

So far, the actual distance, in half-steps, between the two notes has not mattered. But a third made up of three half-steps sounds different from a third made up of four half-steps. And a fifth made up of seven half-steps sounds very different from one of only six half-steps. So in the second step of identifying an interval, clef (Section 1.1.2), key signature (Section 1.1.4), and accidentals (pg 17) become important.

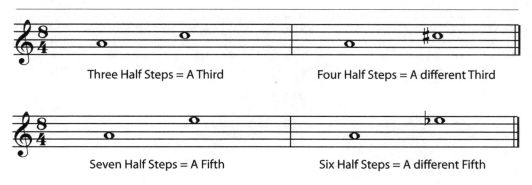

Three Half Steps = A Third   Four Half Steps = A different Third

Seven Half Steps = A Fifth   Six Half Steps = A different Fifth

Figure 4.30: A to C natural and A to C sharp are both thirds, but A to C sharp is a larger interval, with a different sound. The difference between the intervals A to E natural and A to E flat is even more noticeable.

Listen to the differences in the thirds[45] and the fifths[46] in Figure 4.30.

So the second step to naming an interval is to classify it based on the number of half steps (Section 4.2) in the interval. Familiarity with the chromatic scale (pg 123) is necessary to do this accurately.

4.5.3.1 Perfect Intervals

Primes, octaves, fourths, and fifths can be **perfect** intervals.

---

[45] http://cnx.org/content/m10867/latest/twothirds.mid
[46] http://cnx.org/content/m10867/latest/twofifths.mid

NOTE: These intervals *are never classified as major or minor*, although they can be augmented or diminished (see below (Section 4.5.3.3)).

What makes these particular intervals perfect? The physics of sound waves (**acoustics**) shows us that the notes of a perfect interval are very closely related to each other. (For more information on this, see Frequency, Wavelength, and Pitch[47] and Harmonic Series[48].) Because they are so closely related, they sound particularly good together, a fact that has been noticed since at least the times of classical Greece, and probably even longer. (Both the octave and the perfect fifth have prominent positions in most of the world's musical traditions.) Because they sound so closely related to each other, they have been given the name "perfect" intervals.

NOTE: Actually, modern equal temperament (Section 6.2.3.2) tuning does not give the harmonic-series-based pure (Section 6.2.2.1) perfect fourths and fifths. For the music-theory purpose of identifying intervals, this does not matter. To learn more about how tuning affects intervals as they are actually played, see Tuning Systems (Section 6.2).

A perfect prime is also called a **unison**. It is two notes that are the same pitch (Section 1.1.3). A perfect octave is the "same" note an octave (Section 4.1) - 12 half-steps - higher or lower. A **perfect 5th** is 7 half-steps. A **perfect fourth** is 5 half-steps.

Example 4.6:

Perfect Intervals

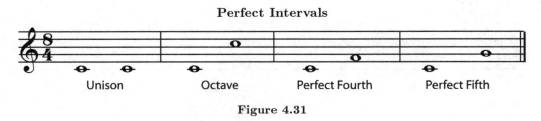

Figure 4.31

Listen to the octave[49], perfect fourth[50], and perfect fifth[51].

4.5.3.2 Major and Minor Intervals

Seconds, thirds, sixths, and sevenths can be **major intervals** or **minor intervals**. The minor interval is always a half-step smaller than the major interval.

Major and Minor Intervals

- 1 half-step = minor second (m2)

- 2 half-steps = major second (M2)

- 3 half-steps = minor third (m3)

- 4 half-steps = major third (M3)

---

[47]"Frequency, Wavelength, and Pitch" <http://cnx.org/content/m11060/latest/>
[48]"Harmonic Series" <http://cnx.org/content/m11118/latest/>
[49]http://cnx.org/content/m10867/latest/P8.mp3
[50]http://cnx.org/content/m10867/latest/P4.mp3
[51]http://cnx.org/content/m10867/latest/P5.mp3

- 8 half-steps = minor sixth (m6)

- 9 half-steps = major sixth (M6)

- 10 half-steps = minor seventh (m7)

- 11 half-steps = major seventh (M7)

Example 4.7:

Major and Minor Intervals

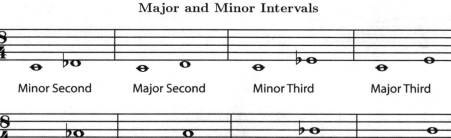

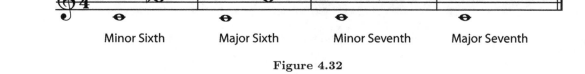

Figure 4.32

Listen to the minor second[52], major second[53], minor third[54], major third[55], minor sixth[56], major sixth[57], minor seventh[58], and major seventh[59].

[52] http://cnx.org/content/m10867/latest/min2.mp3
[53] http://cnx.org/content/m10867/latest/M2.mp3
[54] http://cnx.org/content/m10867/latest/min3.mp3
[55] http://cnx.org/content/m10867/latest/M3.mp3
[56] http://cnx.org/content/m10867/latest/min6.mp3
[57] http://cnx.org/content/m10867/latest/M6.mp3
[58] http://cnx.org/content/m10867/latest/min7.mp3
[59] http://cnx.org/content/m10867/latest/M7.mp3

Exercise 4.12:

Give the complete name for each interval.

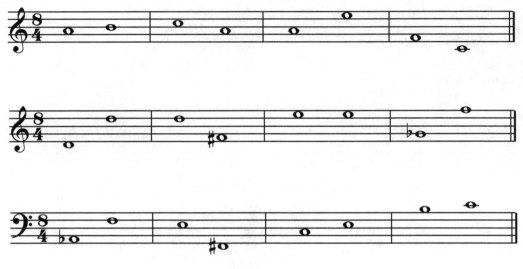

Figure 4.33

(Solution to Exercise 4.12 on p. 168.)

Exercise 4.13:

Fill in the second note of the interval given.

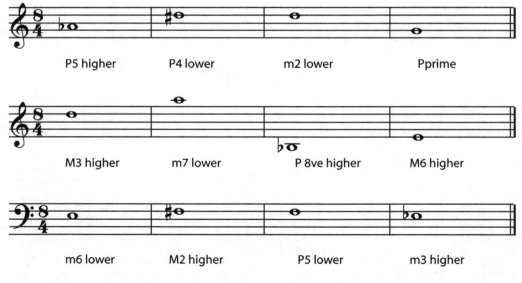

Figure 4.34

(Solution to Exercise 4.13 on p. 169.)

4.5.3.3 Augmented and Diminished Intervals

If an interval is a half-step larger than a perfect or a major interval, it is called **augmented**. An interval that is a half-step smaller than a perfect or a minor interval is called **diminished**. A double sharp (pg 17) or double flat (pg 17) is sometimes needed to write an augmented or diminished interval correctly. Always remember, though, that it is the actual distance in half steps between the notes that determines the type of interval, not whether the notes are written as natural, sharp, or double-sharp.

Example 4.8:

Some Diminished and Augmented Intervals

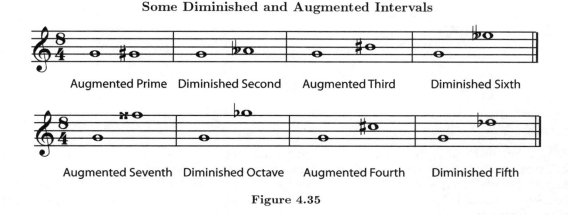

Figure 4.35

Listen to the augmented prime[60], diminished second[61], augmented third[62], diminished sixth[63], augmented seventh[64], diminished octave[65], augmented fourth[66], and diminished fifth[67]. Are you surprised that the augmented fourth and diminished fifth sound the same?

---

[60]http://cnx.org/content/m10867/latest/aug1.mid
[61]http://cnx.org/content/m10867/latest/dim2.mid
[62]http://cnx.org/content/m10867/latest/aug3.mid
[63]http://cnx.org/content/m10867/latest/dim6.mid
[64]http://cnx.org/content/m10867/latest/aug7.mid
[65]http://cnx.org/content/m10867/latest/dim8.mid
[66]http://cnx.org/content/m10867/latest/aug4.mid
[67]http://cnx.org/content/m10867/latest/dim5.mid

Exercise 4.14:

Write a note that will give the named interval.

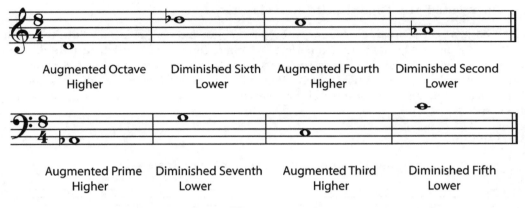

| Augmented Octave | Diminished Sixth | Augmented Fourth | Diminished Second |
| Higher | Lower | Higher | Lower |

| Augmented Prime | Diminished Seventh | Augmented Third | Diminished Fifth |
| Higher | Lower | Higher | Lower |

Figure 4.36

(Solution to Exercise 4.14 on p. 169.)

As mentioned above, the diminished fifth and augmented fourth sound the same. Both are six half-steps, or *three whole tones*, so another term for this interval is a **tritone**. In Western Music (Section 2.8), this unique interval, which cannot be spelled as a major, minor, or perfect interval, is considered unusually dissonant (Section 5.3) and unstable (tending to want to resolve (pg 185) to another interval).

You have probably noticed by now that the tritone is not the only interval that can be "spelled" in more than one way. In fact, because of enharmonic spellings (Section 1.1.5), the interval for any two pitches can be written in various ways. A major third could be written as a diminished fourth, for example, or a minor second as an augmented prime. *Always classify the interval as it is written; the composer had a reason for writing it that way.* That reason sometimes has to do with subtle differences in the way different written notes will be interpreted by performers, but it is mostly a matter of placing the notes correctly in the context of the key (Section 4.3), the chord (Chords), and the evolving harmony (Section 2.5). (Please see Beginning Harmonic Analysis (Section 5.5) for more on that subject.)

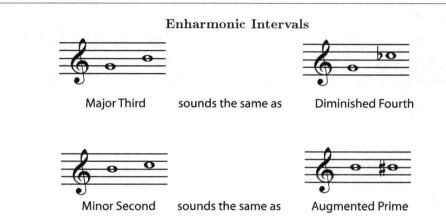

Figure 4.37: Any interval can be written in a variety of ways using enharmonic (Section 1.1.5) spelling. Always classify the interval as it is written.

4.5.4 Inverting Intervals

To **invert** any interval, simply imagine that one of the notes has moved one octave, so that the higher note has become the lower and vice-versa. Because inverting an interval only involves moving one note by an octave (it is still essentially the "same" note in the tonal system), intervals that are **inversions** of each other have a very close relationship in the tonal (Section 4.1) system.

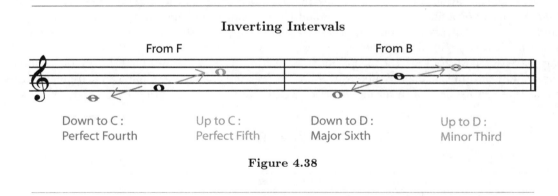

Figure 4.38

To find the inversion of an interval

1. To name the new interval, subtract the name of the old interval from 9.

2. The inversion of a perfect interval is still perfect.

3. The inversion of a major interval is minor, and of a minor interval is major.

4. The inversion of an augmented interval is diminished and of a diminished interval is augmented.

Example 4.9:

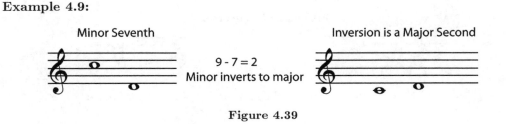

Minor Seventh   Inversion is a Major Second

9 - 7 = 2
Minor inverts to major

Figure 4.39

Exercise 4.15:

What are the inversions of the following intervals?

1. Augmented third
2. Perfect fifth
3. Diminished fifth
4. Major seventh
5. Minor sixth

(Solution to Exercise 4.15 on p. 169.)

4.6 Harmonic Series II: Harmonics, Intervals, and Instruments[68]

4.6.1 Frequency and Interval

The names of the various intervals, and the way they are written on the staff, are mostly the result of a long history of evolving musical notation and theory. But the actual intervals - the way the notes sound - are not arbitrary accidents of history. Like octaves, the other intervals are also produced by the harmonic series. Recall that the frequencies of any two pitches that are one octave (Section 4.1) apart have a 2:1 ratio. (See Harmonic Series I (Section 3.3) to review this.) Every other interval (Section 4.5) that musicians talk about can also be described as having a particular frequency ratio. To find those ratios, look at a harmonic series written in common notation (Section 1.1.1).

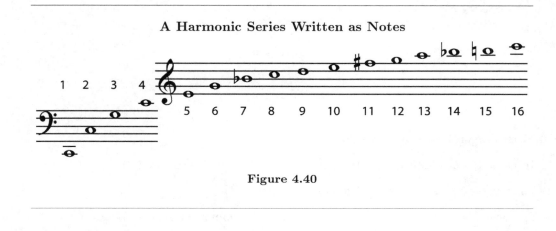

A Harmonic Series Written as Notes

Figure 4.40

[68]This content is available online at <http://cnx.org/content/m13686/1.6/>.

Look at the third harmonic in Figure 4.40. Its frequency is three times the frequency of the first harmonic (ratio 3:1). Remember, the frequency of the second harmonic is two times that of the first harmonic (ratio 2:1). In other words, there are two waves of the higher C for every one wave of the lower C, and three waves of the third-harmonic G for every one wave of the fundamental. So the ratio[69] of the frequencies of the second to the third harmonics is 2:3. (In other words, two waves of the C for every three of the G.) From the harmonic series shown above, you can see that the interval (Section 4.5) between these two notes is a perfect fifth (Section 4.5.3.1). The ratio of the frequencies of all perfect fifths is 2:3.

Exercise 4.16:

1. The interval between the fourth and sixth harmonics (frequency ratio 4:6) is also a fifth. Can you explain this?

2. What other harmonics have an interval of a fifth?

3. Which harmonics have an interval of a fourth?

4. What is the frequency ratio for the interval of a fourth?

(Solution to Exercise 4.16 on p. 170.)

NOTE: If you have been looking at the harmonic series above closely, you may have noticed that some notes that are written to give the same interval have different frequency ratios. For example, the interval between the seventh and eighth harmonics is a major second, but so are the intervals between 8 and 9, between 9 and 10, and between 10 and 11. But 7:8, 8:9, 9:10, and 10:11, although they are pretty close, are not exactly the same. In fact, modern Western (Section 2.8) music uses the equal temperament (Section 6.2.3.2) tuning system, which divides the octave into twelve notes that are equally far apart. (They do have the same frequency ratios, unlike the half steps (Section 4.2) in the harmonic series.) The positive aspect of equal temperament (and the reason it is used) is that an instrument will be equally in tune in all keys. The negative aspect is that it means that all intervals except for octaves are slightly out of tune with regard to the actual harmonic series. For more about equal temperament, see Tuning Systems (Section 6.2.3). Interestingly, musicians have a tendency to revert to true harmonics when they can (in other words, when it is easy to fine-tune each note). For example, an a capella choral group, or a brass ensemble, may find themselves singing or playing perfect fourths and fifths, "contracted" major thirds and "expanded" minor thirds, and half and whole steps of slightly varying sizes.

4.6.2 Brass Instruments

The harmonic series is particularly important for brass instruments. A pianist or xylophone player only gets one note from each key. A string player who wants a different note from a string holds the string tightly in a different place. This basically makes a vibrating string of a new length, with a new fundamental.

But a brass player, without changing the length of the instrument, gets different notes by actually playing the harmonics of the instrument. Woodwinds also do this, although not as much. Most woodwinds can get two different octaves with essentially the same fingering; the lower octave is the fundamental of the column of air inside the instrument at that fingering. The upper octave is the first harmonic.

[69]"Musical Intervals, Frequency, and Ratio" <http://cnx.org/content/m11808/latest/>

NOTE: In some woodwinds, such as the clarinet[70], the upper "octave" may actually be the third harmonic rather than the second, which complicates the fingering patterns of these instruments. Please see Standing Waves and Wind Instruments[71] for an explanation of this phenomenon.

It is the brass instruments that excel in getting different notes from the same length of tubing. The sound of a brass instruments starts with vibrations of the player's lips. By vibrating the lips at different speeds, the player can cause a harmonic of the air column to sound instead of the fundamental. Thus a bugle player can play any note in the harmonic series of the instrument that falls within the player's range. Compare these well-known bugle calls to the harmonic series above (Figure 4.40).

Bugle Calls

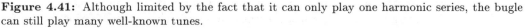

Figure 4.41: Although limited by the fact that it can only play one harmonic series, the bugle can still play many well-known tunes.

For centuries, all brass instruments were valveless. A brass instrument could play only the notes of one harmonic series. (An important exception was the trombone[72] and its relatives, which can easily change their length and harmonic series using a slide.) The upper octaves of the series, where the notes are close enough together to play an interesting melody, were often difficult to play, and some of the harmonics sound quite out of tune to ears that expect equal temperament. The solution to these problems, once brass valves were perfected, was to add a few valves to the instrument; three is usually enough. Each valve opens an extra length of tube, making the instrument a little longer, and making available a whole new harmonic series. Usually one valve gives the harmonic series one half step lower than the valveless intrument; another, one whole step lower; and the third, one and

---

[70]"Clarinets" <http://cnx.org/content/m12604/latest/>
[71]"Standing Waves and Wind Instruments" <http://cnx.org/content/m12589/latest/>
[72]"Trombones" <http://cnx.org/content/m12602/latest/>

a half steps lower. The valves can be used in combination, too, making even more harmonic series available. So a valved brass instrument can find, in the comfortable middle of its range (Section 2.7) (its **middle register**), a valve combination that will give a reasonably in-tune version for every note of the chromatic scale (pg 123). (For more on the history of valved brass, see History of the French Horn[73]. For more on how and why harmonics are produced in wind instruments, please see Standing Waves and Wind Instruments[74])

NOTE: Trombones[75] still use a slide instead of valves to make their instrument longer. But the basic principle is still the same. At each slide "position", the instrument gets a new harmonic series. The notes in between the positions aren't part of the chromatic scale, so they are usually only used for special effects like **glissandos** (sliding notes).

[73]"The French Horn" <http://cnx.org/content/m11617/latest/#s2>
[74]"Standing Waves and Wind Instruments" <http://cnx.org/content/m12589/latest/>
[75]"Trombones" <http://cnx.org/content/m12602/latest/>

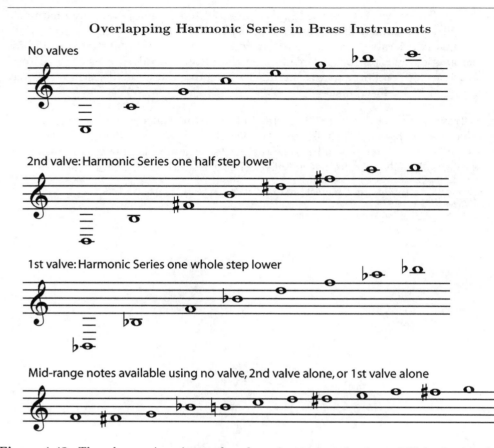

Figure 4.42: These harmonic series are for a brass instrument that has a "C" fundamental when no valves are being used - for example, a C trumpet. Remember, there is an entire harmonic series for every fundamental, and any note can be a fundamental. You just have to find the brass tube with the right length. So a trumpet or tuba can get one harmonic series using no valves, another one a half step lower using one valve, another one a whole step lower using another valve, and so on. By the time all the combinations of valves are used, there is some way to get an in-tune version of every note they need.

Exercise 4.17:

Write the harmonic series for the instrument above when both the first and second valves are open. (You can use this PDF file[76] if you need staff paper.) What new notes are added in the instrument's middle range? Are any notes still missing? *(Solution to Exercise 4.17 on p. 170.)*

NOTE: The French horn[77] has a reputation for being a "difficult" instrument to play. This is also because of the harmonic series. Most brass instruments play in the first few

[76]http://cnx.org/content/m13686/latest/staffpaper1.pdf
[77]"The French Horn" <http://cnx.org/content/m11617/latest/>

octaves of the harmonic series, where the notes are farther apart and it takes a pretty big difference in the mouth and lips (the embouchure[78], pronounced AHM-buh-sher) to get a different note. The range of the French horn is higher in the harmonic series, where the notes are closer together. So very small differences in the mouth and lips can mean the wrong harmonic comes out.

4.6.3 Playing Harmonics on Strings

String players also use harmonics, although not as much as brass players. Harmonics on strings have a very different timbre (Section 2.2) from ordinary string sounds. They give a quieter, thinner, more bell-like tone, and are usually used as a kind of ear-catching special-effect.

Normally a string player holds a string down very tightly. This shortens the length of the vibrating part of the string, in effect making a (temporarily) shorter vibrating string, which has its own full set of harmonics.

To "play a harmonic", the string is touched very, very lightly instead. The length of the string does not change. Instead, the light touch interferes with all of the vibrations that don't have a node (Figure 3.8) at that spot.

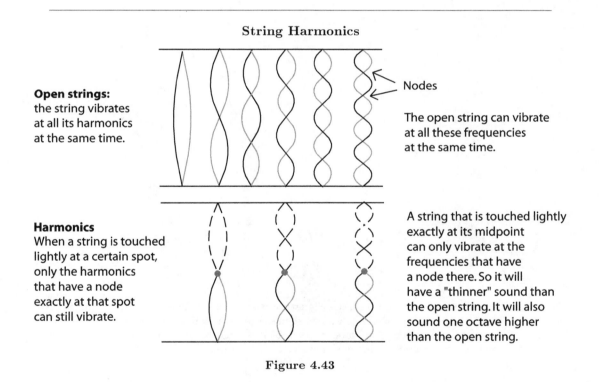

String Harmonics

Open strings:
the string vibrates
at all its harmonics
at the same time.

Nodes

The open string can vibrate
at all these frequencies
at the same time.

Harmonics
When a string is touched
lightly at a certain spot,
only the harmonics
that have a node
exactly at that spot
can still vibrate.

A string that is touched lightly
exactly at its midpoint
can only vibrate at the
frequencies that have
a node there. So it will
have a "thinner" sound than
the open string. It will also
sound one octave higher
than the open string.

Figure 4.43

The thinner, quieter sound of "playing harmonics" is caused by the fact that much of the harmonic series is missing from the sound, which will of course affect the timbre (Section 2.2). Lightly touching the string in most places will result in no sound at all. This technique only works well at places

[78]"Wind Instruments: Some Basics" <http://cnx.org/content/m12364/latest/#p2a>

on the string where a main harmonic (one of the longer, louder lower-numbered harmonics) has a node. Some string players can get more harmonics by both holding the string down in one spot and touching it lightly in another spot, but this is an advanced technique.

4.7 The Circle of Fifths[79]

4.7.1 Related Keys

The circle of fifths is a way to arrange keys to show how closely they are related to each other.

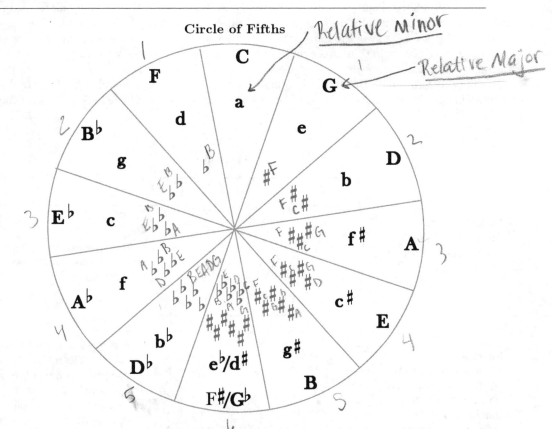

Figure 4.44: The major key for each key signature is shown as a capital letter; the minor key as a small letter. In theory, one could continue around the circle adding flats or sharps (so that B major is also C flat major, with seven flats, E major is also F flat major, with 6 flats and a double flat, and so on), but in practice such key signatures are very rare.

Keys are not considered closely related to each other if they are near each other in the chromatic scale (pg 123) (or on a keyboard). What makes two keys "closely related" is having similar key signatures (Section 1.1.4). So the most closely related key to C major, for example, is A minor, since they have the same key signature (no sharps and no flats). This puts them in the same "slice"

[79]This content is available online at <http://cnx.org/content/m10865/2.11/>.

of the circle. The next most closely related keys to C major would be G major (or E minor), with one sharp, and F major (or D minor), with only one flat. The keys that are most distant from C major, with six sharps or six flats, are on the opposite side of the circle.

The circle of fifths gets its name from the fact that as you go from one section of the circle to the next, you are going up or down by an interval (Section 4.5) of a perfect fifth (Section 4.5.3.1). If you go up a perfect fifth (clockwise in the circle), you get the key that has one more sharp or one less flat; if you go down a perfect fifth (counterclockwise), you get the key that has one more flat or one less sharp. Since going down by a perfect fifth is the same as going up by a perfect fourth (pg 140), the counterclockwise direction is sometimes referred to as a "circle of fourths". (Please review inverted intervals (Section 4.5.4) if this is confusing.)

Example 4.10:

The key of D major has two sharps. Using the circle of fifths, we find that the most closely related major keys (one in each direction) are G major, with only one sharp, and A major, with three sharps. The relative minors of all of these keys (B minor, E minor, and F sharp minor) are also closely related to D major.

Exercise 4.18:

What are the keys most closely related to E flat major? To A minor? *(Solution to Exercise 4.18 on p. 170.)*

Exercise 4.19:

Name the major and minor keys for each key signature.

Figure 4.45

(Solution to Exercise 4.19 on p. 171.)

4.7.2 Key Signatures

If you do not know the order of the sharps and flats, you can also use the circle of fifths to find these. The first sharp in a key signature is always F sharp; the second sharp in a key signature is always (a perfect fifth away) C sharp; the third is always G sharp, and so on, all the way to B sharp.

The first flat in a key signature is always B flat (the same as the last sharp); the second is always E flat, and so on, all the way to F flat. Notice that, just as with the key signatures, you add sharps or subtract flats as you go clockwise around the circle, and add flats or subtract sharps as you go counterclockwise.

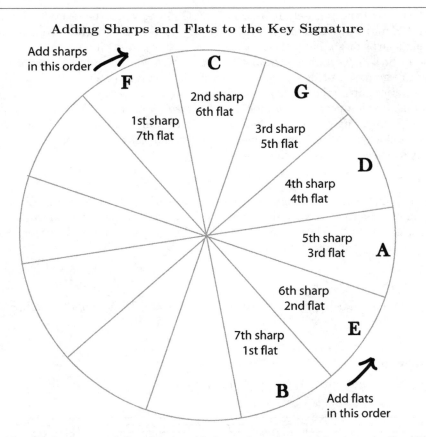

Figure 4.46: Each sharp and flat that is added to a key signature is also a perfect fifth away from the last sharp or flat that was added.

Exercise 4.20:

Figure 4.44 shows that D major has 2 sharps; Figure 4.46 shows that they are F sharp and C sharp. After D major, name the next four sharp keys, and name the sharp that is added with each key.   *(Solution to Exercise 4.20 on p. 171.)*

Exercise 4.21:

E minor is the first sharp minor key; the first sharp added in both major and minor keys is always F sharp. Name the next three sharp minor keys, and the sharp that is added in each key.   *(Solution to Exercise 4.21 on p. 172.)*

Exercise 4.22:

After B flat major, name the next four flat keys, and name the flat that is added with each key.   *(Solution to Exercise 4.22 on p. 172.)*

4.8 Scales that aren't Major or Minor[80]

4.8.1 Introduction

Sounds - ordinary, everyday "noises" - come in every conceivable pitch (Section 1.1.3) and groups of pitches. In fact, the essence of noise, "white noise", is basically every pitch at once, so that no particular pitch is heard.

One of the things that makes music pleasant to hear and easy to "understand" is that only a few of all the possible pitches are used. But not all pieces of music use the same set of pitches. In order to be familiar with the particular notes that a piece of music is likely to use, musicians study scales.

The set of expected pitches for a piece of music can be arranged into a **scale**. In a scale, the pitches are usually arranged from lowest to highest (or highest to lowest), in a pattern that usually repeats within every octave (Section 4.1).

> NOTE: In some kinds of music, the notes of a particular scale are the only notes allowed in a given piece of music. In other music traditions, notes from outside the scale (accidentals (pg 17)) are allowed, but are usually much less common than the scale notes.

The set of pitches, or notes, that are used, and their relationships to each other, makes a big impact on how the music sounds. For example, for centuries, most Western music (Section 2.8) has been based on major (Section 4.3) and minor scales (Section 4.4). That is one of the things that makes it instantly recognizable as Western music. Much (though not all) of the music of eastern Asia, on the other hand, was for many centuries based on pentatonic scales, giving it a much different flavor that is also easy to recognize.

Some of the more commonly used scales that are not major or minor are introduced here. Pentatonic scales are often associated with eastern Asia, but many other music traditions also use them. Blues scales, used in blues, jazz, and other African-American traditions, grew out of a compromise between European and African scales. Some of the scales that sound "exotic" to the Western ear are taken from the musical traditions of eastern Europe, the Middle East, and western Asia. Microtones can be found in some traditional musics (for example, Indian classical music[81]) and in some modern art (pg 92) music.

> NOTE: Some music traditions, such as Indian and medieval European, use modes or ragas, which are not quite the same as scales. Please see Modes and Ragas. (Section 6.3)

4.8.2 Scales and Western Music

The Western (Section 2.8) musical tradition that developed in Europe after the middle ages is based on major and minor scales, but there are other scales that are a part of this tradition.

In the **chromatic scale**, every interval (Section 4.5) is a half step (Section 4.2). This scale gives all the sharp, flat, and natural (Section 1.1.3) notes commonly used in all Western music. It is also the **twelve-tone scale** used by twentieth-century composers to create their atonal music (pg 91). Young instrumentalists are encouraged to practice playing the chromatic scale in order to ensure that they know the fingerings for all the notes. Listen to a chromatic scale[82].

---

[80]This content is available online at <http://cnx.org/content/m11636/1.14/>.

[81]"Indian Classical Music: Tuning and Ragas" <http://cnx.org/content/m12459/latest/>

[82]http://cnx.org/content/m11636/latest/Chromatic.MID

Figure 4.47: The chromatic scale includes all the pitches normally found in Western music. Note that, because of enharmonic (Section 1.1.5) spelling, many of these pitches could be written in a different way (for example, using flats instead of sharps).

In a **whole tone scale**, every interval is a whole step (Section 4.2). In both the chromatic and the whole tone scales, all the intervals are the same. This results in scales that have no tonal center (Section 4.3); no note feels more or less important than the others. Because of this, most traditional and popular Western music uses major or minor scales rather than the chromatic or whole tone scales. But composers who don't want their music to have a tonal center (for example, many composers of "modern classical" music) often use these scales. Listen to a whole tone scale[83].

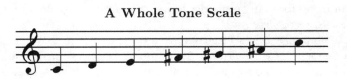

Figure 4.48: Because all the intervals are the same, it doesn't matter much where you begin a chromatic or whole tone scale. For example, this scale would contain the same notes whether you start it on C or E.

Exercise 4.23:

There is basically only one chromatic scale; you can start it on any note, but the pitches will end up being the same as the pitches in any other chromatic scale. There are basically two possible whole tone scales. Beginning on a b, write a whole tone scale that uses a different pitches than the one in Figure 4.48. If you need staff paper, you can download this PDF file[84].   (*Solution to Exercise 4.23 on p. 172.*)

Exercise 4.24:

Now write a whole tone scale beginning on an a flat. Is this scale essentially the same as the one in Figure 4.73 or the one in Figure 4.48?   (*Solution to Exercise 4.24 on p. 173.*)

---

[83]http://cnx.org/content/m11636/latest/WholeTone.mid
[84]http://cnx.org/content/m11636/latest/staffpaper1.pdf

4.8.3 Pentatonic Scales

In Western music, there are twelve pitches within each octave (Section 4.1). (The thirteenth note starts the next octave.) But in a tonal (Section 2.8.3) piece of music only seven of these notes, the seven notes of a major or minor scale, are used often.

In a **pentatonic scale**, only five of the possible pitches within an octave are used. (So the scale will repeat starting at the sixth tone.) The most familiar pentatonic scales are used in much of the music of eastern Asia. You may be familiar with the scale in Figure 4.49 as the scale that is produced when you play all the "black keys" on a piano keyboard.

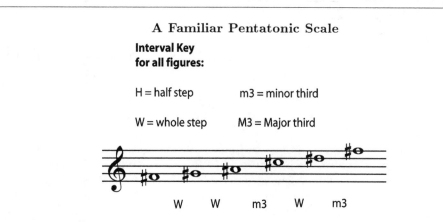

A Familiar Pentatonic Scale

Figure 4.49: This is the pentatonic scale you get when you play the "black keys" on a piano.

Listen to the black key pentatonic scale[85]. Like other scales, this pentatonic scale is transposable (Section 6.4); you can move the entire scale up or down by a half step or a major third or any interval (Section 4.5) you like. The scale will sound higher or lower, but other than that it will sound the same, because the pattern of intervals between the notes (half steps, whole steps, and minor thirds) is the same. (For more on intervals, see Half Steps and Whole Steps (Section 4.2) and Interval (Section 4.5). For more on patterns of intervals within scales, see Major Scales (Section 4.3) and Minor Scales (Section 4.4).) Now listen to a transposed pentatonic scale[86].

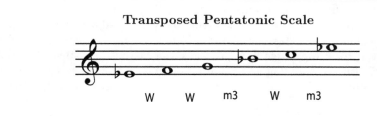

Transposed Pentatonic Scale

Figure 4.50: This is simply a transposition of the scale in Figure 4.49

[85]http://cnx.org/content/m11636/latest/pentatonic1.mid
[86]http://cnx.org/content/m11636/latest/pentatonic2.mid

But this is not the only possible type of pentatonic scale. Any scale that uses only five notes within one octave is a pentatonic scale. The following pentatonic scale, for example, is not simply another transposition of the "black key" pentatonic scale; the pattern of intervals between the notes is different. Listen to this different pentatonic scale[87].

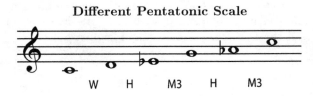

Different Pentatonic Scale

W   H   M3   H   M3

Figure 4.51: This pentatonic scale is not a transposed version of Figure 4.49.It has a different set of intervals.

The point here is that music based on the pentatonic scale in Figure 4.49 will sound very different from music based on the pentatonic scale in Figure 4.51, because the relationships between the notes are different, much as music in a minor key is noticeably different from music in a major key. So there are quite a few different possible pentatonic scales that will produce a recognizably "unique sound", and many of these possible five-note scales have been named and used in various music traditions around the world.

Exercise 4.25:

To get a feeling for the concepts in this section, try composing some short pieces using the pentatonic scales given in Figure 4.49 and in Figure 4.51. You may use more than one octave of each scale, but use only one scale for each piece. As you are composing, listen for how the constraints of using only those five notes, with those pitch relationships, affect your music. See if you can play your Figure 4.49 composition in a different key, for example, using the scale in Figure 4.50.   *(Solution to Exercise 4.25 on p. 173.)*

4.8.4 Dividing the Octave, More or Less

Any scale will list a certain number of notes within an octave. For major and minor scales, there are seven notes; for pentatonic, five; for a chromatic scale, twelve. Although some divisions are more common than others, any division can be imagined, and many are used in different musical traditions around the world. For example, the classical music of India recognizes twenty-two different possible pitches within an octave; each raga uses five, six, or seven of these possible pitches. (Please see Indian Classical Music: Tuning and Ragas[88] for more on this.) And there are some traditions in Africa that use six or eight notes within an octave. Listen to one possible eight-tone, or octatonic scale[89].

[87]http://cnx.org/content/m11636/latest/penta3.mid
[88]"Indian Classical Music: Tuning and Ragas" <http://cnx.org/content/m12459/latest/>
[89]http://cnx.org/content/m11636/latest/Octatonic.mid

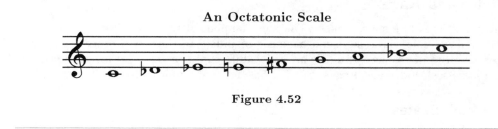

An Octatonic Scale

Figure 4.52

Many Non-Western traditions, besides using different scales, also use different tuning systems (Section 6.2); the intervals in the scales may involve **quarter tones** (a half of a half step), for example, or other intervals we don't use. Even trying to write them in common notation can be a bit misleading.

Microtones are intervals smaller than a half step. Besides being necessary to describe the scales and tuning systems of many Non-Western traditions, they have also been used in modern Western classical music, and are also used in African-American traditions such as jazz and blues. As of this writing, the Huygens-Fokker Foundation[90] was a good place to start looking for information on microtonal music.

4.8.5 The Blues Scale

Blues scales are closely related to pentatonic scales. (Some versions are pentatonic.) Rearrange the pentatonic scale in Figure 4.50 above so that it begins on the C, and add an F sharp in between the F and G, and you have a commonly used version of the blues scale. Listen to this blues scale[91].

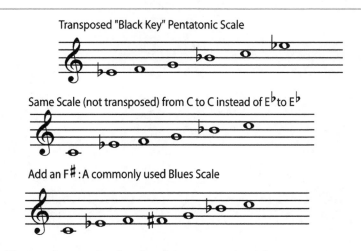

Figure 4.53: Blues scales are closely related to pentatonic scales.

---

[90] http://www.xs4all.nl/~huygensf/english/index.html
[91] http://cnx.org/content/m11636/latest/BlueScale.mid

4.8.6 Modes and Ragas

Many music traditions do not use scales. The most familiar of these to the Western (Section 2.8) listener are medieval chant and the classical music of India. In these and other modal traditions, the rules for constructing a piece of music are quite different than the rules for music that is based on a scale. Please see Modes and Ragas (Section 6.3) for more information.

4.8.7 "Exotic" Scales

There are many other possible scales that are not part of the major-minor system; these are sometimes called **"exotic" scales**, since they are outside the usual Western (Section 2.8) system. Some, like pentatonic and octatonic scales, have fewer or more notes per octave, but many have seven tones, just as a major scale does. Some, like the whole tone scale, are invented by composers exploring new ideas. Others, which may be given appellations such as "Persian" or "Hungarian" by the person using or studying them, are loosely based on the music of other cultures. These scales are sometimes borrowed from music that is actually modal (Section 6.3), but then they are used in Western classical, jazz or "world" music simply as unusual scales. Since they usually ignore the tuning, melodic forms, and other aesthetic principles of the traditions that they are borrowed from, these "exotic" scales should not be considered accurate representations of those traditions.

If you want to compose or improvise music, you can experiment with making up new scales, unusual combinations of notes to be used in your music. Or you can look up some of the many "exotic" scales already in use. (Try a web search for "exotic scales".) Here (Figure 4.54) are just a few examples of the many possibilities. Listen to the "symmetrical" scale[92], "enigmatic" scale[93], "Arabian" Scale[94], and "Hungarian Major" Scale[95].

---

[92]http://cnx.org/content/m11636/latest/Symmetrical.mid
[93]http://cnx.org/content/m11636/latest/Enigmatic.mid
[94]http://cnx.org/content/m11636/latest/Arabian.mid
[95]http://cnx.org/content/m11636/latest/HungarianMajor.mid

Some "Exotic" Scales

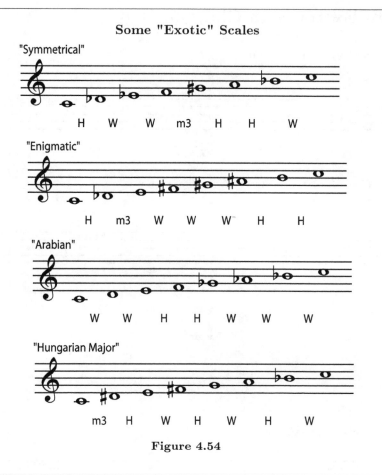

Figure 4.54

Solutions to Exercises in Chapter 4

Solution to Exercise 4.1 (p. 121):

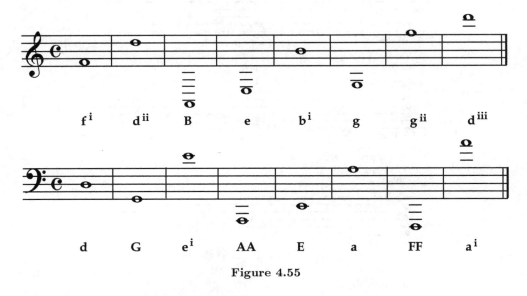

Figure 4.55

Solution to Exercise 4.2 (p. 125):

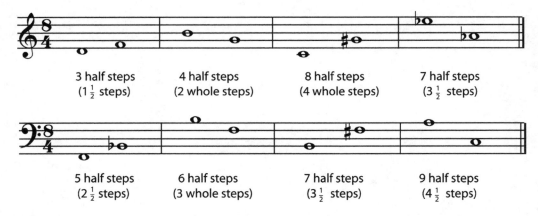

Figure 4.56

Solution to Exercise 4.3 (p. 126):

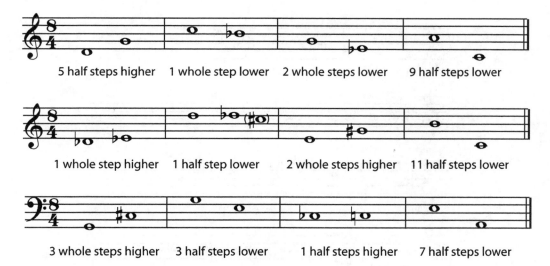

Figure 4.57: If your answer is different, check to see if you have written a different enharmonic spelling (Section 1.1.5) of the note in the answer. For example, the B flat could be written as an A sharp.

Solution to Exercise 4.4 (p. 126):

1. Major

2. Major

3. Minor

4. Major

5. Minor

Solution to Exercise 4.5 (p. 128):

Figure 4.58

Notice that although they look completely different, the scales of F sharp major and G flat major (numbers 5 and 6) sound exactly the same when played, on a piano as shown in Figure 4.59, or on any other instrument using equal temperament (Section 6.2.3.2) tuning. If this surprises you, please read more about enharmonic (Section 1.1.5) scales.

Enharmonic Scales

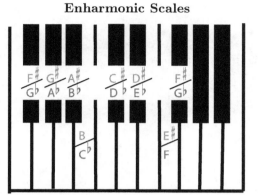

Figure 4.59: Using this figure of a keyboard, or the fingerings from your own instrument, notice that the notes for the F sharp major scale and the G flat major scale in Figure 4.58, although spelled differently, will sound the same.

Solution to Exercise 4.6 (p. 131):

Figure 4.60

Solution to Exercise 4.7 (p. 133):

1. A minor: C major

2. G minor: B flat major

3. B flat minor: D flat major

4. E minor: G major

5. F minor: A flat major

6. F sharp minor: A major

Solution to Exercise 4.8 (p. 134):

Figure 4.61

Solution to Exercise 4.9 (p. 134):

1. A melodic minor

2. G melodic minor

3. B flat melodic minor

4. E melodic minor

5. F melodic minor

6. F sharp melodic minor

Figure 4.62

Solution to Exercise 4.10 (p. 138):

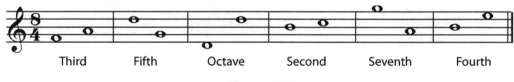

Third   Fifth   Octave   Second   Seventh   Fourth

Figure 4.63

Solution to Exercise 4.11 (p. 138):

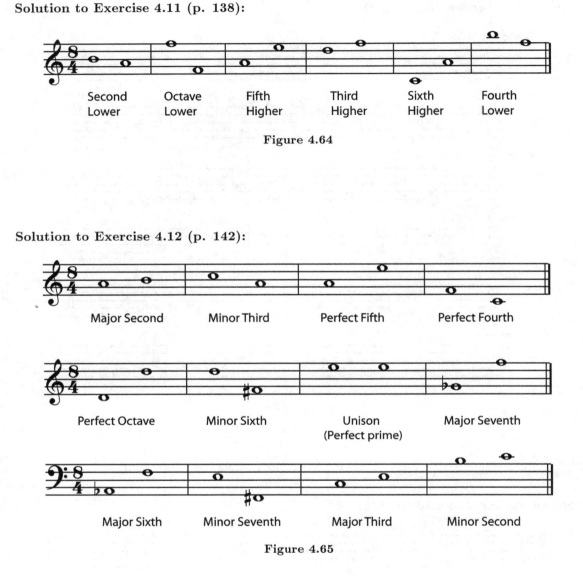

Figure 4.64

Solution to Exercise 4.12 (p. 142):

Figure 4.65

Solution to Exercise 4.13 (p. 142):

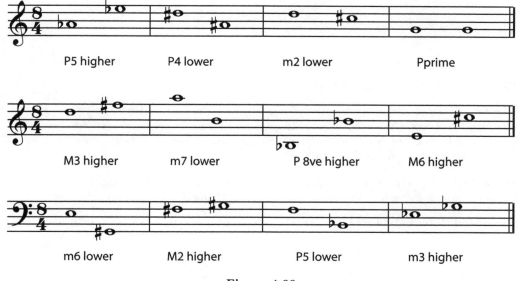

Figure 4.66

Solution to Exercise 4.14 (p. 144):

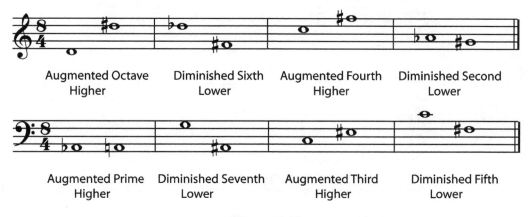

Figure 4.67

Solution to Exercise 4.15 (p. 146):

1. Diminished sixth
2. Perfect fourth

3. Augmented fourth

4. Minor second

5. Major third

Solution to Exercise 4.16 (p. 147):

1. The ratio 4:6 reduced to lowest terms is 2:3. (In other words, they are two ways of writing the same mathematical relationship. If you are more comfortable with fractions than with ratios, think of all the ratios as fractions instead. 2:3 is just two-thirds, and 4:6 is four-sixths. Four-sixths reduces to two-thirds.)

2. Six and nine (6:9 also reduces to 2:3); eight and twelve; ten and fifteen; and any other combination that can be reduced to 2:3 (12:18, 14:21 and so on).

3. Harmonics three and four; six and eight; nine and twelve; twelve and sixteen; and so on.

4. 3:4

Solution to Exercise 4.17 (p. 150):
Opening both first and second valves gives the harmonic series one-and-a-half steps lower than "no valves".

Harmonic Series on **A**

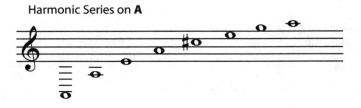

New midrange notes:

The only midrange note still missing is the G♯,
which can be played by adding a third valve, and
holding down the second and third valves at the same time.

Figure 4.68

Solution to Exercise 4.18 (p. 153):

E flat major (3 flats):

- B flat major (2 flats)

- A flat major (4 flats)

- C minor (3 flats)

- G minor (2 flats)

- F minor (4 flats)

A minor (no sharps or flats):

- E minor (1 sharp)

- D minor (1 flat)

- C major (no sharps or flats)

- G major (1 sharp)

- F major (1 flat)

Solution to Exercise 4.19 (p. 153):

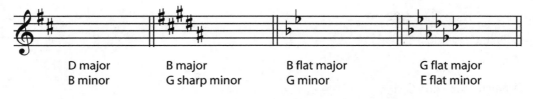

| D major | B major | B flat major | G flat major |
| B minor | G sharp minor | G minor | E flat minor |

Figure 4.69

Solution to Exercise 4.20 (p. 154):

- A major adds G sharp

- E major adds D sharp

- B major adds A sharp

- F sharp major adds E sharp

G major   D major   A major   E major   B major   F sharp major

Figure 4.70

Solution to Exercise 4.21 (p. 154):

- B minor adds C sharp

- F sharp minor adds G sharp

- C sharp minor adds D sharp

Figure 4.71

Solution to Exercise 4.22 (p. 154):

- E flat major adds A flat

- A flat major adds D flat

- D flat major adds G flat

- G flat major adds C flat

Figure 4.72

Solution to Exercise 4.23 (p. 156):

Figure 4.73: This whole tone scale contains the notes that are not in the whole tone scale in Figure 4.48.

Solution to Exercise 4.24 (p. 156):

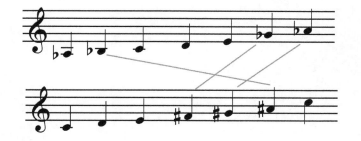

Figure 4.74: The flats in one scale are the enharmonic (Section 1.1.5) equivalents of the sharps in the other scale.

Assuming that octaves don't matter - as they usually don't in Western (Section 2.8) music theory, this scale shares all of its possible pitches with the scale in Figure 4.48.

Solution to Exercise 4.25 (p. 158):
If you can, have your teacher listen to your compositions.

Chapter 5

Harmony and Form

5.1 Triads[1]

Harmony (Section 2.5) in Western music (Section 2.8) is based on triads. **Triads** are simple three-note chords (Chords) built of thirds (pg 137).

5.1.1 Triads in Root Position

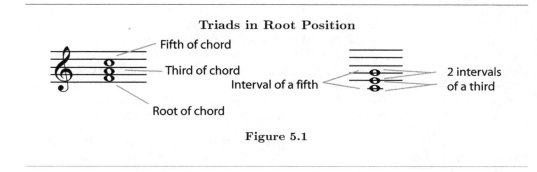

Figure 5.1

The chords in Figure 5.1 are written in root position, which is the most basic way to write a triad. In **root position**, the **root**, which is the note that names the chord, is the lowest note. The **third of the chord** is written a third (Figure 4.26) higher than the root, and the **fifth of the chord** is written a fifth (Figure 4.26) higher than the root (which is also a third higher than the third of the chord). So the simplest way to write a triad is as a stack of thirds, in root position.

> NOTE: The type of interval or chord - major, minor, diminished, etc., is not important when you are determining the position of the chord. To simplify things, all notes in the examples and exercises below are natural, but it would not change their position at all if some notes were sharp or flat. It would, however, change the name of the triad - see Naming Triads (Section 5.2).

---

[1]This content is available online at <http://cnx.org/content/m10877/2.14/>.

Exercise 5.1:

Write a triad in root position using each root given. If you need some staff paper for exercises you can print this PDF file[2].

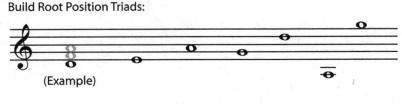

Build Root Position Triads:

(Example)

Figure 5.2

(Solution to Exercise 5.1 on p. 210.)

5.1.2 First and Second Inversions

Any other chord that has the same-named notes as a root position chord is considered to be essentially the same chord in a different **position**. In other words, all chords that have only D naturals, F sharps, and A naturals, are considered D major chords.

> NOTE: *But* if you change the pitch (Section 1.1.3) or spelling (Section 1.1.5) of any note in the triad, you have changed the chord (see Naming Triads (Section 5.2)). For example, if the F sharps are written as G flats, or if the A's are sharp instead of natural, you have a different chord, not an inversion of the same chord. If you add notes, you have also changed the name of the chord (see Beyond Triads (Section 5.4)). *You cannot call one chord the inversion of another if either one of them has a note that does not share a name (for example "F sharp" or "B natural") with a note in the other chord.*

If the third of the chord is the lowest note, the chord is in **first inversion**. If the fifth of the chord is the lowest note, the chord is in **second inversion**. A chord in second inversion may also be called a **six-four chord**, because the intervals (Section 4.5) in it are a sixth and a fourth.

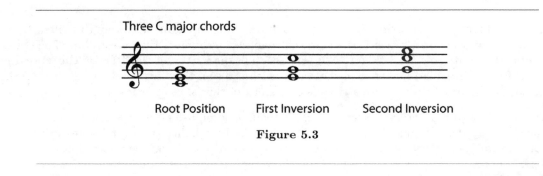

Three C major chords

Root Position   First Inversion   Second Inversion

Figure 5.3

It does not matter how far the higher notes are from the lowest note, or how many of each note there are (at different octaves or on different instruments); all that matters is which note is lowest.

---

[2]http://cnx.org/content/m10877/latest/staffpaper1.pdf

(In fact, one of the notes may not even be written, only implied by the context of the chord in a piece of music. A practiced ear will tell you what the missing note is; we won't worry about that here.) To decide what position a chord is in, move the notes to make a stack of thirds and identify the root.

Example 5.1:

Notes are G, D, and B. Rewrite as thirds:

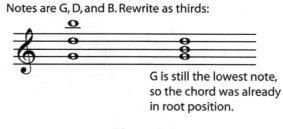

G is still the lowest note, so the chord was already in root position.

Figure 5.4

Example 5.2:

Notes are a G, 2 C's, and an E. Rewrite G, C, and E as thirds:

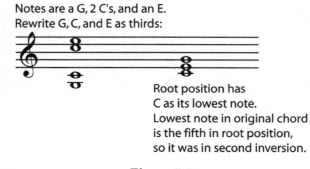

Root position has C as its lowest note. Lowest note in original chord is the fifth in root position, so it was in second inversion.

Figure 5.5

Exercise 5.2:

Rewrite each chord in root position, and name the original position of the chord.

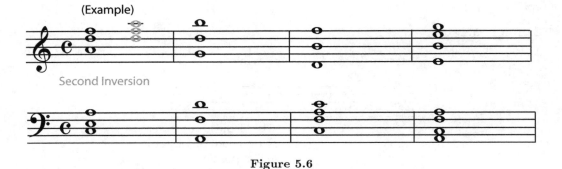

Figure 5.6

(Solution to Exercise 5.2 on p. 210.)

5.2 Naming Triads[3]

The position (Section 5.1) that a chord is in does make a difference in how it sounds, but it is a fairly small difference. Listen[4] to a G major chord in three different positions.

Figure 5.7: G major chord in three different positions.

A much bigger difference in the chord's sound comes from the intervals (Section 4.5) between the root-position notes of the chord. For example, if the B in one of the chords above was changed to a B flat, you would still have a G triad (Section 5.1), but the chord would now sound very different. So chords are named according to the intervals between the notes when the chord is in root position (Section 5.1). Listen[5] to four different G chords.

---

[3]This content is available online at <http://cnx.org/content/m10890/2.13/>.
[4]http://cnx.org/content/m10890/latest/Inversions.MID
[5]http://cnx.org/content/m10890/latest/GChords.MID

Figure 5.8: These are also all G chords, but they are four different G chords. The intervals between the notes are different, so the chords sound very different.

5.2.1 Major and Minor Chords

The most commonly used triads (Section 5.1) form major (Section 4.3) chords and minor (Section 4.4) chords. All major chords and minor chords have an interval (Section 4.5) of a perfect fifth (pg 140) between the root and the fifth of the chord (Section 5.1). A perfect fifth (7 half-steps) can be divided into a major third (Major and Minor Intervals) (4 half-steps) plus a minor third (Major and Minor Intervals) (3 half-steps). If the interval between the root and the third of the chord is the major third (with the minor third between the third and the fifth of the chord), the triad is a **major chord**. If the interval between the root and the third of the chord is the minor third (and the major third is between the third and fifth of the chord), then the triad is a **minor chord**. Listen closely to a major triad[6] and a minor triad[7].

Example 5.3:

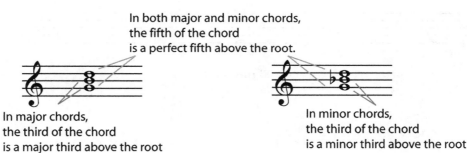

In both major and minor chords,
the fifth of the chord
is a perfect fifth above the root.

In major chords,
the third of the chord
is a major third above the root

In minor chords,
the third of the chord
is a minor third above the root

Figure 5.9

[6]http://cnx.org/content/m10890/latest/chomj.mp3
[7]http://cnx.org/content/m10890/latest/chomin.mp3

Example 5.4:

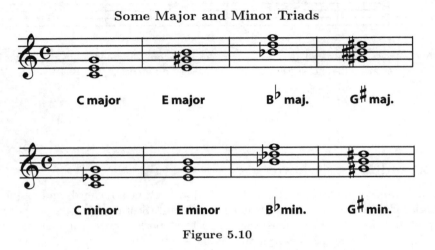

Figure 5.10

Exercise 5.3:

Write the major chord for each root given.

Figure 5.11

(Solution to Exercise 5.3 on p. 210.)

Exercise 5.4:

Write the minor chord for each root given.

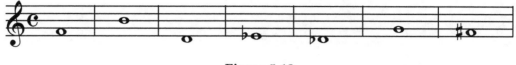

Figure 5.12

(Solution to Exercise 5.4 on p. 211.)

5.2.2 Augmented and Diminished Chords

Because they don't contain a perfect fifth, augmented and diminished chords have an unsettled feeling and are normally used sparingly. An **augmented chord** is built from two major thirds, which adds up to an augmented fifth. A **diminished chord** is built from two minor thirds, which add up to a diminished fifth. Listen closely to an augmented triad[8] and a diminished triad[9].

Example 5.5:

Some Augmented and Diminished Triads

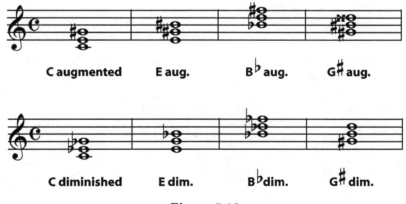

Figure 5.13

---

[8]http://cnx.org/content/m10890/latest/choaug.mp3
[9]http://cnx.org/content/m10890/latest/chodim.mp3

Exercise 5.5:

Write the augmented triad for each root given.

Figure 5.14

(Solution to Exercise 5.5 on p. 211.)

Exercise 5.6:

Write the diminished triad for each root given.

Figure 5.15

(Solution to Exercise 5.6 on p. 211.)

Notice that you can't avoid double sharps or double flats by writing the note on a different space or line. *If you change the spelling (Section 1.1.5) of a chord's notes, you have also changed the chord's name.* For example, if, in an augmented G sharp major chord, you rewrite the D double sharp as an E natural, the triad becomes an E augmented chord.

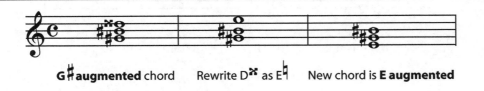

G♯ **augmented** chord   Rewrite D𝄪 as E♮   New chord is **E augmented**

Figure 5.16: Changing the spelling of any note in a chord also changes the chord's name.

You can put the chord in a different position (Section 5.1) or add more of the same-named notes at other octaves without changing the name of the chord. But changing the note names or adding different-named notes, will change the name of the chord. Here is a summary of the intervals in triads in root position.

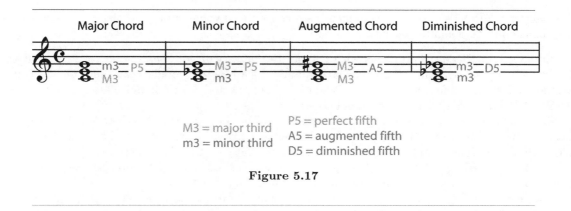

M3 = major third
m3 = minor third

P5 = perfect fifth
A5 = augmented fifth
D5 = diminished fifth

Figure 5.17

Exercise 5.7:

Now see if you can identify these chords that are not necessarily in root position. Rewrite them in root position first if that helps.

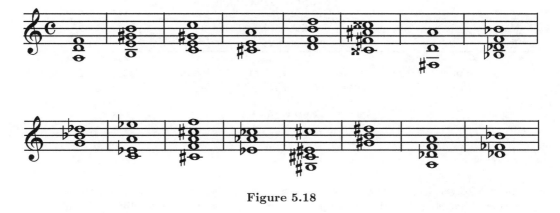

Figure 5.18

(Solution to Exercise 5.7 on p. 212.)

5.3 Consonance and Dissonance[10]

Notes that sound good together when played at the same time are called **consonant**. Chords built only of consonances sound pleasant and "stable"; you can listen to one for a long time without feeling that the music needs to change to a different chord. Notes that are **dissonant** can sound harsh or unpleasant when played at the same time. Or they may simply feel "unstable"; if you hear a chord with a dissonance in it, you may feel that the music is pulling you towards the chord that **resolves** the dissonance. Obviously, what seems pleasant or unpleasant is partly a matter of opinion. This discussion only covers consonance and dissonance in Western (Section 2.8) music.

---

[10]This content is available online at <http://cnx.org/content/m11953/1.9/>.

NOTE: For activities that introduce these concepts to young students, please see Consonance and Dissonance Activities[11].

Of course, if there are problems with tuning, the notes will not sound good together, but this is not what consonance and dissonance are about. (Please note, though, that the choice of tuning system can greatly affect which intervals sound consonant and which sound dissonant! Please see Tuning Systems (pg 226) for more about this.)

Consonance and dissonance refer to intervals (Section 4.5) and chords (Chords). The **interval** between two notes is the number of half steps (Section 4.2) between them, and all intervals have a name that musicians commonly use, like major third (Major and Minor Intervals) (which is 4 half steps), perfect fifth (pg 140) (7 half steps), or octave (Section 4.1). (See Interval (Section 4.5) to learn how to determine and name the interval between any two notes.)

An interval is measured between two notes. When there are more than two notes sounding at the same time, that's a **chord**. (See Triads (Section 5.1), Naming Triads (Section 5.2), and Beyond Triads (Section 5.4) for some basics on chords.) Of course, you can still talk about the interval between any two of the notes in a chord.

The simple intervals (pg 137) that are considered to be consonant are the minor third[12], major third[13], perfect fourth[14], perfect fifth[15], minor sixth[16], major sixth[17], and the octave[18].

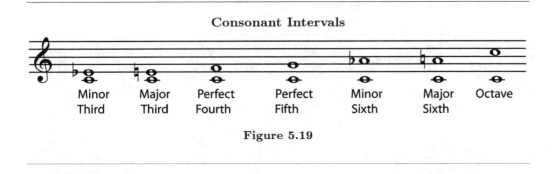

Consonant Intervals

Minor Third   Major Third   Perfect Fourth   Perfect Fifth   Minor Sixth   Major Sixth   Octave

Figure 5.19

In modern Western Music (Section 2.8), all of these intervals are considered to be pleasing to the ear. Chords that contain only these intervals are considered to be "stable", restful chords that don't need to be resolved (pg 185). When we hear them, we don't feel a need for them to go to other chords.

The intervals that are considered to be dissonant are the minor second[19], the major second[20], the minor seventh[21], the major seventh[22], and particularly the tritone[23], which is the interval in between the perfect fourth and perfect fifth.

---

[11]"Consonance and Dissonance Activities" <http://cnx.org/content/m11999/latest/>
[12]http://cnx.org/content/m11953/latest/minorthird.mid
[13]http://cnx.org/content/m11953/latest/majorthird.mid
[14]http://cnx.org/content/m11953/latest/fourth.mid
[15]http://cnx.org/content/m11953/latest/fifth.mid
[16]http://cnx.org/content/m11953/latest/minorsixth.mid
[17]http://cnx.org/content/m11953/latest/majorsixth.mid
[18]http://cnx.org/content/m11953/latest/octave.mid
[19]http://cnx.org/content/m11953/latest/minorsecond.mid
[20]http://cnx.org/content/m11953/latest/majorsecond.mid
[21]http://cnx.org/content/m11953/latest/minorseventh.mid
[22]http://cnx.org/content/m11953/latest/majorseventh.mid
[23]http://cnx.org/content/m11953/latest/tritone.mid

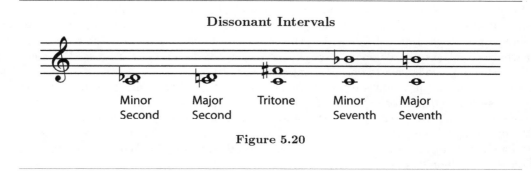

Dissonant Intervals

Figure 5.20

These intervals are all considered to be somewhat unpleasant or tension-producing. In tonal music (pg 91), chords containing dissonances are considered "unstable"; when we hear them, we expect them to move on to a more stable chord. Moving from a dissonance to the consonance that is expected to follow it is called **resolution**, or **resolving** the dissonance. The pattern of tension and release created by resolved dissonances is part of what makes a piece of music exciting and interesting. Music that contains no dissonances can tend to seem simplistic or boring. On the other hand, music that contains a lot of dissonances that are never resolved (for example, much of twentieth-century "classical" or "art" music) can be difficult for some people to listen to, because of the unreleased tension.

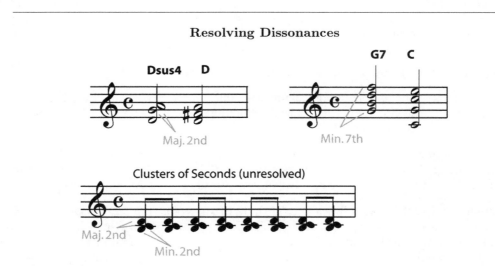

Resolving Dissonances

Figure 5.21: In most music a dissonance will resolve; it will be followed by a consonant chord that it naturally leads to, for example a G seventh chord resolves to a C major chord[24], and a D suspended fourth resolves to a D major chord[25]. A series of unresolved dissonances[26], on the other hand, can produce a sense of unresolved tension.

---

[24]http://cnx.org/content/m11953/latest/GseventhC.mid
[25]http://cnx.org/content/m11953/latest/DsusD.mid
[26]http://cnx.org/content/m11953/latest/dissonant.mid

Why are some note combinations consonant and some dissonant? Preferences for certain sounds is partly cultural; that's one of the reasons why the traditional musics of various cultures can sound so different from each other. Even within the tradition of Western music (Section 2.8), opinions about what is unpleasantly dissonant have changed a great deal over the centuries. But consonance and dissonance do also have a strong physical basis in nature.

In simplest terms, the sound waves of consonant notes "fit" together much better than the sound waves of dissonant notes. For example, if two notes are an octave apart, there will be exactly two waves of one note for every one wave of the other note. If there are two and a tenth waves or eleven twelfths of a wave of one note for every wave of another note, they don't fit together as well. For much more about the physical basis of consonance and dissonance, see Acoustics for Music Theory (Section 3.1), Harmonic Series[27], and Tuning Systems (Section 6.2).

5.4 Beyond Triads: Naming Other Chords[28]

5.4.1 Introduction

Once you know how to name triads (please see Triads (Section 5.1) and Naming Triads (Section 5.2)), you need only a few more rules to be able to name all of the most common chords.

This skill is necessary for those studying music theory. It's also very useful at a "practical" level for composers, arrangers, and performers (especially people playing chords, like pianists and guitarists), who need to be able to talk to each other about the chords that they are reading, writing, and playing.

Chord manuals, fingering charts, chord diagrams, and notes written out on a staff are all very useful, especially if the composer wants a very particular sound on a chord. But all you really need to know are the name of the chord, your major scales (Section 4.3) and minor scales (Section 4.4), and a few rules, and you can figure out the notes in any chord for yourself.

What do you need to know to be able to name most chords?

1. You must know your major, minor, augmented and diminished triads. Either have them all memorized, or be able to figure them out following the rules for triads. (See Triads (Section 5.1) and Naming Triads (Section 5.2).)

2. You must be able to find intervals from the root (Section 5.1) of the chord. One way to do this is by using the rules for intervals. (See Interval (Section 4.5).) *Or if you know your scales and don't want to learn about intervals, you can use the method in #3 instead.*

3. If you know all your scales (always a good thing to know, for so many reasons), you can find all the intervals from the root using scales. For example, the "4" in Csus4 is the 4th note in a C (major or minor) scale, and the "minor 7th" in Dm7 is the 7th note in a D (natural) minor scale. If you would prefer this method, but need to brush up on your scales, please see Major Keys and Scales (Section 4.3) and Minor Keys and Scales (Section 4.4).

4. You need to know the rules for the common seventh chords (Section 5.4.3), for extending (Section 5.4.4) and altering (Section 5.4.6) chords, for adding notes (Section 5.4.4), and for naming bass notes (Section 5.4.5). The basic rules for these are all found below.

NOTE: Please note that the modern system of chord symbols, discussed below, is very different from the **figured bass** shorthand popular in the seventeenth century (which is not discussed here). For example, the "6" in figured bass notation implies the first inversion

---

[27]"Harmonic Series" <http://cnx.org/content/m11118/latest/>
[28]This content is available online at <http://cnx.org/content/m11995/1.10/>.

(Section 5.1) chord, not an added 6. (As of this writing, there was a very straightforward summary of figured bass at Ars Nova Software[29].)

5.4.2 Chord Symbols

Some instrumentalists, such as guitarists and pianists, are sometimes expected to be able to play a named chord, or an accompaniment (Accompaniment) based on that chord, without seeing the notes written out in common notation (Section 1.1.1). In such cases, a **chord symbol** above the staff (Section 1.1.1) tells the performer what chord should be used as accompaniment to the music until the next symbol appears.

Chord Symbols

He'd ne'er leave the girl with the straw -ber- ry curls and the band played on.

Figure 5.22: A chord symbol above the staff is sometimes the only indication of which notes should be used in the accompaniment (Accompaniment). Chord symbols also may be used even when an accompaniment is written out, so that performers can read either the chord symbol or the notated music, as they prefer.

There is widespread agreement on how to name chords, but there are several different systems for writing chord symbols. Unfortunately, this can be a little confusing, particularly when different systems use the same symbol to refer to different chords. If you're not certain what chord is wanted, you can get useful clues both from the notes in the music and from the other chord symbols used. (For example, if the "minus" chord symbol is used, check to see if you can spot any chords that are clearly labelled as either minor or diminished.)

---

[29]http://www.ars-nova.com/cpmanual/realizeharmony.htm

Examples of Chord Symbol Variety

Major chord	**C**	**CMaj**	C△		
Minor chord	**Cm**	**Cmin**	C −		
Augmented Chord	**Caug**	C +			
Diminished Chord*	**Cdim**	C −			
Major Seventh	**CM7**	**CMaj7**	C△	C△7	C 7
Minor Seventh	**Cm7**	**Cmin7**	C−7		
Diminished Seventh*	**Cdim7**	C ○			

*It is so common to add the (diminished) seventh to the diminished chord, that the symbol for the diminished chord may be used with the assumption that you will add the diminished seventh.

Figure 5.23: There is unfortunately a wide variation in the use of chord symbols. In particular, notice that some symbols, such as the "minus" sign and the triangle, can refer to different chords, depending on the assumptions of the person who wrote the symbol.

5.4.3 Seventh Chords

If you take a basic triad (Section 5.1) and add a note that is a seventh (pg 137) above the root (Section 5.1), you have a **seventh chord**. There are several different types of seventh chords, distinguished by both the type of triad and the type of seventh used. Here are the most common.

Seventh Chords

- Seventh (or "dominant seventh") chord = major triad + minor seventh

- Major Seventh chord = major triad + major seventh

- Minor Seventh chord = minor triad + minor seventh

- Diminished Seventh chord = diminished triad + diminished seventh (half step lower than a minor seventh)

- Half-diminished Seventh chord = diminished triad + minor seventh

An easy way to remember where each seventh is:

- The *major seventh* is one half step below the octave (Section 4.1).

- The *minor seventh* is one half step below the major seventh.

- The *diminished seventh* is one half step below the minor seventh.

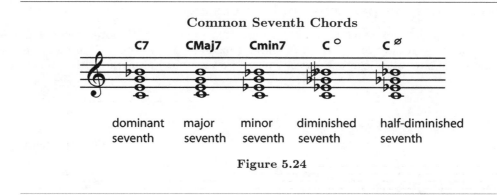

Common Seventh Chords

dominant seventh · major seventh · minor seventh · diminished seventh · half-diminished seventh

Figure 5.24

Listen to the differences between the C seventh[30], C major seventh[31], C minor seventh[32], C diminished seventh[33], and C half-diminished seventh[34].

Exercise 5.8:

Write the following seventh chords. If you need staff paper, you can print this PDF file[35]

1. G minor seventh

2. E (dominant) seventh

3. B flat major seventh

4. D diminished seventh

5. F (dominant) seventh

6. F sharp minor seventh

7. G major seventh

8. B half-diminished seventh

(Solution to Exercise 5.8 on p. 212.)

Exercise 5.9:

Write a Ddim7, Fdim7, G#dim7, and Bdim7. Look closely at the chords you have written and see if you can notice something surprising about them. (Hint: try rewriting the chords enharmonically (Section 1.1.5) so that all the notes are either natural or (single) flat. *(Solution to Exercise 5.9 on p. 213.)*

---

[30] http://cnx.org/content/m11995/latest/chodom7.mp3

[31] http://cnx.org/content/m11995/latest/choM7.mp3

[32] http://cnx.org/content/m11995/latest/chomin7.mp3

[33] http://cnx.org/content/m11995/latest/chodim7.mp3

[34] http://cnx.org/content/m11995/latest/chohalfdim.mp3

[35] http://cnx.org/content/m11995/latest/staffpaper1.pdf

5.4.4 Added Notes, Suspensions, and Extensions

The seventh is not the only note you can add to a basic triad to get a new chord. You can continue to *extend* the chord by adding to the stack of thirds (Section 5.1), or you can *add* any note you want. The most common additions and extensions add notes that are in the scale named by the chord.

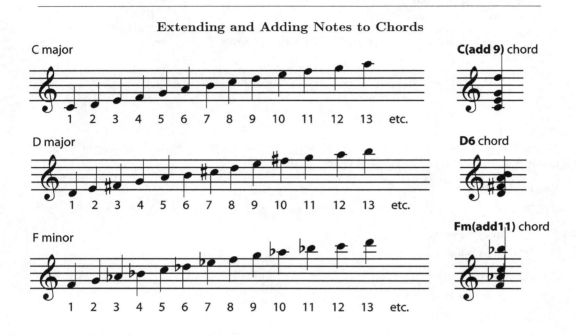

Figure 5.25: To find out what to call a note added to a chord, count the notes of the scale named by the chord.

The first, third, and fifth (1, 3, and 5) notes of the scale are part of the basic triad. So are any other notes in other octaves that have the same name as 1, 3, or 5. In a C major chord, for example, that would be any C naturals, E naturals, and G naturals. If you want to add a note with a different name, just list its number (its **scale degree**) after the name of the chord.

Adding to and Extending Chords

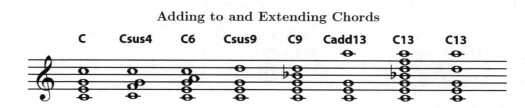

Figure 5.26: Labelling a number as "sus" (suspended) implies that it replaces the chord tone immediately below it. Labelling it "add" implies that only that note is added. In many other situations, the performer is left to decide how to play the chord most effectively. Chord tones may or may not be left out. In an extended chord, all or some of the notes in the "stack of thirds" below the named note may also be added.

Many of the higher added notes are considered **extensions** of the "stack of thirds" begun in the triad. In other words, a C13 can include (it's sometimes the performer's decision which notes will actually be played) the seventh, ninth, and eleventh as well as the thirteenth. Such a chord can be dominant, major, or minor; the performer must take care to play the correct third and seventh. If a chord symbol says to "add13", on the other hand, this usually means that only the thirteenth is added.

A Variety of Ninth Chords

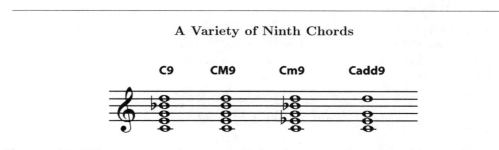

Figure 5.27: Take care to use the correct third and seventh - dominant, major, or minor - with extended chords. If the higher note is labelled "add", don't include the chord extensions that aren't named.

NOTE: All added notes and extensions, including sevenths, introduce dissonance (Section 5.3) into the chord. In some modern music, many of these dissonances are heard as pleasant or interesting or jazzy and don't need to be resolved. However, in other styles of music, dissonances need to be resolved (pg 185), and some chords may be altered to make the dissonance sound less harsh (for example, by leaving out the 3 in a chord with a 4).

You may have noticed that, once you pass the octave (8), you are repeating the scale. In other words, C2 and C9 both add a D, and C4 and C11 both add an F. It may seem that C4 and C11 should therefore be the same chords, but in practice these chords usually do sound different; for example, performers given a C4 chord will put the added note near the bass note and often use it as a temporary replacement for the third (the "3") of the chord. On the other hand, they will put the added note of a C11 at the top of the chord, far away from the bass note and piled up on top of all the other notes of the chord (including the third), which may include the 7 and 9 as well as the 11. The result is that the C11 - an **extension** - has a more diffuse, jazzy, or impressionistic sound. The C4, on the other hand, has a more intense, needs-to-be-resolved, classic **suspension** sound. In fact, 2, 4, and 9 chords are often labelled **suspended** (sus), and follow the same rules for resolution (pg 185) in popular music as they do in classical.

Figure 5.28: Low-number added notes and high-number added notes are treated differently. So even though they both add an F, a C4 suspension[36] will sound quite different from a C11[37] extended chord.

5.4.5 Bass Notes

The bass line (Accompaniment) of a piece of music is very important, and the composer/arranger often will want to specify what note should be the lowest-sounding in the chord. At the end of the chord name will be a slash followed by a note name, for example C/E. The note following the slash should be the bass note.

Naming the Bass Note

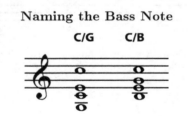

Figure 5.29: The note following the slash is the bass note of the chord. It can be a note that is already in the chord - making the chord a first or second inversion (pg 176) - or it can be an added note, following the same basic rules as other added notes (including using it to replace other notes in the chord).

The note named as the bass note can be a note normally found in the chord - for example, C/E or C/G - or it can be an added note - for example C/B or C/A. If the bass note is not named, it is best to use the tonic (pg 127) as the primary bass note.

---

[36]http://cnx.org/content/m11995/latest/C4C.mid
[37]http://cnx.org/content/m11995/latest/C11.mid

Exercise 5.10:

Name the chords. (Hint: Look for suspensions, added notes, extensions, and basses that are not the root. Try to identify the main triad or root first.)

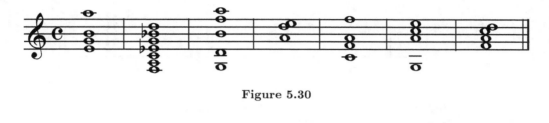

Figure 5.30

(Solution to Exercise 5.10 on p. 213.)

Exercise 5.11:

For guitarists, pianists, and other chord players: Get some practical practice. Name some chords you don't have memorized (maybe F6, Am/G, Fsus4, BM7, etc.). Chords with fingerings that you don't know but with a sound that you would recognize work best for this exercise. Decide what notes must be in those chords, find a practical fingering for them, play the notes and see what they sound like. *(Solution to Exercise 5.11 on p. 213.)*

5.4.6 Altering Notes and Chords

If a note in the chord is not in the major or minor scale of the root (Section 5.1) of the chord, it is an **altered note** and makes the chord an **altered chord**. The alteration - for example "flat five" or "sharp nine" - is listed in the chord symbol. Any number of alterations can be listed, making some chord symbols quite long. *Alterations are not the same as accidentals (pg 17).* Remember, a chord symbol always names notes in the scale of the chord root (Section 5.1), ignoring the key signature (Section 1.1.4) of the piece that the chord is in, so the alterations are from the scale of the chord, not from the key of the piece.

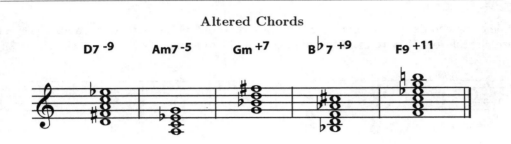

The "half-diminished seventh" may be written as a
"minor seventh with flat five" as here.

The "minor chord with sharp seventh" is also sometimes referred to
as a "minor, major seventh" chord, for example **Gm 7**

Figure 5.31: There is some variation in the chord symbols for altered chords. Plus/minus or sharp/flat symbols may appear before or after the note number. When sharps and flats are used, remember that the alteration is always from the scale of the chord root, not from the key signature.

Exercise 5.12:

On a treble clef staff, write the chords named. You can print this PDF file[38] if you need staff paper for this exercise.

    1.D (dominant) seventh with a flat nine

    2.A minor seventh with a flat five

    3.G minor with a sharp seven

    4.B flat (dominant) seventh with a sharp nine

    5.F nine sharp eleven

(Solution to Exercise 5.12 on p. 214.)

5.5 Beginning Harmonic Analysis[39]

5.5.1 Introduction

It sounds like a very technical idea, but basic **harmonic analysis** just means understanding how a chord is related to the key and to the other chords in a piece of music. This can be such useful information that you will find many musicians who have not studied much music theory, and even some who don't read music, but who can tell you what the I ("one") or the V ("five") chord are in a certain key.

    Why is it useful to know how chords are related?

- Many standard forms (Section 5.7) (for example, a "twelve bar blues") follow very specific chord progressions (Chords), which are often discussed in terms of harmonic relationships.

[38]http://cnx.org/content/m11995/latest/staffpaper1.pdf
[39]This content is available online at <http://cnx.org/content/m11643/1.15/>.

- If you understand chord relationships, you can transpose (Section 6.4) any chord progression you know to any key (Section 4.3) you like.

- If you are searching for chords to go with a particular melody (Section 2.3) (in a particular key), it is very helpful to know what chords are most likely in that key, and how they might be likely to progress from one to another.

- Improvisation requires an understanding of the chord progression.

- Harmonic analysis is also necessary for anyone who wants to be able to compose reasonable chord progressions or to study and understand the music of the great composers.

5.5.2 Basic Triads in Major Keys

Any chord might show up in any key, but some chords are much more likely than others. The most likely chords to show up in a key are the chords that use only the notes in that key (no accidentals (pg 17)). So these chords have both names and numbers that tell how they fit into the key. (We'll just discuss basic triads (Section 5.1) for the moment, not seventh chords (pg 188) or other added-note (Section 5.4.4) or altered (pg 193) chords.) The chords are numbered using Roman numerals from I to vii.

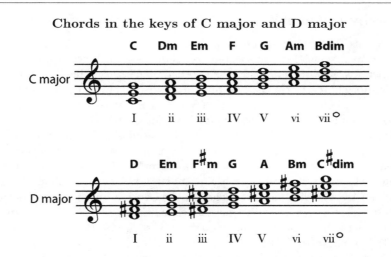

Figure 5.32: To find all the basic chords in a key, build a simple triad (in the key) on each note of the scale. You'll find that although the chords change from one key to the next, the *pattern* of major and minor chords is always the same.

Exercise 5.13:

Write and name the chords in G major and in B flat major. (Hint: Determine the key signature (Section 1.1.4) first. Make certain that each chord begins on a note in the major scale (Section 4.3) and contains only notes in the key signature.) If you need some staff paper, you can print this PDF file[40]   *(Solution to Exercise 5.13 on p. 214.)*

---

[40]http://cnx.org/content/m11643/latest/staffpaper1.pdf

You can find all the basic triads that are possible in a key by building one triad, in the key, on each note of the scale (each **scale degree**). One easy way to name all these chords is just to number them: the chord that starts on the first note of the scale is "I", the chord that starts on the next scale degree is "ii", and so on. Roman numerals are used to number the chords. Capital Roman numerals are used for major chords (Section 5.2.1) and small Roman numerals for minor chords (Section 5.2.1). The diminished chord (Section 5.2.2) is in small Roman numerals followed by a small circle. Because major scales always follow the same pattern, the pattern of major and minor chords is also the same in any major key. The chords built on the first, fourth, and fifth degrees of the scale are always major chords (I, IV, and V). The chords built on the second, third, and sixth degrees of the scale are always minor chords (ii, iii, and vi). The chord built on the seventh degree of the scale is a diminished chord.

> NOTE: Notice that IV in the key of B flat is an E flat major chord, not an E major chord, and vii in the key of G is F sharp diminished, not F diminished. If you can't name the scale notes in a key, you may find it difficult to predict whether a chord should be based on a sharp, flat, or natural note. This is only one reason (out of many) why it is a good idea to memorize all the scales. (See Major Keys and Scales (Section 4.3).) However, if you don't plan on memorizing all the scales at this time, you'll find it useful to memorize at least the most important chords (start with I, IV, and V) in your favorite keys.

5.5.3 A Hierarchy of Chords

Even among the chords that naturally occur in a key signature, some are much more likely to be used than others. In most music, the most common chord is I. In Western music (Section 2.8), I is the tonal center (Section 4.3) of the music, the chord that feels like the "home base" of the music. As the other two major chords in the key, IV and V are also likely to be very common. In fact, the most common added-note chord in most types of Western music is a V chord (the dominant chord (Section 5.5.4)) with a minor seventh (Major and Minor Intervals) added (V7). It is so common that this particular flavor of seventh (Section 5.4.3) (a major chord with a minor seventh added) is often called a **dominant seventh**, regardless of whether the chord is being used as the V (the dominant) of the key. Whereas the I chord feels most strongly "at home", V7 gives the strongest feeling of "time to head home now". This is very useful for giving music a satisfying ending. Although it is much less common than the V7, the diminished vii chord (often with a diminished seventh (Section 5.2.2) added), is considered to be a harmonically unstable chord that strongly wants to resolve to I. Listen to these very short progressions and see how strongly each suggests that you must be in the key of C: C (major) chord(I)[41]; F chord to C chord (IV - I)[42]; G chord to C chord (V - I)[43]; G seventh chord to C chord (V7 - I)[44]; B diminished seventh chord to C chord (viidim7 - I)[45] (Please see Cadence (Section 5.6) for more on this subject.)

Many folk songs and other simple tunes can be accompanied using only the I, IV and V (or V7) chords of a key, a fact greatly appreciated by many beginning guitar players. Look at some chord progressions from real music.

---

[41]http://cnx.org/content/m11643/latest/Cchord.mid
[42]http://cnx.org/content/m11643/latest/FchordCchord.mid
[43]http://cnx.org/content/m11643/latest/GchordCchord.mid
[44]http://cnx.org/content/m11643/latest/G7chordCchord.mid
[45]http://cnx.org/content/m11643/latest/BdimchordCchord.MID

Some chord progressions

A Common Twelve Bar Blues:

I	I	I	I7
IV7	IV7	I	I
V7	V7	I	I

Verse of "Jingle Bells"

I	I	I	IV
IV	V7	V7	I
I	I	I	IV
IV	V7	V7	I

Chorus of "Bye Bye, Love"

IV	I	IV	I
IV	I	V7	I

Figure 5.33: Much Western music is harmonically pretty simple, so it can be very useful just to know I, IV, and V in your favorite keys. This figure shows progressions as a list of chords (read left to right as if reading a paragraph), one per measure.

A lot of folk music, blues, rock, marches, and even some classical music is based on simple chord progressions, but of course there is plenty of music that has more complicated harmonies. Pop and jazz in particular often include many chords with added (Section 5.4.4) or altered (pg 193) notes. Classical music also tends to use more complex chords in greater variety, and is very likely to use chords that are not in the key.

More Complex Chord Progressions

Chorus of "Love Me Tender"

I	III7	vi	I7
IVM7	iv	I	I
v6	VI7	II7	II7
V7sus4	V7	I	I

Beginning of Liszt's "Liebestraum"

I	III7	Vi7	II7
ii7	V7	I	Idim I

Figure 5.34: Some music has more complex harmonies. This can include more unusual chords such as major sevenths, and chords with altered (pg 193) notes such as sharp fives. It may also include more basic chords that aren't in the key, such as I diminished and II (major), or even chords based on notes that are not in the key such as a sharp IV chord. (Please see Beyond Triads (Section 5.4.2) to review how to read chord symbols.)

Extensive study and practice are needed to be able to identify and understand these more complex progressions. It is not uncommon to find college-level music theory courses that are largely devoted to harmonic analysis and its relationship to musical forms. This course will go no further than to encourage you to develop a basic understanding of what harmonic analysis is about.

5.5.4 Naming Chords Within a Key

So far we have concentrated on identifying chord relationships by number, because this system is commonly used by musicians to talk about every kind of music from classical to jazz to blues. There is another set of names that is commonly used, particularly in classical music, to talk about harmonic relationships. Because numbers are used in music to identify everything from beats to intervals to harmonics to what fingering to use, this naming system is sometimes less confusing.

I	=	Tonic
ii	=	Supertonic
iii	=	Mediant
IV	=	Subdominant
V	=	Dominant
vi	=	Submediant
vii°	=	Subtonic, or Leading Tone

Figure 5.35

Exercise 5.14:

Name the chord.

1. Dominant in C major
2. Subdominant in E major
3. Tonic in G sharp major
4. Mediant in F major
5. Supertonic in D major
6. Submediant in C major
7. Dominant seventh in A major

(Solution to Exercise 5.14 on p. 215.)

Exercise 5.15:

The following chord progression is in the key of G major. Identify the relationship of each chord to the key by both name and number. Which chord is not in the key? Which chord in the key has been left out of the progression?

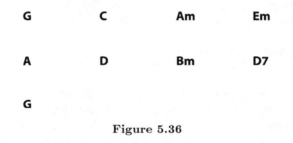

Figure 5.36

(Solution to Exercise 5.15 on p. 215.)

5.5.5 Minor Keys

Since minor scales (Section 4.4) follow a different pattern of intervals (Section 4.5) than major keys, they will produce chord progressions with important differences from major key progressions.

Exercise 5.16:

Write (triad) chords that occur in the keys of a minor, e minor, and d minor. Remember to begin each triad on a note of the natural minor scale and to include only notes in the scale in each chord. Which chord relationships are major? Which minor? Which diminished? If you need staff paper, print this PDF file[46]   *(Solution to Exercise 5.16 on p. 216.)*

Exercise 5.17:

In the harmonic minor (Section 4.4.4) scale, the seventh scale degree (pg 196) is raised by a half step (Section 4.2). Which chords would this change? How would it change them? Why does the harmonic minor scale (so-called because it is useful in harmony) do this? Which altered chords would be used most often?   *(Solution to Exercise 5.17 on p. 216.)*

---

[46]http://cnx.org/content/m11643/latest/staffpaper1.pdf

5.5.6 Modulation

Sometimes a piece of music temporarily moves into a new key. This is called **modulation**. It is very common in traditional classical music; long symphony and concerto movements almost always spend at least some time in a different key (usually a closely related key (Section 4.7) such as the dominant (Section 5.5.4) or subdominant (Section 5.5.4), or the relative minor or relative major (Section 4.4.3)), to keep things interesting. Shorter works, even in classical style, are less likely to have complete modulations. In most styles of music, a slow, gradual modulation to the new key (and back) seems more natural, and abrupt modulations can seem unpleasant and jarring. But implied modulations, in which the tonal center seems to suddenly shift for a short time, can be very common in some shorter works (jazz standards, for example). As in longer works, modulation, with its new set of chords, is a good way to keep a piece interesting. If you find that the chord progression in a piece of music suddenly contains many chords that you would not expect in that key, it may be that the piece has modulated. Lots of accidentals, or even an actual change of key signature (Section 1.1.4), are other clues that the music has modulated.

A new key signature (Section 1.1.4) may help you to identify the modulation key. If there is not a change of key signature, remember that the new key is likely to contain whatever accidentals (pg 17) are showing up. It is also likely that many of the chords in the progression will be chords that are common in the new key. Look particularly for tonic chords and dominant sevenths. The new key is likely to be closely related (Section 4.7) to the original key, but another favorite trick in popular music is to simply move the key up one whole step (Section 4.2), for example from C major to D major.

5.5.7 Further Study

Although the concept of harmonic analysis is pretty basic, actually analyzing complex pieces can be a major challenge. This is one of the main fields of study for those who are interested in studying music theory at a more advanced level. One next step for those interested in the subject is to become familiar with all the ways notes may be added to basic triads. (Please see Beyond Triads (Section 5.4) for an introduction to that subject.) At that point, you may want to spend some time practicing analyzing some simple, familiar pieces. As of this writing, the site Music Theory for Songwriters[47] featured "chord maps" that help the student predict likely chord progressions. For more advanced practice, look for music theory books that focus entirely on harmony or that spend plenty of time analyzing harmonies in real music. (Some music history textbooks are in this category.) You will progress more quickly if you can find books that focus on the music genre that you are most interested in (there are books on jazz harmony, for example).

5.6 Cadence[48]

A **cadence** is any place in a piece of music that has the feel of an ending point. This can be either a strong, definite stopping point - the end of the piece, for example, or the end of a movement or a verse - but it also refers to the "temporary-resting-place" pauses that round off the ends of musical ideas within each larger section.

A musical phrase (Section 2.3.4), like a sentence, usually contains an understandable idea, and then pauses before the next idea starts. Some of these musical pauses are simply take-a-breath-type pauses, and don't really give an "ending" feeling. In fact, like questions that need answers, many phrases leave the listener with a strong expectation of hearing the next, "answering", phrase. Other phrases, though, end with a more definite "we've arrived where we were going" feeling. The

---

[47]http://www.chordmaps.com

[48]This content is available online at <http://cnx.org/content/m12402/1.9/>.

composer's expert control over such feelings of expectation and arrival are one of the main sources of the listener's enjoyment of the music.

Like a story, a piece of music can come to an end by simply stopping, but most listeners will react to such abruptness with dissatisfaction: the story or music simply "stopped" instead of "ending" properly. A more satisfying ending, in both stories and music, is usually provided by giving clues that an end is coming, and then ending in a commonly-accepted way. Stories are also divided into paragraphs, chapters, stanzas, scenes, or episodes, each with their own endings, to help us keep track of things and understand what is going on. Music also groups phrases and motifs (Section 2.3.5) into verses, choruses, sections, and movements, marked off by strong cadences to help us keep track of them. In good stories, there are clues in the plot and the pacing - in the Western (Section 2.8) tradition, the chase gets more exciting, characters good and bad get what they deserve, the inevitable tragedy occurs, or misunderstandings get resolved - that signal that the end of the story is nearing. Similarly, in music there are clues that signal to the listener that the end is coming up. These clues may be in the form (Section 5.7); in the development of the musical ideas; in the music's tempo (Section 1.2.8), texture (Section 2.4), or rhythmic (Section 2.1) complexity; in the chord progression (Chords); even in the number and length of the phrases (Section 2.3.4) (Western listeners are fond of powers of two[49]). Like the ending of a story, an ending in music is more satisfying if it follows certain customs that the listener expects to hear. If you have grown up listening to a particular musical tradition, you will automatically have these expectations for a piece of music, even if you are not aware of having them. And like the customs for storytelling, these expectations can be different in different musical traditions.

Some things that produce a feeling of cadence

- *Harmony* - In most Western (Section 2.8) and Western-influenced music (including jazz and "world" musics), harmony (Section 2.5) is by far the most important signal of cadence. One of the most fundamental "rules" of the major-minor harmony system is that music ends on the tonic (pg 127). A tonal (pg 91) piece of music will almost certainly end on the tonic chord, although individual phrases or sections may end on a different chord (the dominant (pg 198) is a popular choice). But a composer cannot just throw in a tonic chord and expect it to sound like an ending; the harmony must "lead up to" the ending and make it feel inevitable (just as a good story makes the ending feel inevitable, even if it's a surprise). So the term **cadence**, in tonal music, usually refers to the "ending" chord plus the short chord progression (Chords) that led up to it. There are many different terms in use for the most common tonal cadences; you will find the most common terms below (Some Tonal Cadence Terms). Some (but not all) modal (Section 6.3) musics also use harmony to indicate cadence, but the cadences used can be quite different from those in tonal harmony.

- *Melody* - In the major/minor tradition, the melody will normally end on some note of the tonic chord triad (Section 5.1), and a melody ending on the tonic will give a stronger (more final-sounding) cadence than one ending on the third or fifth of the chord. In some modal (Section 6.3) musics, the melody plays the most important role in the cadence. Like a scale, each mode also has a home note, where the melody is expected to end. A mode often also has a formula that the melody usually uses to arrive at the ending note. For example, it may be typical of one mode to go to the final note from the note one whole tone (pg 124) below it; whereas in another mode the penultimate note may be a minor third (pg 137) above the final note. (Or a mode may have more than one possible melodic cadence, or its typical cadence may be more complex.)

- *Rhythm* - Changes in the rhythm (Section 2.1), a break or pause in the rhythm, a change in the tempo (Section 1.2.8), or a slowing of or pause in the harmonic rhythm (Chords) are also commonly found at a cadence.

---

[49]"Powers, Roots, and Equal Temperament" <http://cnx.org/content/m11809/latest/>

- *Texture* - Changes in the texture (Section 2.4) of the music also often accompany a cadence. For example, the music may momentarily switch from harmony (Section 2.5) to unison or from counterpoint (Section 2.6) to a simpler block-chord homophony (Section 2.4.2.2).

- *Form* - Since cadences mark off phrases and sections, form (Section 5.7) and cadence are very closely connected, and the overall architecture of a piece of music will often indicate where the next cadence is going to be - every eight measures for a certain type of dance, for example. (When you listen to a piece of music, you actually expect and listen for these regularly-spaced cadences, at least subconsciously. An accomplished composer may "tease" you by seeming to lead to a cadence in the expected place, but then doing domething unexpected instead.)

Harmonic analysis (Section 5.5), form (Section 5.7), and cadence in Western (Section 2.8) music are closely interwoven into a complex subject that can take up an entire course at the college-music-major level. Complicating matters is the fact that there are several competing systems for naming cadences. This introductory course cannot go very deeply into this subject, and so will only touch on the common terms used when referring to cadences. Unfortunately, the various naming systems may use the same terms to mean different things, so even a list of basic terms is a bit confusing.

Some Tonal Cadence Terms

- **Authentic** - A dominant (Section 5.5.4) chord followed by a tonic (pg 127) chord (V-I, or often V7-I).

- **Complete Cadence** - same as authentic cadence.

- **Deceptive Cadence** - This refers to any time that the music seems to lead up to a cadence, but then doesn't actually land on the expected tonic, and also often does not bring the expected pause in the music.

- **False Cadence** - Same as deceptive cadence.

- **Full Close** - Same as authentic cadence.

- **Half-cadence** - May refer to a cadence that ends on the dominant chord (V). This type of cadence is more common at pause-type cadences than at full-stop ones. OR may have same meaning as plagal cadence.

- **Half close** - Same as plagal cadence.

- **Imperfect Cadence** - May refer to an authentic (V-I) cadence in which the chord is not in root position, or the melody does not end on the tonic. *OR* may mean a cadence that ends on the dominant chord (same as one meaning of half-cadence).

- **Interrupted Cadence** - Same as deceptive cadence.

- **Perfect Cadence** - Same as authentic cadence. As its name suggests, this is considered the strongest, most final-sounding cadence. Some do not consider a cadence to be completely perfect unless the melody ends on the tonic and both chords (V and I) are in root position (Section 5.1).

- **Plagal Cadence** - A subdominant (Section 5.5.4) chord followed by a tonic chord (IV-I). For many people, this cadence will be familiar as the "Amen" chords at the end of many traditional hymns.

- **Semi-cadence** - Same possible meanings as half cadence.

You can listen to a few simple cadences here: Perfect Cadence[50], Plagal Cadence[51], Half-cadence[52], Deceptive Cadence[53]. The figure below also shows some very simple forms of some common cadences. The first step in becoming comfortable with cadences is to start identifying them in music that is very familiar to you. Find the pauses and stops in the music. Do a harmonic analysis (Section 5.5) of the last few chords before each stop, and identify what type of cadence it is. Then see if you can begin to recognize the type of cadence just by listening to the music.

Examples of Common Cadences

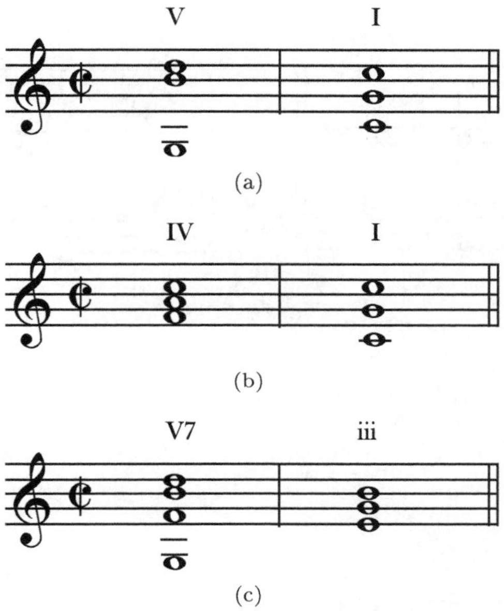

Figure 5.37: (a) Perfect Cadence in C major (b) Plagal Cadence in C major (c) Deceptive Cadence in C major

---

[50]http://cnx.org/content/m12402/latest/PerfectCadence.swf
[51]http://cnx.org/content/m12402/latest/PlagalCadence.swf
[52]http://cnx.org/content/m12402/latest/HalfCadence.swf
[53]http://cnx.org/content/m12402/latest/FalseCadence.swf

Exercise 5.18:

Identify the type of cadence in each excerpt. (Hint: First identify the key and then do a harmonic analysis (Section 5.5) of the progression.

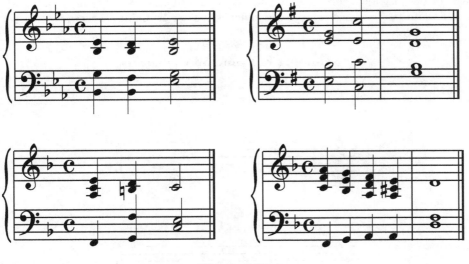

Figure 5.38

(Solution to Exercise 5.18 on p. 217.)

5.7 Form[54]

5.7.1 Form is the Basic Structure

Every piece of music has an overall plan or structure, the "big picture", so to speak. This is called the **form** of the music.

It is easy to recognize and grasp the form of some things, because they are small and simple, like a grain of salt, or repetitive, like a wall made of bricks of the same size. Other forms are easy to understand because they are so familiar; if you see dogs more often than you do sea cucumbers, it should be easier for you to recognize the form of an unfamiliar dog than of an unfamiliar sea cucumber. Other things, like a forest ecosystem, or the structure of a government, are so complex that they have to be explored or studied before their structure can be understood.

Musical forms offer a great range of complexity. Most listeners will quickly grasp the form of a short and simple piece, or of one built from many short repetitions. It is also easier to recognize familiar musical forms. The average American, for example, can distinguish easily between the verses and refrain of any pop song, but will have trouble recognizing what is going on in a piece of music for Balinese gamelan. Classical music traditions around the world tend to encourage longer, more complex forms which may be difficult to recognize without the familiarity that comes from study or repeated hearings.

You can enjoy music without recognizing its form, of course. But understanding the form of a piece helps a musician put together a more credible performance of it. Anyone interested in music

---

[54]This content is available online at <http://cnx.org/content/m10842/2.11/>.

theory or history, or in arranging or composing music, must have a firm understanding of form. And being able to "see the big picture" does help the listener enjoy the music even more.

5.7.2 Describing Form

Musicians traditionally have two ways to describe the form of a piece of music. One way involves labelling each large section with a letter. The other way is to simply give a name to a form that is very common.

5.7.2.1 Labelling Form With Letters

Letters can be used to label the form of any piece of music, from the simplest to the most complex. Each major section of the music is labelled with a letter; for example, the first section is the A section. If the second section (or third or fourth) is exactly the same as the first, it is also labelled A. If it is very much like the A section, but with some important differences, it can be labelled A' (pronounced "A prime"). The A' section can also show up later in the piece, or yet another variation of A, A" (pronounced "A double prime") can show up, and so on.

The first major section of the piece that is very different from A is labelled B, and other sections that are like it can be labelled B, B', B", and so on. Sections that are not like A or B are labelled C, and so on.

How do you recognize the sections? With familiar kinds of music, this is pretty easy. (See Figure 5.39 for some examples of forms that will be familiar to most listeners.) With unfamiliar types of music, it can be more of a challenge. Whether the music is classical, modern, jazz, or pop, listen for repeated sections of music. Also, listen for big changes, in the rhythm (Section 2.1), melody (Section 2.3), harmony (Section 2.5), texture (Section 2.4), and timbre (Section 2.2). A new section that is not a repetition will usually have noticeable differences in more than one of these areas. For an excellent discussion of form, with plenty of chances to practice hearing the beginnings of new sections, please see Professor Brandt's Sound Reasoning[55] course. In particular, Musical Form[56] deals with recognizing when something new is being introduced (A/B instead of A only), and Time's Effect on the Material[57] deals with recognizing when a section reappears changed (A', B', or A").

---

[55]*Sound Reasoning* <http://cnx.org/content/col10214/latest/>
[56]"Musical Form" <http://cnx.org/content/m11629/latest/>
[57]"" <http://cnx.org/content/m11434/latest/>

Some Familiar Forms

Typical Children's Nursery Rhyme:	A	
	One short section with no major changes in the sound of the music	A
Typical Hymn (no refrain):	A A' A"	
First Verse	Everyone sings the melody	A
Second Verse	Choir adds harmonies	A'
Third Verse	Organ adds more complex accompaniment	A"
Typical Pop Song:	A B A' B A" B' OR A B A' B C B'	
First verse	Solo singer with quiet instrumental backup	A
Refrain	Different melody, different chord progression, often a "bigger", more complex texture than verse.	B
Second verse	Different words, but the music is very similar to the first verse (usually with small differences)	A'
Refrain	Same as first refrain (no noticeable differences)	B
Third verse OR Bridge	Same comments as second verse OR New melody with new chord progression	A" OR C
Final Refrain	May add more vocal or instrumental parts, for most complex texture yet	B'

Figure 5.39: Most folk and popular music features simple forms that encourage participation.

Exercise 5.19:

Practice identifying some easy musical forms. Pick some favorite songs and listen to each repeatedly until you are satisfied that you have identified its full form using letters and primes. Compare the forms of the tunes to spot similarities and differences.

Listen for:

- *Verses* have the same melody but different words.

- *Refrains* have the same melody and the same words.

- *Bridge Sections* are new material that appears late in the song, usually appearing only once or twice, often in place of a verse and usually leading into the refrain. (You may want to note the differences - and the similarity - in the use of the term **bridge** by popular musicians and jazz musicians; see below (Some Common Forms)).

- *Instrumentals* are important sections that have no vocals. They can come at the beginning or end, or in between other sections. Is there more than one? Do they have the same melody as a verse or refrain? Are they similar to each other?

(Solution to Exercise 5.19 on p. 217.)

While discussing a piece of music in detail, musicians may also use letters to label smaller parts of the piece within larger sections, even down to labelling individual phrases (Section 2.3.4). For example, the song "The Girl I Left Behind" has many verses with no refrain, an A A' A"- type form. However, a look (Figure 5.40) at the tune of one verse shows that within that overall form is an A A' B A" phrase structure.

Phrase Structure in "The Girl I Left Behind"

Figure 5.40: In detailed discussions of a piece of music, smaller sections, and even individual phrases, may also be labelled with letters, in order to discuss the piece in greater detail. The A A B A form of this verse is very common, found in verses of everything from folk to jazz to pop music. Verses of blues songs are more likely to have an A A' B form.

Exercise 5.20:

Now try labeling the phrases of a verse or a refrain of some of the songs you listened to in Exercise 5.19. Listen for phrases that use similar melodies. (Sometimes, but not always, they even use the same words.) How many of your refrains and verses were basically A A B A? What were the others?   *(Solution to Exercise 5.20 on p. 217.)*

5.7.2.2 Naming Forms

Often a musical form becomes so popular with composers that it is given a name. For example, if a piece of music is called a "theme and variations", it is expected to have an overall plan quite different from a piece called a "rondo". (Specifically, the theme and variations would follow an A A' A" A"'... plan, with each section being a new variation on the theme in the first section. A rondo follows an A B A C A ... plan, with a familiar section returning in between sections of new music.)

Also, many genres of music tend to follow a preset form, like the "typical pop song form" in Figure 5.39. A **symphony**, for example, is usually a piece of music written for a fairly large number of instruments. It is also associated with a particular form, so knowing that a piece of music is called a symphony should lead you to expect certain things about it. For example, listeners familiar with the symphonic form expect a piece called a symphony to have three or four (depending on when it was written) main sections, called **movements**. They expect a moment of silence in between movements, and also expect the movements to sound very different from each other; for example if the first movement is fast and loud, they might expect that the second movement would be slow and quiet. If they have heard many symphonies, they also would not be at all surprised if the first movement is in sonata form and the third movement is based on a dance.

> NOTE: Although a large group of people who play classical music together is often called a symphony, the more accurate term for the group is **orchestra**. The confusion occurs because many orchestras call themselves "symphony orchestras" because they spend so much time playing symphonies (as opposed to, for example, an "opera orchestra" or a "pops orchestra").

Other kinds of music are also so likely to follow a particular overall plan that they have become associated with a particular form. You can hear musicians talk about something being concerto form or sonata form, for example (even if the piece is not technically a concerto or sonata). Particular dances (a minuet, for example), besides having a set tempo (Section 1.2.8) and time signature (Section 1.2.3), will sometimes have a set form that suits the dance steps. And many marches are similar enough in form that there are names for the expected sections (first strain, second strain, trio, break strain).

But it is important to remember that forms are not sets of rules that composers are required to follow. Some symphonies don't have silence between movements, and some don't use the sonata form in any of their movements. Plenty of marches have been written that don't have a trio section, and the development section of a sonata movement can take unexpected turns. And hybrid forms, like the sonata rondo, can become popular with some composers. After all, in architecture, "house" form suggests to most Americans a front and back door, a dining room off the kitchen, and bedrooms with closets, but an architect is free to leave out the dining room, and put the main door at the side of the house and the closets in the bathrooms. Whether a piece of music is a march, a sonata, or a theme and variations, the composer is always free to experiment with the overall architecture of the piece.

Being able to spot that overall architecture as we listen - knowing, so to speak, which room we are in right now - gives us important clues that help us understand and appreciate the music.

Some Common Forms

- *Through-composed* - One section (usually not very long) that does not contain any large repetitions. If a short piece includes repeated phrases, it may be classified by the structure of its phrases.

- *Strophic* - Composed of verses. The music is repeated sections with fairly small changes. May or may not include a refrain (pg 207).

- *Variations* - One section repeated many times. Most commonly, the melody remains recognizable in each section, and the underlying harmonic structure (Section 5.5) remains basically the same, but big changes in rhythm (Section 2.1), tempo (Section 1.2.8), texture (Section 2.4), or timbre (Section 2.2) keep each section sounding fresh and interesting. Writing a set of variations is considered an excellent exercise for students interested in composing, arranging, and orchestration.

- *Jazz standard song form* - Jazz utilizes many different forms, but one very common form is closely related to the strophic and variation forms. A chord progression (Chords) in A A B A form (with the B section called the bridge (pg 207)) is repeated many times. On the first and last repetition, the melody is played or sung, and soloists improvise during the other repetitions. The overall form of verse-like repetition, with the melody played only the first and final times, and improvisations on the other repetitions, is very common in jazz even when the A A B A song form is not being used.

- *Rondo* - One section returns repeatedly, with a section of new music before each return. (A B A C A ; sometimes A B A C A B A)

- *Dance forms* - Dance forms usually consist of repeated sections (so there is plenty of music to dance to), with each section containing a set number of measures (Section 1.2.3.1) (often four, eight, sixteen, or thirty-two) that fits the dance steps. Some very structured dance forms (Minuet, for example) are associated even with particular phrase (Section 2.3.4) structures and harmonic progressions (Section 5.5) within each section.

- *Binary Form* - Two different main sections (A B). Commonly in Western (Section 2.8) classical music, the A section will move away from the tonic (pg 127), with a strong cadence (Section 5.6) in another key, and the B section will move back and end strongly in the tonic.

- *Ternary Form* - Three main sections, usually A B A or A B A'.

- *Cyclic Form* - There are two very different uses of this term. One refers to long multimovement works (a "song cycle", for example) that have an overarching theme and structure binding them together. It may also refer to a single movement or piece of music with a form based on the constant repetition of a single short section. This may be an exact repetition (**ostinato**) in one part of the music (for example, the bass line, or the rhythm section), while development, variation, or new melodies occur in other parts. Or it may be a repetition that gradually changes and evolves. This intense-repetition type of cyclic form is very common in folk musics around the world and often finds its way into classical and popular musics, too.

- *Sonata form* - may also be called sonata-allegro or first-movement form. It is in fact often found in the first movement of a sonata, but it has been an extremely popular form with many well-known composers, and so can be found anywhere from the first movement of a quartet to the final movement of a symphony. In this relatively complex form (too complex to outline here), repetition and development of melodic themes within a framework of expected key changes allow the composer to create a long movement that is unified enough that it makes sense to the listener, but varied enough that it does not get boring.

Solutions to Exercises in Chapter 5

Solution to Exercise 5.1 (p. 176):

Build Root Position Triads:

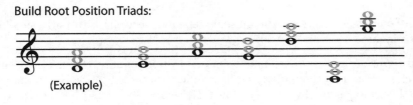

(Example)

Figure 5.41

Solution to Exercise 5.2 (p. 178):

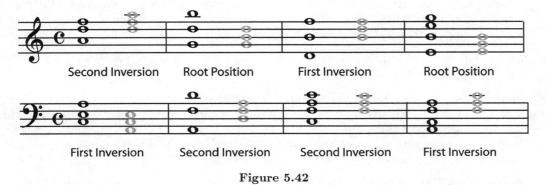

Second Inversion   Root Position   First Inversion   Root Position

First Inversion   Second Inversion   Second Inversion   First Inversion

Figure 5.42

Solution to Exercise 5.3 (p. 180):

Figure 5.43

Solution to Exercise 5.4 (p. 181):

Figure 5.44

Solution to Exercise 5.5 (p. 182):

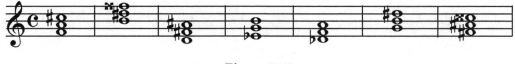

Figure 5.45

Solution to Exercise 5.6 (p. 182):

Figure 5.46

Solution to Exercise 5.7 (p. 183):

Chords are rewritten in root position.

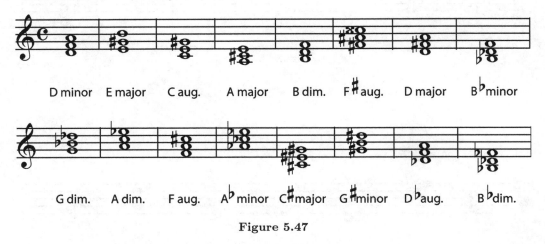

Figure 5.47

Solution to Exercise 5.8 (p. 189):

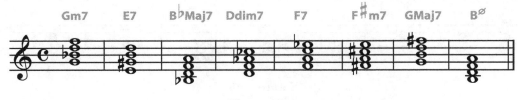

Figure 5.48

Solution to Exercise 5.9 (p. 189):

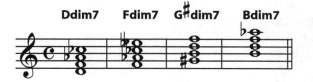

Respell each chord so that you are only using
natural and (single) flat notes:

All of the chords contain the (enharmonic) equivalent
of the same four notes: D , F , A♭, and B ,
so these chords sound like inversions of each other.
There are two other sets of enharmonically
equivalent diminished seventh chords;
how quickly can you find them?

Figure 5.49

Solution to Exercise 5.10 (p. 192):

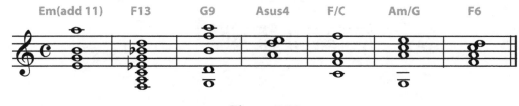

Figure 5.50

Solution to Exercise 5.11 (p. 193):

You can check your work by

- listening to the chords to see if they sound correct

- playing your chords for your teacher or other trained musician

- checking your answers using a chord manual or chord diagrams

Solution to Exercise 5.12 (p. 194):

Notice that a half-diminished seventh (Seventh Chords) can be (and sometimes is) written as it is here, as a minor seventh with flat five.

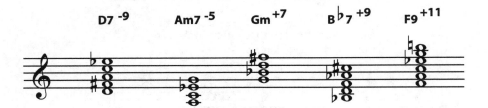

Note that a "half-diminished seventh" may be written as a "minor seventh with flat five", as it is here.

The "minor chord with sharp seventh" is sometimes referred to as a "minor, major seventh" chord, for example   **Gm7**

Figure 5.51

Solution to Exercise 5.13 (p. 195):

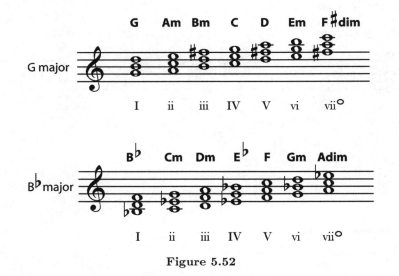

Figure 5.52

Solution to Exercise 5.14 (p. 199):

1. G major (G)

2. A major (A)

3. G sharp major (G#)

4. A minor (Am)

5. E minor (Em)

6. A minor (Am)

7. E seventh (E7)

Solution to Exercise 5.15 (p. 199):

I	IV	ii	vi
G	**C**	**Am**	**Em**
tonic	subdominant	supertonic	submediant
II	V	iii	V7
A	**D**	**Bm**	**D7**
not in key*	dominant	mediant	dominant seventh

I
G
tonic

There is no subtonic in this progression.

*It is A minor (with a C natural), not A major (with a C sharp)
that belongs in this key. An A major chord can sound good in the key of G major,
however. It is the dominant of the dominant (D major), so playing an
A major chord can sometimes make the music feel like it has temporarily moved
to the (closely related) key of D major. This type of harmonic complexity helps
keep a piece of music interesting.

Figure 5.53

Solution to Exercise 5.16 (p. 199):

The tonic, subdominant, and dominant are minor (i, iv, and v). The mediant, submediant, and subtonic are major (III, VI, and VII). The supertonic (ii) is diminished.

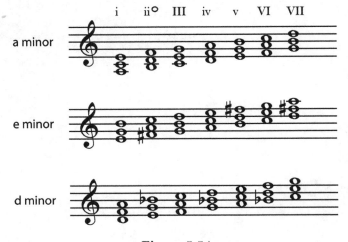

Figure 5.54

Solution to Exercise 5.17 (p. 199):

The III chord would become augmented; the v chord would become major; and the vii chord would become a diminished sharp seven chord. The major dominant chord would be most useful in establishing the tonal center (pg 127) of the piece, although the diminished sharp seven might also sometimes be used for cadences (Section 5.6).

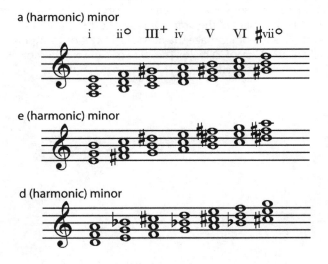

Figure 5.55

Solution to Exercise 5.18 (p. 204):

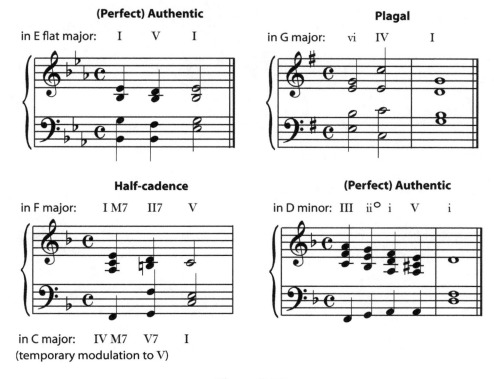

Figure 5.56

Notice that the half cadence looks like (and in fact is) a modulation (Section 5.5.6) to the dominant. In this very common progression, the dominant seventh of the dominant (which requires an accidental) makes the dominant feel like a very strong resting point, and the piece will continue on in the dominant key for a while, before returning to the tonic key. Also notice the accidental required in the minor key to make the (major) dominant chord.

Solution to Exercise 5.19 (p. 206):

Your answers will depend on the songs you choose. Check them with a teacher if you can. (Bring the music so the teacher can listen to it while checking your answers.)

Solution to Exercise 5.20 (p. 208):

If one is available, have a music teacher check your answers.

Chapter 6

Challenges

6.1 Ear Training[1]

6.1.1 What is Ear Training?

When musicians talk about **ear**, they don't mean the sense organ itself so much as the brain's ability to perceive, distinguish, and understand what the ear has heard. The term **ear training** refers to teaching musicians to recognize information about notes (Section 1.2.1) and chords (Chords) just by hearing them. (You can check your "ear" by trying this ear training game[2].)

A few people have what is called **perfect pitch** or **absolute pitch**. These people, when they hear music, can tell you exactly what they are hearing: the G above middle C (pg 120), for example, or the first inversion (Section 5.1.2) of an F minor chord (Section 5.2.1). A few musicians with particularly perceptive ears can even tell you that a piano is tuned a few cents (pg 231) higher than the one that they play at home. This is an unusual skill that even most trained musicians do not have, and research seems to suggest that if you don't have it at a very early age, you cannot develop it. (For more on this subject, you may want to look up Robert Jourdain's *Music, the Brain, and Ecstasy: How Music Captures our Imagination.*)

However, most musicians can be trained to recognize **relative pitch**. In other words, if you play two notes, they can tell you that one of them is a major third (Major and Minor Intervals) higher than the other. If you play four chords (Chords) in a row, they can tell you that you played a tonic-subdominant-dominant seventh-tonic (I-IV-V7-I) chord progression (Chords).

Fortunately, having relative pitch is good enough, and for many musicians may even be more useful than perfect pitch, because of the way Western (Section 2.8) music is conceived. Since all major keys (Section 4.3) are so similar, a piece in a major key will sound almost exactly the same whether you play it in C major or D major. The thing that matters is not what note you start on, but how all the notes are related to each other and to the "home" note (the tonic (pg 127)) of the key. If someone really wants the piece to be in a different key (because it's easier to sing or play in that key, or just because they want it to sound higher or lower), the whole thing can be transposed (Section 6.4), but the only difference that would make (in the sound) is that the entire piece will sound higher or lower. Most listeners would not even notice the difference, unless you played it in both keys, one right after the other.

> NOTE: All minor keys (Section 4.4) are also heard by most listeners as interchangeable, but there are important differences between major keys and minor keys. In fact, the differences in sound between a major key and a minor key is one of the first differences

---

[1]This content is available online at <http://cnx.org/content/m12401/1.11/>.
[2]http://cnx.org/content/m12401/latest/EarTraining.exe

that a musician should be able to hear. If you would like to see whether your "ear" can recognize the difference between major and minor keys, please try the listening exercise (Exercise 4.4) in Major Keys and Scales (Exercise 4.4).

So, you often don't need to know exactly what notes or chords are being played. Simply having an ear well-trained in "relative pitch" is extremely useful in many ways. Guitar and piano players can figure out chord progressions (Chords) just by listening to them, and then play the progressions in their favorite keys. Other instrumentalists can play a favorite tune without a written copy of it, just by knowing what the interval to the next note must be. Composers and music arrangers can jot down a piece of music without having to "pick it out" on an instrument to find the notes and chords they want. And of course, ear training is crucial to any musician who wants to play jazz or any type of improvisation. Given a well-trained "ear", any musical idea that you "hear" in your head, you can play. And ear training is also crucial for those interested in music theory, musicology, or just being able to write down a tune accurately.

As with all other musical skills, there are many different levels and kinds of proficiency. One musician may be very good at "playing by ear", but may not even read music and cannot name intervals (Section 4.5) or write the music down. Another may be very good at "taking dictation" (writing down the music they hear), and yet feel unable to do jazz improvisation. As always, the key is to practice the particular skills that you want to develop.

6.1.2 Ear Training Skills

6.1.2.1 Tuning

This is the most basic ear training skill, crucial to being able to play music that people will want to hear.

Suggestions

- At the beginner level, work with a skilled musician who can teach you how to tune your instrument and help you identify and fix tuning problems.

- Play with other musicians often. (Playing along with recordings does not teach good tuning skills.) Don't just tune at the beginning of rehearsals and performances. Listen at all times and be ready to retune any note whenever necessary.

- Spend as much time as necessary tuning whenever you play. Do not (knowingly) practice while out of tune; if you do, it will slow down your ear training tremendously. Whenever possible, until you are good at tuning, get someone else to help you tune every time you play.

- Practice tuning quickly and accurately. Learn any alternate fingerings and other "tricks" available on your instrument for fine-tuning each note as you play.

6.1.2.2 Playing Chords By Ear

For instruments that play chordal accompaniments, this is an incredibly useful skill.

Suggestions

- You do not have to learn to read music to be able to do this, but it is very helpful to know a little bit about music theory so that you can predict which chords are most likely to happen in a song. Try starting with Beginning Harmonic Analysis (Section 5.5).

- Really listen to the chord progressions to the songs you do know. What do they sound like? Play the same progressions in different keys and listen to how that does and also does not change the sound of the progression. Change the bass notes of the chords to see how that changes the sound of the progression to your ears. Change fingerings and chord voicings, and again listen carefully to how that changes the sound to your ears.

- Practice figuring out the chords to familiar songs (that you don't know the chords to). For songs that you do know the chords to, try playing them in an unfamiliar key, or see if you can change or add chords to make a new harmony that still fits the melody.

- A teacher who understands harmony can help tremendously with this particular skill. Even if you don't normally take lessons, you might want to consider having a series of lessons on this. Find a teacher who is willing and able to teach you specifically about harmony and typical chord progressions.

6.1.2.3 Playing Tunes by Ear

This is fun to be able to do, makes it easy to increase your repertoire, and is an important step in being able to improvise.

Suggestions

- Just do it! The best way to learn this skill is to spend some of your practice time trying to play tunes you know and like.

- Once you start getting good at this, see how quickly you can get a new tune down. How few mistakes can you make the first time you try it? Can you "recover" quickly from a mistake by making it sound like a bit of improvisation?

- If you play a melody instrument (one that plays only one note at a time), there are different bits of information that help you recognize what the next note will be: how far it is from the note you are on (see Interval (Section 4.5)), where it is in the key (see Beginning Harmonic Analysis (Section 5.5)) or where it is in the chord (see Triads (Section 5.1)). These three things are all related to each other, of course - and a musician with a well-trained ear will be aware of all of them, at least subconsciously - but you may find at first that one works better for you than the others. You may want to experiment: is it easier for you to think of the next note as being a perfect fourth higher than the note you are on, or as being the root of the chord, or as being the fifth note in the scale of the key?

- As of this writing, petersax-online[3] had many exercises graded from simple to more difficult to help the beginner practice playing what you hear.

6.1.2.4 Improvisation

This is *the* skill you need for jazz. Blues, rock, and many Non-Western (Section 2.8) traditions also use improvisation.

Suggestions

- Know your scales and arpeggios. A good improviser, given the name of a chord, can quickly play not only the notes of the chord but also the scale implied by the chord. Any decent book on playing jazz, or any teacher familiar with jazz, will introduce the student to these chords and scales.

---

[3]http://www.petersax.com

- There are now many book/CD combinations available to help the beginning improviser in many different genres and on many different instruments. A good book of this type will give the student a chance to improvise on many familiar tunes, and some also introduce the music theory involved. At the time of this writing, one source of a large variety of such books was jazzbooks.com[4] .

- The exercises at the petersax[5] site mentioned above would also be useful for the beginning improviser.

- Listen to jazz often. Listen to the improvisers you admire, and if a particular solo really appeals to you, listen to it many times, find the notes on your instrument, and then try writing it down as accurately as you can. Many famous improvisors, when interviewed, mention how useful it was to them to learn from other soloists by **transcribing** their solos in this way.

- Figure out how to play your favorite jazz (or blues or rock) **licks** (short motives (Section 2.3.5) that show up in many pieces in the same genre) on your instrument. Practice stringing them together in ways that make sense to you, but are different from what you've heard. Add your own variations.

- Find a teacher who is familiar with the type of improvisation you want to learn, join a jazz band, and/or get together with other musicians who also want to practise improvisation and take turns playing background/rhythm for each other.

6.1.2.5 Recognizing Intervals and Writing Music Down

This is the skill that allowed Beethoven to continue composing masterpieces even after he became deaf. If you are interested in composing, arranging, music theory, musicology, or just being able to write down a tune quickly and accurately, you'll want to be able to make that quick connection between what you hear and written music.

Suggestions

- Before you can do this, you must know your major (Section 4.3) and minor (Section 4.4) keys and scales and your Intervals (Section 4.5). You may also want to understand Transposition (Section 6.4), since you may find it easier to work in some keys than in others.

- Here is a game[6] you can play to practice identifying intervals when you hear them. It's an application (.exe file) that you can play in Windows. Or you can play the same game with a friend. Sit back-to-back and take turns playing intervals and guessing what was just played. If you get good at guessing intervals, see if you can guess the exact notes that were played. (You may be surprised at how well you can guess the exact notes if they are played on an instrument that you play often.)

- Once again, practice is the best way to become good at this. Start with tunes that you know well, but don't know what the (written) notes are. Listen to them in your head (or play a recording) while trying to write them down. Then play what you have written, noticing where you were correct and where you made mistakes. Which intervals are you good at hearing? Which do you have trouble identifying? Do you often mistake one particular interval for another? Do you tend to identify a note by its interval from the previous note or by its place in the chord or in the key? Answering these questions will help you improve more quickly.

---

[4]http://www.jazzbooks.com
[5]http://www.petersax.com
[6]http://cnx.org/content/m12401/latest/EarTraining.exe

- Some people find it easier to learn to recognize intervals if they associate each interval with a familiar tune. (For example, in the familiar song from *The Sound of Music* that begins "Do, a deer, a female deer...", all the intervals in the phrase "a female deer" are major thirds, and every interval in the phrase "someday I'll wish upon a star" in the song "Somewhere Over the Rainbow" is a minor third.) The tune should be very familiar, so when trying to hear a tritone (pg 144), some people will prefer thinking of the beginning of "The Simpsons" theme; others will prefer the beginning of "Maria" from *West Side Story*. If you think this method will work for you, try playing the interval you are having trouble hearing, and see what tune it reminds you of.

6.2 Tuning Systems[7]

6.2.1 Introduction

The first thing musicians must do before they can play together is "tune". For musicians in the standard Western music (Section 2.8) tradition, this means agreeing on exactly what pitch (Section 1.1.3) (what frequency (Section 3.1.4)) is an "A", what is a "B flat" and so on. Other cultures not only have different note names and different scales, they may even have different notes - different pitches - based on a different tuning system. In fact, the modern Western tuning system, which is called **equal temperament**, replaced (relatively recently) other tuning systems that were once popular in Europe. All tuning systems are based on the physics of sound (Section 3.1). But they all are also affected by the history of their music traditions, as well as by the tuning peculiarities of the instruments used in those traditions.

NOTE: To understand all of the discussion below, you must be comfortable with both the musical concept of interval and the physics concept of frequency. If you wish to follow the whole thing but are a little hazy on the relationship between pitch and frequency, the following may be helpful: Pitch (Section 1.1.3); Acoustics for Music Theory (Section 3.1); Harmonic Series I: Timbre and Octaves (Section 3.3); and Octaves and the Major-Minor Tonal System (Section 4.1). If you do not know what intervals are (for example, major thirds and perfect fourths), please see Interval (Section 4.5) and Harmonic Series II: Harmonics, Intervals and Instruments (Section 4.6). If you need to review the mathematical concepts, please see Musical Intervals, Frequency, and Ratio[8] and Powers, Roots, and Equal Temperament[9]. Meanwhile, here is a reasonably nontechnical summary of the information below: Modern Western music uses the equal temperament (Section 6.2.3.2) tuning system. In this system, an octave (Section 4.1) (say, from C to C) is divided into twelve equally-spaced notes. "Equally-spaced" to a musician basically means that each of these notes is one half step (Section 4.2) from the next, and that all half steps sound like the same size pitch change. (To a scientist or engineer, "equally-spaced" means that the ratio of the frequencies of the two notes in any half step is always the same.) This tuning system is very convenient for some instruments, such as the piano, and also makes it very easy to change key (Section 4.3) without retuning instruments. But a careful hearing of the music, or a look at the physics of the sound waves involved, reveals that equal-temperament pitches are not based on the harmonics (Section 3.3) physically produced by any musical sound. The "equal" ratios of its half steps are the twelfth root of two, rather than reflecting the simpler ratios produced by the sounds themselves, and the important intervals that build harmonies can sound slightly out of tune. This often leads to some "tweaking" of the tuning

[7]This content is available online at <http://cnx.org/content/m11639/1.16/>.
[8]"Musical Intervals, Frequency, and Ratio" <http://cnx.org/content/m11808/latest/>
[9]"Powers, Roots, and Equal Temperament" <http://cnx.org/content/m11809/latest/#s4>

in real performances, away from equal temperament. It also leads many other music traditions to prefer tunings other than equal temperament, particularly tunings in which some of the important intervals are based on the pure, simple-ratio intervals of physics. In order to feature these favored intervals, a tuning tradition may: use scales in which the notes are not equally spaced; avoid any notes or intervals which don't work with a particular tuning; change the tuning of some notes when the key (Section 4.3) or mode (Section 6.3) changes; or any combination of these techniques.

6.2.2 Tuning based on the Harmonic Series

Almost all music traditions recognize the octave (Section 4.1). When one note has a frequency (Section 3.1.4) that is exactly two times the frequency of a second note, then the first note is one octave higher than the second note. A simple mathematical way to say this is that the ratio[10] of the frequencies is 2:1. Two notes that are exactly one octave apart sound good together because their frequencies are related in such a simple way. If a note had a frequency, for example, that was 2.11 times the frequency of another note (instead of exactly 2 times), the two notes would not sound so good together. In fact, most people would find the effect very unpleasant and would say that the notes are not "in tune" with each other.

To find other notes that sound "in tune" with each other, we look for other sets of pitches that have a "simple" frequency relationship. These sets of pitches with closely related frequencies are often written in common notation (Section 1.1.1) as a harmonic series (Section 3.3). The harmonic series is not just a useful idea constructed by music theory; it is often found in "real life", in the real-world physics of musical sounds. For example, a bugle can play only the notes of a specific harmonic series. And every musical note you hear is not a single pure frequency, but is actually a blend of the pitches of a particular harmonic series. (The relative strengths of the harmonics are what gives the note its timbre (Section 2.2). See Harmonic Series II: Harmonics, Intervals and Instruments (Section 4.6); Standing Waves and Musical Instruments (Section 3.2); and Standing Waves and Wind Instruments[11] for more about how and why musical sounds are built from harmonic series.)

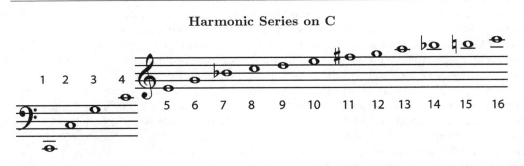

Figure 6.1: Here are the first sixteen pitches in a harmonic series that starts on a C natural. The series goes on indefinitely, with the pitches getting closer and closer together. A harmonic series can start on any note, so there are many harmonic series, but *every harmonic series has the same set of intervals and the same frequency ratios*.

---

[10]"Musical Intervals, Frequency, and Ratio" <http://cnx.org/content/m11808/latest/>
[11]"Standing Waves and Wind Instruments" <http://cnx.org/content/m12589/latest/>

What does it mean to say that two pitches have a "simple frequency relationship"? It doesn't mean that their frequencies are almost the same. Two notes whose frequencies are almost the same - say, the frequency of one is 1.005 times the other - sound bad together. Again, when we hear them, we say they are "out of tune". Notes with a close relationship have frequencies that can be written as a ratio[12] of two small whole numbers; the smaller the numbers, the more closely related the notes are. Two notes that are exactly the same pitch, for example, have a frequency ratio of 1:1, and octaves, as we have already seen, are 2:1. Notice that when two pitches are related in this simple-ratio way, it means that they can be considered part of the same harmonic series, and in fact the actual harmonic series of the two notes may also overlap and reinforce each other. The fact that the two notes are complementing and reinforcing each other in this way, rather than presenting the human ear with two completely different harmonic series, may be a major reason why they sound consonant (Section 5.3) and "in tune".

> NOTE: Notice that the actual frequencies of the notes do not matter. What matters is how they compare to each other - basically, how many waves of one note go by for each wave of the other note. Although the actual frequencies of the notes will change for every harmonic series, the comparison between the notes will be the same.

For more examples, look at the harmonic series in Figure 6.1. The number beneath a note tells you the relationship of that note's frequency to the frequency of the first note in the series - the **fundamental**. For example, the frequency of the note numbered 3 in Figure 6.1 is three times the frequency of the fundamental, and the frequency of the note numbered fifteen is fifteen times the frequency of the fundamental. In the example, the fundamental is a C. That note's frequency times 2 gives you another C; times 2 again (4) gives another C; times 2 again gives another C (8), and so on. Now look at the G's in this series. The first one is number 3 in the series. 3 times 2 is 6, and number 6 in the series is also a G. So is number 12 (6 times 2). Check for yourself the other notes in the series that are an octave apart. You will find that the ratio for one octave (Section 4.1) is always 2:1, just as the ratio for a unison is always 1:1. Notes with this small-number ratio of 2:1 are so closely related that we give them the same name, and most tuning systems are based on this octave relationship.

The next closest relationship is the one based on the 3:2 ratio, the interval (Section 4.5) of the perfect fifth (pg 140) (for example, the C and G in the example harmonic series). The next lowest ratio, 4:3, gives the interval of a perfect fourth (pg 140). Again, these pitches are so closely related and sound so good together that their intervals have been named "perfect". The perfect fifth figures prominently in many tuning systems, and, in Western music, all major and minor chords are based on the perfect fifth. (See Triads (Section 5.1) and Naming Triads (Section 5.2) for more about the intervals in major and minor chords.)

6.2.2.1 Pythagorean Intonation

The Pythagorean system is so named because it was actually discussed by Pythagoras, the famous Greek mathematician and philosopher, who in the sixth century B.C. already recognized the simple arithmetical relationship involved in intervals of octaves, fifths, and fourths. He and his followers believed that numbers were the ruling principle of the universe, and that musical harmonies were a basic expression of the mathematical laws of the universe. Their model of the universe involved the "celestial spheres" making a kind of harmony as they moved in circles dictated by the same arithmetical relationships as musical harmonies.

In the Pythagorean system, all tuning is based on the interval of the pure fifth. **Pure intervals** are the ones found in the harmonic series, with very simple frequency ratios. So a pure fifth will have a frequency ratio of exactly 3:2. Using a series of perfect fifths (and assuming perfect octaves,

---

[12]"Musical Intervals, Frequency, and Ratio" <http://cnx.org/content/m11808/latest/>

too, so that you are filling in every octave as you go), you can eventually fill in an entire chromatic scale.

Pythagorean Intonation

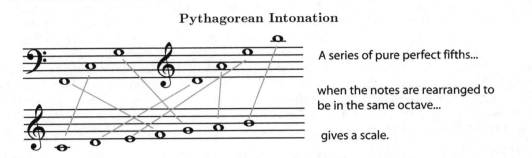

A series of pure perfect fifths...

when the notes are rearranged to be in the same octave...

gives a scale.

Figure 6.2: You can continue this series of perfect fifths to get the rest of the notes of a chromatic scale; the series would continue F sharp, C sharp, and so on.

The main weakness of the Pythagorean system is that a series of pure perfect fifths will never take you to a note that is a pure octave above the note you started on. To see why this is a problem, imagine beginning on a C. A series of perfect fifths would give: C, G, D, A, E, B, F sharp, C sharp, G sharp, D sharp, A sharp, E sharp, and B sharp. In equal temperament (which doesn't use pure fifths), that B sharp would be exactly the same pitch as the C seven octaves above where you started (so that the series can, in essence, be turned into a closed loop, the Circle of Fifths (Section 4.7)). Unfortunately, the B sharp that you arrive at after a series of pure fifths is a little higher than that C.

So in order to keep pure octaves, instruments that use Pythagorean tuning have to use eleven pure fifths and one smaller fifth . The smaller fifth has traditionally been called a **wolf** fifth because of its unpleasant sound. Keys that avoid the wolf fifth sound just fine on instruments that are tuned this way, but keys in which the wolf fifth is often heard become a problem. To avoid some of the harshness of the wolf intervals, some harpsichords and other keyboard instruments were built with split keys for D sharp/E flat and for G sharp/A flat. The front half of the key would play one note, and the back half the other (differently tuned) note.

Pythagorean tuning was widely used in medieval and Renaissance times. Major seconds and thirds are larger in Pythagorean intonation than in equal temperament, and minor seconds and thirds are smaller. Some people feel that using such intervals in medieval music is not only more authentic, but sounds better too, since the music was composed for this tuning system.

More modern Western music, on the other hand, does not sound pleasant using Pythagorean intonation. Although the fifths sound great, the thirds (Major and Minor Intervals) are simply too far away from the pure major and minor thirds of the harmonic series. In medieval music, the third was considered a dissonance and was used sparingly - and actually, when you're using Pythagorean tuning, it really is a dissonance - but modern harmonies are built mainly on thirds (see Triads (Section 5.1)).

Some modern Non-Western music traditions, which have a very different approach to melody and harmony, still base their tuning on the perfect fifth. Wolf fifths and ugly thirds are not a problem in these traditions, which build each mode (Section 6.3) within the framework of the perfect fifth, retuning for different modes as necessary. To read a little about one such tradition, please see Indian Classical Music: Tuning and Ragas[13].

[13]"Indian Classical Music: Tuning and Ragas" <http://cnx.org/content/m12459/latest/>

6.2.2.2 Mean-tone System

The mean-tone system, in order to have pleasant-sounding thirds, takes rather the opposite approach from the Pythagorean. It uses the pure major third (Major and Minor Intervals). In this system, the whole tone (or whole step (Section 4.2)) is considered to be exactly half of the pure major third (this is the "mean", or average, tone, that gives the system its name). A semitone (or half step (Section 4.2)) is exactly half of a whole tone.

These smaller intervals all work out well in mean-tone tuning, but the result is a fifth that is noticeably smaller than a pure fifth. And a series of pure thirds will also eventually not line up with pure octaves, so an instrument tuned this way will also have a problem with wolf (pg 226) intervals.

As mentioned above, Pythagorean tuning made sense in medieval times, when music was dominated by fifths. Once the concept of harmony in thirds took hold, thirds became the most important interval (Section 4.5); simple perfect fifths were now heard as "austere" and, well, medieval-sounding. So mean-tone tuning was very popular in Europe in the 16th through 18th centuries.

But fifths can't be avoided entirely. A basic major or minor chord, for example, is built of two thirds, but it also has a perfect fifth between its outer two notes (see triads (Section 5.1)). So even while mean-tone tuning was enjoying great popularity, some composers and musicians were searching for other solutions.

6.2.2.3 Just Intonation

Just intonation is the system of tuning that is often used (sometimes unconsciously) by musicians who can make small tuning adjustments quickly. This includes vocalists, most wind instruments, and many string instruments. Look again at the harmonic series (Figure 6.1).

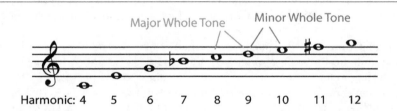

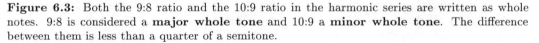

Figure 6.3: Both the 9:8 ratio and the 10:9 ratio in the harmonic series are written as whole notes. 9:8 is considered a **major whole tone** and 10:9 a **minor whole tone**. The difference between them is less than a quarter of a semitone.

As the series goes on, the ratios get smaller and the notes closer together. Standard notation writes all of these "close together" intervals as whole steps (whole tones) or half steps (semitones), but they are of course all slightly different from each other. For example, the notes with frequency ratios of 9:8 and 10:9 and 11:10 are all written as whole steps. To compare how close (or far) they actually are, turn the ratios into decimals.

Whole Step Ratios Written as Decimals

- $9/8 = 1.125$

- $10/9 = 1.111$

- $11/10 = 1.1$

NOTE: In case you are curious, the size of the whole tone of the "mean tone" system is also the mean, or average, of the major and minor whole tones.

These are fairly small differences, but they can still be heard easily by the human ear. Just intonation uses both the 9:8 whole tone, which is called a **major whole tone** and the 10:9 whole tone, which is called a **minor whole tone**, in order to construct both pure thirds and pure fifths. Because chords are constructed of thirds and fifths (see Triads (Section 5.1)), this tuning makes typical Western harmonies particularly pleasing to the ear.

The problem with just intonation is that it matters which steps of the scale are major whole tones and which are minor whole tones, so an instrument tuned exactly to play with just intonation in the key of C major will have to retune to play in C sharp major or D major. For instruments that can tune almost instantly, like voices, violins, and trombones, this is not a problem; but it is unworkable for pianos, harps, and other other instruments that cannot make small tuning adjustments quickly.

As of this writing, there was useful information about various tuning systems at several different websites, including The Development of Musical Tuning Systems[14], where one could hear what some intervals sound like in the different tuning systems, and Kyle Gann's Just Intonation Explained[15], which included some audio samples of works played in just intonation.

6.2.3 Temperament

There are times when tuning is not much of an issue. When a good choir sings in harmony without instruments, they will tune without even thinking about it. All chords will tend towards pure fifths and thirds, as well as seconds, fourths, sixths, and sevenths that reflect the harmonic series. Instruments that can bend most pitches enough to fine-tune them during a performance - and this includes most orchestral instruments - also tend to play the "pure" intervals. This can happen unconsciously, or it can be deliberate, as when a conductor asks for an interval to be "expanded" or "contracted".

But for many instruments, such as piano, organ, harp, bells, harpsichord, xylophone - any instrument that cannot be fine-tuned quickly - tuning is a big issue. A harpsichord that has been tuned using the Pythagorean system or just intonation may sound perfectly in tune in one key - C major, for example - and fairly well in tune in a related key (Section 4.7) - G major - but badly out of tune in a "distant" key like D flat major. Adding split keys or extra keys can help (this was a common solution for a time), but also makes the instrument more difficult to play. In Western music (Section 2.8), the tuning systems that have been invented and widely used that directly address this problem are the various temperaments, in which the tuning of notes is "tempered" slightly from pure intervals. (Non-Western music traditions have their own tuning systems, which is too big a subject to address here.)

6.2.3.1 Well Temperaments

As mentioned above (pg 226), the various tuning systems based on pure intervals eventually have to include "wolf" intervals that make some keys unpleasant or even unusable. The various **well temperament** tunings that were very popular in the 18th and 19th centuries tried to strike a balance between staying close to pure intervals and avoiding wolf intervals. A well temperament might have several pure fifths, for example, and several fifths that are smaller than a pure fifth, but not so small that they are "wolf" fifths. In such systems, tuning would be noticeably different in each key (Section 4.3), but every key would still be pleasant-sounding and usable. This made well temperaments particularly welcome for players of difficult-to-tune instruments like the harpsichord and piano.

---

[14]http://www.midicode.com/tunings/index.shtml
[15]http://www.kylegann.com/tuning.html

NOTE: Historically, there has been some confusion as to whether or not well temperament and equal temperament are the same thing, possibly because well temperaments were sometimes referred to at the time as "equal temperament". But these well temperaments made all keys equally useful, not equal-sounding as modern equal temperament does.

As mentioned above (Section 6.2.2.2), mean-tone tuning was still very popular in the eighteenth century. J. S. Bach wrote his famous "Well-Tempered Klavier" in part as a plea and advertisement to switch to a well temperament system. Various well temperaments did become very popular in the eighteenth and nineteenth centuries, and much of the keyboard-instrument music of those centuries may have been written to take advantage of the tuning characteristics of particular keys in particular well temperaments. It is interesting to note that the different keys in a well temperament tuning were sometimes considered to be aligned with specific colors and emotions. In this way they may have had more in common with various modes and ragas (Section 6.3) than do keys in equal temperament.

6.2.3.2 Equal Temperament

In modern times, well temperaments have been replaced by equal temperament, so much so in Western music (Section 2.8) that equal temperament is considered standard tuning even for voice and for instruments that are more likely to play using just intonation when they can (see above (Section 6.2.2.3)). In equal temperament, only octaves (Section 4.1) are pure (Section 6.2.2.1) intervals. The octave is divided into twelve equally spaced half steps (Section 4.2), and all other intervals (Section 4.5) are measured in half steps. This gives, for example, a fifth (pg 140) that is a bit smaller than a pure fifth, and a major third (Major and Minor Intervals) that is larger than the pure major third. The differences are smaller than the wolf tones (pg 226) found in other tuning systems, but they are still there.

Equal temperament is well suited to music that changes key (Section 4.3) often, is very chromatic (pg 91), or is harmonically complex (Section 5.5). It is also the obvious choice for atonal (pg 91) music that steers away from identification with any key or tonality at all. Equal temperament has a clear scientific/mathematical basis, is very straightforward, does not require retuning for key changes, and is unquestioningly accepted by most people. However, because of the lack of pure intervals, some musicians find it unsatisfying. As mentioned above, just intonation is sometimes substituted for equal temperament when practical. Some musicians would also like to reintroduce well temperaments, at least for performances of the music which was written for well-tempered instruments.

6.2.4 A Comparison of Equal Temperament with the Harmonic Series

In a way, equal temperament is a compromise between the Pythagorean approach and the mean-tone approach. Neither the third nor the fifth is pure, but neither of them is terribly far off, either. Because equal temperament divides the octave into twelve equal semi-tones (half steps), the frequency ratio of each semi-tone is the twelfth root of 2. If you do not understand why it is the twelfth root of 2 rather than, say, one twelfth, please see the explanation below (pg 231). (There is a review of powers and roots in Powers, Roots, and Equal Temperament[16] if you need it.)

---

[16]"Powers, Roots, and Equal Temperament" <http://cnx.org/content/m11809/latest/#s4>

$$\sqrt[12]{2} \quad = \text{ a semitone (half step)}$$

$$\left(\sqrt[12]{2}\ \right)^2 = \text{ a whole tone (whole step)}$$

$$\left(\sqrt[12]{2}\ \right)^4 = \text{ a major third (four semitones)}$$

$$\left(\sqrt[12]{2}\ \right)^7 = \text{ a perfect fifth (seven semitones)}$$

$$\left(\sqrt[12]{2}\ \right)^{12} = 2 = \text{ an octave (twelve semitones)}$$

Figure 6.4: In equal temperament, the ratio of frequencies in a semitone (half step) is the twelfth root of two. Every interval is then simply a certain number of semitones. Only the octave (the twelfth power of the twelfth root) is a pure interval.

In equal temperament, the only pure interval is the octave. (The twelfth power of the twelfth root of two is simply two.) All other intervals are given by irrational numbers based on the twelfth root of two, not nice numbers that can be written as a ratio of two small whole numbers. In spite of this, equal temperament works fairly well, because most of the intervals it gives actually fall quite close to the pure intervals. To see that this is so, look at Figure 6.5. Equal temperament and pure intervals are calculated as decimals and compared to each other. (You can find these decimals for yourself using a calculator.)

Comparing the Frequency Ratios for Equal Temperament and Pure Harmonic Series

Interval	Equal Temperament Frequency Ratio		Approximate Difference		Harmonic Series Frequency Ratio	
Unison	$(\sqrt[12]{2})^0$	$\simeq$ 1.0000	0.0	1.0000	$\simeq$	1/1
Minor Second	$(\sqrt[12]{2})^1$	$\simeq$ 1.0595	0.0314	1.0909	$\simeq$	12/11
Major Second	$(\sqrt[12]{2})^2$	$\simeq$ 1.1225	0.0025	1.1250	$\simeq$	9/8
Minor Third	$(\sqrt[12]{2})^3$	$\simeq$ 1.1892	0.0108	1.2000	$\simeq$	6/5
Major Third	$(\sqrt[12]{2})^4$	$\simeq$ 1.2599	0.0099	1.2500	$\simeq$	5/4
Perfect Fourth	$(\sqrt[12]{2})^5$	$\simeq$ 1.3348	0.0015	1.3333	$\simeq$	4/3
Tritone	$(\sqrt[12]{2})^6$	$\simeq$ 1.4142	0.0142	1.4000	$\simeq$	7/5
Perfect Fifth	$(\sqrt[12]{2})^7$	$\simeq$ 1.4983	0.0017	1.5000	$\simeq$	3/2
Minor Sixth	$(\sqrt[12]{2})^8$	$\simeq$ 1.5874	0.0126	1.6000	$\simeq$	8/5
Major Sixth	$(\sqrt[12]{2})^9$	$\simeq$ 1.6818	0.0151	1.6667	$\simeq$	5/3
Minor Seventh	$(\sqrt[12]{2})^{10}$	$\simeq$ 1.7818	0.0318	1.7500	$\simeq$	7/4
Major Seventh	$(\sqrt[12]{2})^{11}$	$\simeq$ 1.8897	0.0564	1.8333	$\simeq$	11/6
Octave	$(\sqrt[12]{2})^{12}$	$\simeq$ 2.0000	0.0	2.0000	$\simeq$	2/1

Figure 6.5: Look again at Figure 6.1 to see where pure interval ratios come from. The ratios for equal temperament are all multiples of the twelfth root of two. Both sets of ratios are converted to decimals (to the nearest ten thousandth), so you can easily compare them.

Except for the unison and the octave, none of the ratios for equal temperament are exactly the same as for the pure interval. Many of them are reasonably close, though. In particular, perfect fourths and fifths and major thirds are not too far from the pure intervals. The intervals that are the furthest from the pure intervals are the major seventh, minor seventh, and minor second (intervals that are considered dissonant (Section 5.3) anyway).

Because equal temperament is now so widely accepted as standard tuning, musicians do not usually even speak of intervals in terms of ratios. Instead, tuning itself is now defined in terms of equal-temperament, with tunings and intervals measured in cents. A **cent** is 1/100 (the hundredth root) of an equal-temperament semitone. In this system, for example, the major whole tone discussed above measures 204 cents, the minor whole tone 182 cents, and a pure fifth is 702 cents.

Why is a cent the hundredth root of a semitone, and why is a semitone the twelfth root of an octave? If it bothers you that the ratios in equal temperament are roots, remember the pure octaves and fifths of the harmonic series.

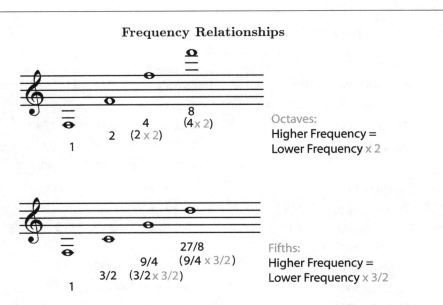

Figure 6.6: Remember that, no matter what note you start on, the note one octave higher has 2 times its frequency. Also, no matter what note you start on, the note that is a perfect fifth higher has exactly one and a half times its frequency. Since each of these intervals is so many "times" in terms of frequencies, when you *add* intervals, you *multiply* their frequencies. For example, a series of two perfect fifths will give a frequency that is 3/2 x 3/2 (or 9/4) the beginning frequency.

Every octave has the same frequency ratio; the higher note will have 2 *times* the frequency of the lower note. So if you go up another octave from there (another 2 times), that note must have 2 x 2, or 4 times the frequency of the lowest note. The next octave takes you up 2 times higher than that, or 8 times the frequency of the first note, and so on.

In just the same way, in every perfect fifth, the higher note will have a frequency one and a half (3/2) times the lower note. So to find out how much higher the frequency is after a series of perfect fifths, you would have to multiply (not add) by one and a half (3/2) every time you went up another perfect fifth.

All intervals work in this same way. So, in order for twelve semitones (half steps) to equal one octave, the size of a half step has to be a number that gives the answer "2" (the size of an octave) when you multiply it twelve times: in other words, the twelfth root of two. And in order for a hundred cents to equal one semitone, the size of a cent must be the number that, when you multiply it 100 times, ends up being the same size as a semitone; in other words, the hundredth root of the twelfth root of two. This is why most musicians prefer to talk in terms of cents and intervals instead of frequencies.

6.2.5 Beats and Wide Tuning

One well-known result of tempered tunings is the aural phenomenon known as **beats**. As mentioned above (pg 224), in a pure interval (Section 6.2.2.1) the sound waves have frequencies that are related to each other by very simple ratios. Physically speaking, this means that the two smooth waves line up together so well that the combined wave - the wave you hear when the two are played at the same time - is also a smooth wave. Tunings that are slightly off from the pure interval, however, will result in a combined wave that has a bumpiness in it. Because the two waves are each very even, the bump itself is very even and regular, and can be heard as a "beat" - a very regular change in the intensity of the sound. The beats are so regular, in fact, that they can be timed; for equal temperament they are on the order of a beat per second in the mid range of a piano. A piano tuner works by listening to and timing these beats, rather than by being able to "hear" equal temperament intervals precisely.

It should also be noted that some music traditions around the world do not use the type of precision tunings described above, not because they can't, but because of an aesthetic preference for **wide tuning**. In these traditions, the sound of many people playing precisely the same pitch is considered a thin, uninteresting sound; the sound of many people playing near the same pitch is heard as full, lively, and more interesting.

Some music traditions even use an extremely precise version of wide tuning. The *gamelan* orchestras of southeast Asia, for example, have an aesthetic preference for the "lively and full" sounds that come from instruments playing near, not on, the same pitch. In some types of gamelans, pairs of instruments are tuned very precisely so that each pair produces beats, and the rate of the beats is the same throughout the entire range (Section 2.7) of that gamelan. This impressive feat of tuning can only be reliably produced by a few instrument makers with long-standing traditions.

6.2.6 Further Study

As of this writing:

- The Just Intonation Network[17] had much information about Just Intonation, including some audio examples.

- Kyle Gann's An Introduction to Historical Tunings[18] was a good source about both the historical background and more technical information about various tunings. It also includes some audio examples.

- The Huygens-Fokker Foundation had a very large on-line bibliography[19] of tuning and temperament.

- Musemath[20] had several animations illustrating equal temperament and the math necessary to understand it.

6.3 Modes and Ragas[21]

6.3.1 Introduction

In many music traditions, including Western music (Section 2.8), the list of all the notes that are expected or allowed in a particular piece of music is a scale (Section 4.3). A long tradition of using scales in particular ways has trained listeners to expect certain things from a piece of music. If you hear a song in C major, for example, not only will your ear/brain expect to hear the notes from the C major scale (Section 4.3), it will expect to hear them grouped into certain chords (Chords), and it will expect the chords to follow each other in certain patterns (chord progressions (Chords)) and to end in a certain way (a cadence (Section 5.6)). You don't have to have any musical training at

---

[17]http://www.justintonation.net/
[18]http://www.kylegann.com/histune.html
[19]http://www.xs4all.nl/~huygensf/doc/bib.html
[20]http://www.musemath.com
[21]This content is available online at <http://cnx.org/content/m11633/1.9/>.

all to have these expectations; you only need to have grown up in a culture that listens to this kind of music.

The expectations for music in a minor key are a little different than for music in a major key. But it is important to notice that you can move that song in C major to E major, G flat major, or any other major key. It will sound basically the same, except that it will sound higher or lower. In the same way, all minor keys are so alike that music can easily be **transposed** from one minor key to another. (For more on this subject, see Major Scales (Section 4.3), Minor Scales (Section 4.4), Scales that aren't Major or Minor (Section 4.8), and Transposition (Section 6.4).)

This sameness is not true for musical traditions that use modes instead of scales. In these traditions, *the* **mode**, *like a scale, lists the notes that are used in a piece of music. But each mode comes with a different set of expectations in how those notes will be used and arranged.*

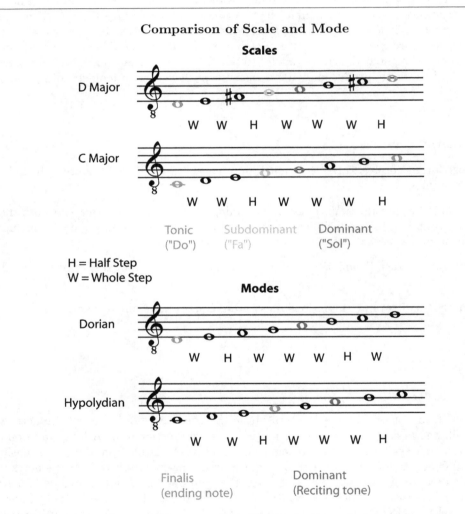

Figure 6.7: Compare the differences and similarities between the two major scales, and the differences and similarities between the two medieval church modes.

Figure 6.7 shows two scales and two modes. The two major scales (Section 4.3) use different notes, but the relationship of the notes to each other is very similar. For example, the pattern of half steps and whole steps (Section 4.2) in each one is the same, and the interval (Section 4.5) (distance) between the tonic (pg 127) and the dominant (Section 5.5.4) is the same. Compare this to the two church modes. The pattern of whole steps and half steps within the octave (Section 4.1) is different; this would have a major effect on a chant, which would generally stay within the one octave range. Also, the interval between the finalis (pg 236) and the dominant (pg 236) is different, and they are in different places within the range (Section 2.7) of the mode. The result is that music in one mode would sound quite different than music in the other mode. You can't simply transpose (Section 6.4) music from one mode to another as you do with scales and keys; modes are too different.

6.3.2 The Classical Greek Modes

We can only guess what music from ancient Greek and Roman times really sounded like. They didn't leave any recordings, of course, nor did they write down their music. But they did write about music, so we know that they used modes based on tetrachords. A **tetrachord** is a mini-scale of four notes, in descending pitch (Section 1.1.3) order, that are contained within a perfect fourth (Section 4.5.3.1) (five half steps (Section 4.2)) instead of an octave (Section 4.1) (twelve half steps).

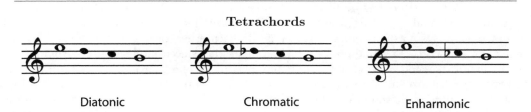

Figure 6.8: Here are three possible Greek tetrachords, as nearly as they can be written in modern notation. The outer notes are a perfect fourth apart; we can be pretty certain of that, since the perfect fourth is a natural interval playable, for example, on many ancient wind instruments (See Harmonic Series II (Section 4.6) and Interval (Section 4.5)). The actual tuning of the inner notes can only be guessed, however, since our equal temperament (Section 6.2.3.2) is a relatively modern invention.

Since a tetrachord fills the interval of a perfect fourth (pg 140), two tetrachords with a whole step (Section 4.2) between the end of one and the beginning of the other will fill an octave. Different Greek modes were built from different combinations of tetrachords.

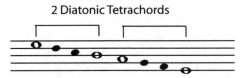

Figure 6.9: Each Greek mode was built of two tetrachords in a row, filling an octave.

We have very detailed descriptions of tetrachords and of Greek music theory (for example, *Harmonics*, written by Aristoxenus in the fourth century B.C.), but there is still no way of knowing exactly what the music really sounded like. The enharmonic, chromatic, and diatonic tetrachords mentioned in ancient descriptions are often now written as in the figure above. But references in the old texts to "shading" suggest that the reality was more complex, and that they probably did not use the same intervals we do. It is more likely that ancient Greek music sounded more like other traditional Mediterranean and Middle Eastern musics than that it sounded anything like modern Western (Section 2.8) music.

Western (Section 2.8) composers often consistently choose minor (Section 4.4) keys over major (Section 4.3) keys (or vice versa) to convey certain moods (minor for melancholy, for example, and major for serene). One interesting aspect of Greek modes is that different modes were considered to have very different effects, not only on a person's mood, but even on character and morality. This may also be another clue that ancient modes may have had more variety of tuning and pitch than modern keys do.

6.3.3 The Medieval Church Modes

Sacred music in the middle ages in Western Europe - Gregorian chant, for example - was also modal, and the medieval **Church modes** were also considered to have different effects on the listener. (As of this writing the site Ricercares by Vincenzo Galilei[22] had a list of the "ethos" or mood associated with each medieval mode.) In fact, the names of the church modes were borrowed from the Greek modes, but the two systems don't really correspond to each other, or use the same name to indicate the same set of intervals. So some books prefer to name the church modes using a Roman numeral system. Each of these modes can easily be found by playing its one octave range, or **ambitus**, on the "white key" notes on a piano. But the Dorian mode, for example, didn't have to start on the pitch we call a D. The important thing was the pattern of half steps and whole steps within that octave, and their relationship to the notes that acted as the modal equivalent of tonal centers (Section 4.3), the *finalis* and the *dominant*. Generally, the last note of the piece was the **finalis**, giving it the same "resting place" function as a modern tonal center. The **dominant**, also called the **reciting tone** or **tenor**, was the note most often used for long recitations on the same pitch.

---

[22]http://www.recorderhomepage.net/galilei.html

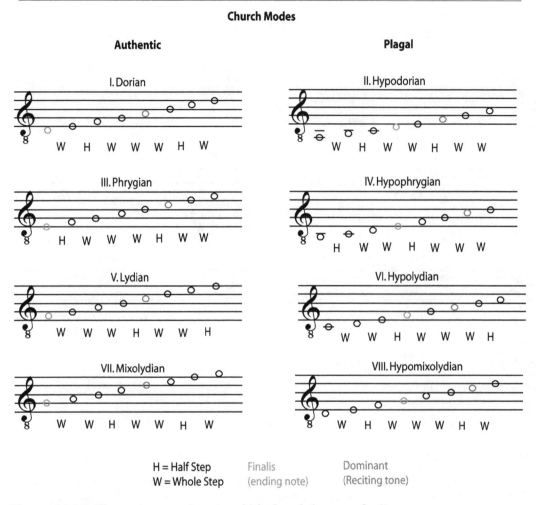

Figure 6.10: The modes came in pairs which shared the same *finalis*.

A mode can be found by playing all the "white key" notes on a piano for one octave. From D to D, for example is Dorian; from F to F is Lydian. Notice that no modes begin on A, B, or C. This is because a B flat was allowed, and the modes beginning on D, E, and F, when they use a B flat, have the same note patterns and relationships as would modes beginning on A, B, and C. After the middle ages, modes beginning on A, B, and C were named, but they are still not considered Church modes. Notice that the Aeolian (or the Dorian using a B flat) is the same as an A (or D) natural minor (pg 131) scale and the Ionian (or the Lydian using a B flat) is the same as a C (or F) major scale.

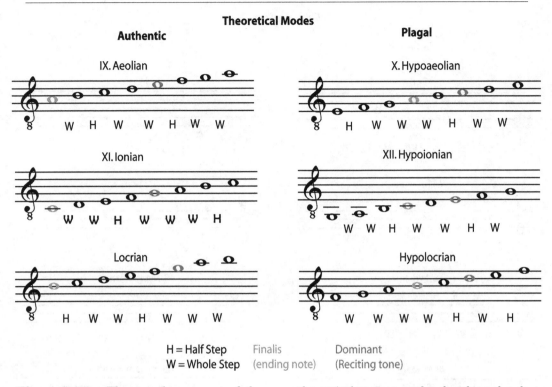

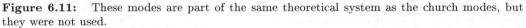

Figure 6.11: These modes are part of the same theoretical system as the church modes, but they were not used.

In our modern tonal system, any note may be sharp, flat, or natural (Section 1.1.3), but in this modal system, only the B was allowed to vary. The symbols used to indicate whether the B was "hard" (our B natural) or "soft" (our B flat) eventually evolved into our symbols for sharps, flats, and naturals. All of this may seem very arbitrary, but it's important to remember that medieval mode theory, just like our modern music theory, was not trying to invent a logical system of music. It was trying to explain, describe, and systematize musical practices that were already flourishing because people liked the way they sounded.

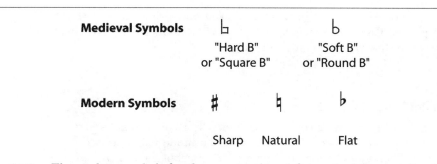

Figure 6.12: The modern symbols for sharp, natural, and flat evolved from medieval notation indicating what type of B should be used.

The tuning system (Section 6.2) used in medieval Europe was also not our familiar equal temperament (Section 6.2.3.2) system. It was a just intonation (pg 227) system, based on a pure (Section 6.2.2.1) perfect fifth (pg 139). In this system, half steps (Section 4.2) are not all equal to each other. Slight adjustments are made in tuning and intervals to make them more pleasant to the ear; and the medieval ear had different preferences than our modern ears. This is another reason that modes sounded very different from each other, although that particular difference may be missing today when chant is sung using equal temperament.

6.3.4 Modal Jazz and Folk Music

Some jazz and folk music is also considered modal and also uses the Greek/medieval mode names. In this case, the scales used are the same as the medieval church modes, but they do not have a reciting tone and are used much more like modern major and minor scales. Modal European (and American) folk music tends to be older tunes that have been around for hundreds of years. Modal jazz, on the other hand, is fairly new, having developed around 1960.

It is important to remember when discussing these types of music that it does not matter what specific note the modal scale starts on. What matters is the pattern of notes within the scale, and the relationship of the pattern to the tonic (pg 127)/finalis (pg 236). For example, note that the Dorian "scale" as written above starts on a D but basically has a C major key signature, resulting in the third and seventh notes of the scale being a half step (Section 4.2) lower than in a D major scale. (A jazz musician would call this **flatted** or **flat** thirds and sevenths.) So *any scale with a flatted third and seventh can be called a Dorian scale.*

Exercise 6.1:

You need to know your major keys (Section 4.3) and intervals (Section 4.5) to do this problem. Use the list of "white key" modes in Figure 6.10 to figure out the following information for each of the four modes below. Before looking at the solutions, check your own answers to make sure that the answers you get for step 2 and step 4 are in agreement with each other.

1. List the flats and sharps you would use if this were a major scale rather than a mode.

2. In this mode, which scale tones are raised or lowered from the major key?

3. What is the interval between the mode and the major key with the same key signature?

4. List the flats or sharps in this key signature.

5.Write one octave of notes in this mode. You may print out this PDF file[23] if you need staff paper. Check to make sure that your "modal scale" agrees with all the things that you have written about it already.

Example

1.D major has 2 sharps: F sharp and C sharp.

2.Looking at Figure 6.10, you can see that the Lydian mode starts on an F. The key of F major would have a B flat, but in the mode this is raised one half step, to B natural. Therefore *the fourth degree of the Lydian mode is raised one half step.*

3.F lydian has the same key signature as C major, which is a perfect fourth lower. So all Lydian modes have the same key signature as the major key a perfect fourth below them.

4.We want D Lydian. The major scale beginning a perfect fourth below D major is A major. A major has three sharps: F sharp, C sharp and G sharp. Adding a G sharp does raise the fourth degree of the scale by one half step, just as predicted in step 2.

Example: D Lydian

If you start with a D major scale, and raise the fourth tone a half step
(raise G natural to G sharp),
you get D Lydian, which has the same key signature as A major,
the key a perfect fourth lower than D major.

Figure 6.13

1.A Dorian

2.C Lydian

3.B flat Mixolydian

4.D Phrygian

(Solution to Exercise 6.1 on p. 256.)

---

[23]http://cnx.org/content/m11633/latest/staffpaper1.pdf

6.3.5 The Ragas of Classical Indian Music

The ragas[24] of classical India and other, similar traditions, are more like modes than they are like scales. Like modes, different *ragas* sound very different from each other, for several reasons. They may have different interval patterns between the "scale" notes, have different expectations for how each note of the *raga* is to be used, and may even use slightly different tunings. Like the modal musics discussed above, individual Indian *ragas* are associated with specific moods.

In fact, in practice, *ragas* are even more different from each other than the medieval European modes were. The *raga* dictates how each note should be used, more specifically than a modal or major-minor system does. Some pitches will get more emphasis than others; some will be used one way in an ascending melody and another way in a descending melody; some will be used in certain types of ornaments. And these rules differ from one *raga* to the next. The result is that each *raga* is a collection of melodic scales, phrases, motifs, and ornaments, that may be used together to construct music in that *raga*. The number of possible ragas is practically limitless, and there are hundreds in common use. A good performer will be familiar with dozens of *ragas* and can improvise music - traditional classical music in India is improvised - using the accepted format for each *raga*.

The *raga* even affects the tuning of the notes. Indian classical music is usually accompanied by a *tanpura*, which plays a drone background. The *tanpura* is usually tuned to a pure (Section 6.2.2.1) perfect fifth (pg 139), so, just as in medieval European music, the tuning system is a just intonation (pg 227) system. As in Western (Section 2.8) just intonation, the octave is divided into twelve possible notes, only some of which are used in a particular *raga* (just as Westerners use only some of the twelve notes in each key). But as was true for the church modes (Section 6.3.3), using the pure perfect fifth means that some "half steps" will be larger than others. (If you would like to understand why this is so, please see Harmonic Series II (Section 4.6) and Tuning Systems (Section 6.2).) Even though the variations between these different "half steps" are small, they strongly affect the sound of the music. So, the tuning of some of the notes (not the ones dictated by the *tanpura*) may be adjusted to better suit a particular *raga*. (Please see Listening to Indian Classical Music[25] and Indian Classical Music: Tuning and Ragas[26] for more information on this subject.)

6.3.6 Other Non-Western Modal Musics

To the average Western listener, medieval European chant and classical Indian music are the two most familiar traditions that are not based on major and minor scales. But many other musical traditions around the world are not based on Western scales. Some of these have modes similar to the medieval Church modes; they also tend to be a list of notes (or a pattern of intervals (Section 4.5)) used with a specific *finalis*, which may encourage certain types of melodies. While the church mode/jazz mode tradition features diatonic (pg 91) modes (which can be played using only the white keys of a piano), non-Western modes may use other types of scales (Section 4.8).

In other music traditions, modes are much more like Indian *ragas*, featuring important variations in tuning and melodic expectations from one mode to the next, so that each mode may be seen as a collection of related melodic ideas, phrases, and ornamentations that are traditionally played with a certain set of notes tuned in a certain way. (Some non-Indian traditions even use the term *raga*.) All of these musics have long traditions that are very different from the familiar major-minor tonal system, and usually also have a different approach to harmony, rhythm, and performance practice.

6.3.7 Bibliography

Donald Jay Grout's *A History of Western Music* introduces both Greek and medieval modes. Lee Evans's *Modes and Their Use in Jazz* is both comprehensive and accessible for any musician who

[24]"Indian Classical Music: Tuning and Ragas" <http://cnx.org/content/m12459/latest/>
[25]"Listening to Indian Classical Music" <http://cnx.org/content/m12502/latest/>
[26]"Indian Classical Music: Tuning and Ragas" <http://cnx.org/content/m12459/latest/>

wants to begin to study that subject. For Western musicians, an introduction to *ragas*, that is neither too vague nor too technical, does not seem to be available as of this writing.

6.4 Transposition: Changing Keys[27]

Changing the key (Section 4.3) of a piece of music is called **transposing** the music. Music in a major key (Section 4.3) can be transposed to any other major key; music in a minor key (Section 4.4) can be transposed to any other minor key. (Changing a piece from minor to major or vice-versa requires many more changes than simple transposition.) A piece will also sound higher or lower once it is transposed. There are some ways to avoid having to do the transposition yourself, but learning to transpose can be very useful for performers, composers, and arrangers.

6.4.1 Why Transpose?

Here are the most common situations that may require you to change the key of a piece of music:

- To put it in the right key for your *vocalists*. If your singer or singers are struggling with notes that are too high or low, changing the key to put the music in their range (Section 2.7) will result in a much better performance.

- Instrumentalists may also find that a piece is *easier to play* if it is in a different key. Players of both bowed and plucked strings generally find fingerings and tuning to be easier in sharp keys, while woodwind and brass players often find flat keys more comfortable and in tune.

- Instrumentalists with *transposing instruments* will usually need any part they play to be properly transposed before they can play it. Clarinet[28], French horn[29], saxophone[30], trumpet, and cornet[31] are the most common transposing instruments[32].

6.4.2 Avoiding Transposition

In some situations, you can avoid transposition, or at least avoid doing the work yourself. Some stringed instruments - guitar for example - can use a capo[33] to play in higher keys. A good electronic keyboard will transpose for you. If your music is already stored as a computer file, there are programs that will transpose it for you and display and print it in the new key. However, if you only have the music on paper, it may be easier to transpose it yourself than to enter it into a music program to have it transposed. So if none of these situations apply to you, it's time to learn to transpose.

> NOTE: If you play a chordal instrument (guitar, for example), you may not need to write down the transposed music. There are instructions below (Section 6.4.6) for transposing just the names of the chords.

---

[27]This content is available online at <http://cnx.org/content/m10668/2.13/>.
[28]"Clarinets" <http://cnx.org/content/m12604/latest/>
[29]"The French Horn" <http://cnx.org/content/m11617/latest/>
[30]"Saxophones" <http://cnx.org/content/m12611/latest/>
[31]"Trumpets and Cornets" <http://cnx.org/content/m12606/latest/>
[32]"Transposing Instruments" <http://cnx.org/content/m10672/latest/>
[33]"Guitars" <http://cnx.org/content/m12745/latest/#p9c>

6.4.3 How to Transpose Music

There are four steps to transposition:

1. Choose your transposition.

2. Use the correct key signature (Section 1.1.4).

3. Move all the notes the correct interval (Section 4.5).

4. Take care with your accidentals (pg 17).

6.4.3.1 Step 1: Choose Your Transposition

In many ways, this is the most important step, and the least straightforward. The transposition you choose will depend on why you are transposing. If you already know what transposition you need, you can go to step two. If not, please look at the relevant sections below first:

- Are you rewriting the music for a transposing instrument (Section 6.4.4.2)?

- Are you looking for a key that is in the range of your vocalist (Section 6.4.4.1)?

- Are you looking for a key that is more playable (Section 6.4.4.3) on your instrument?

6.4.3.2 Step 2: Write the New Key Signature

If you have chosen the transposition because you want a particular key, then you should already know what key signature to use. (If you don't, see Key Signature (Section 1.1.4).) If you have chosen the transposition because you wanted a particular interval (say, a whole step lower or a perfect fifth higher), then the key changes by the same interval. For example, if you want to transpose a piece in D major up one whole step (Section 4.2), the key also moves up one whole step, to E major. Transposing a piece in B minor down a major third (Major and Minor Intervals) will move the key signature down a major third to G minor. For more information on and practice identifying intervals, see Interval (Section 4.5). For further information on how moving music up or down changes the key signature, see The Circle of Fifths (Section 4.7).

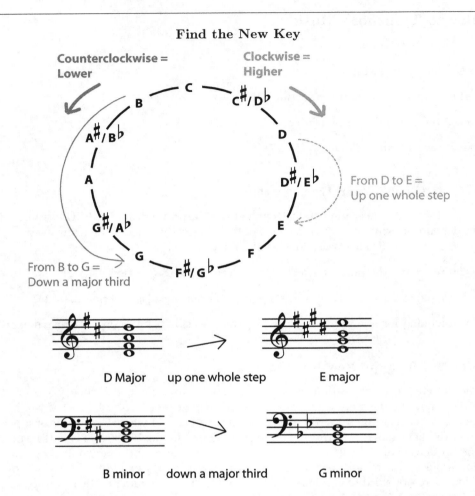

Figure 6.14: You must know the interval between the old and new keys, and you must know the new key signature. This step is very important; if you use the wrong key signature, the transposition will not work.

6.4.3.3 Step 3: Transpose the Notes

Now rewrite the music, changing all the notes by the correct interval. You can do this for all the notes in the key signature simply by counting lines and spaces. As long as your key signature is correct, you do not have to worry about whether an interval is major, minor, or perfect.

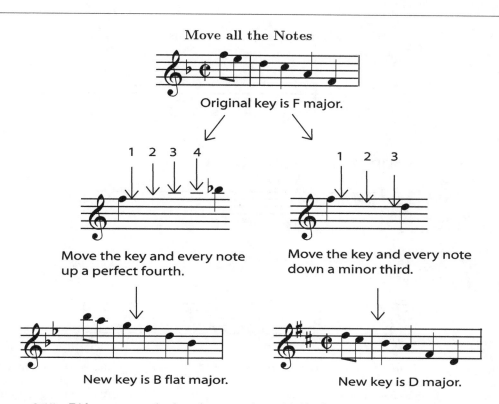

Figure 6.15: Did you move the key down a minor third? Simply move all the notes down a third in the new key; count down three lines-or-spaces to find the new spot for each note. Did you move the key up a perfect fourth? Then move all the notes up four lines-and-spaces. Remember to count every line and every space, including the ones the notes start on and end on. Once you get the hang of it, this step is very straightforward, but it may take a while if you have a lot of music.

6.4.3.4 Step 4: Be Careful with Accidentals

Most notes can simply be moved the correct number of lines and spaces. Whether the interval is minor, major, or perfect will take care of itself if the correct key signature has been chosen. But some care must be taken to correctly transpose accidentals. Put the note on the line or space where it would fall if it were not an accidental, and then either lower or raise it from your new key signature. For example, an accidental B natural in the key of E flat major has been raised a half step from the note in the key (which is B flat). In transposing down to the key of D major, you need to raise the A natural in the key up a half step, to A sharp. If this is confusing, keep in mind that the interval between the old and new (transposed) notes (B natural and A sharp) must be one half step, just as it is for the notes in the key.

> NOTE: If you need to raise a note which is already sharp in the key, or lower a note that is already flat, use double sharps or double flats (Figure 1.20)

Transposing Accidentals

Original E flat major

Transposed to D major

Transposed to E major

Figure 6.16:   Flats don't necessarily transpose as flats, or sharps as sharps. For example, if the accidental originally raised the note one half step out of the key, by turning a flat note into a natural, the new accidental may raise the note one half step out of the key by turning a natural into a sharp.

Exercise 6.2:

The best practice for transposing is to transpose a piece you know well into a new key. *(Solution to Exercise 6.2 on p. 256.)*

6.4.4 Choosing Your New Key

Before you can begin transposing, you must decide what your new key (Section 4.3) will be. This will depend on why you are transposing, and what kinds of vocalists and instrumentalists you are working with.

6.4.4.1 Working with Vocalists

If you are trying to accomodate singers, your main concern in choosing a key is finding their range (Section 2.7). Is the music you are working with too high or too low? Is it only a step too high, or does it need to be changed by a third or a fifth? Once you determine the interval (Section 4.5) needed, check to make certain this will be a comfortable key for your instrumentalists.

Example 6.1:

A church choir director wants to encourage the congregation to join in on a particular hymn. It is written in four parts with the melody in the soprano part, in a range slightly too high for untrained singers. The hymn is written in the key of E flat. Lowering it by a minor third (one and a half steps) will allow the congregation to sing with gusto.

Figure 6.17: The hymn is originally in E flat. The melody that goes up to an F is too high for most untrained vocalists (male and female).

Figure 6.18: The same hymn in C is more easily singable by a congregation.

Example 6.2:

An alto vocalist would like to perform a blues standard originally sung by a soprano or tenor in B flat. She needs the song to be at least a whole step (Section 4.2) lower. Lowering it by a whole step would put it in the key of A flat. The guitar, bass, and harmonica players don't like to play in A flat, however, and the vocalist wouldn't mind singing even lower. So the best solution is to lower it by a minor third (Major and Minor Intervals), and play in the key of G.

(a)

(b)

Figure 6.19: (a) The key of this blues standard is comfortable for a soprano or tenor, as shown in this excerpt. (b) An alto or baritone can deliver a more powerful performance if the music is transposed down a minor third.

Exercise 6.3:

You're accompanying a soprano who feels that this folk tune in C minor is too low for her voice. The guitar player would prefer a key with no flats and not too many sharps.

Figure 6.20: Tune in C minor too low for some sopranos voices.

(Solution to Exercise 6.3 on p. 257.)

6.4.4.2 Transposing Instruments

Transposing instruments are instruments for which standard parts are written higher or lower than they sound. A very accomplished player of one of these instruments may be able to transpose at sight, saving you the trouble of writing out a transposed part, but most players of these instruments will need a transposed part written out for them. Here is a short list of the most common transposing instruments. For a more complete list and more information, see Transposing Instruments[34].

---

[34]"Transposing Instruments" <http://cnx.org/content/m10672/latest/>

Transposing Instruments

- Clarinet[35] is usually (but not always) a B flat instrument. Transpose C parts up one whole step for B flat instruments. (In other words, write a B flat part one whole step higher than you want it to sound.)

- Trumpet and Cornet[36] parts can be found in both B flat and C, but players with B flat instruments will probably want a B flat (transposed) part.

- French Horn[37] parts are usually in F these days. However, because of the instrument's history, older orchestral parts may be in any conceivable transposition, even changing transpositions in the middle of the piece. Because of this, some horn players learn to transpose at sight. Transpose C parts up a perfect fifth to be read in F.

- Alto and Baritone Saxophone[38] are E flat instruments. Transpose parts up a major sixth for alto sax, and up an octave plus a major sixth for bari sax.

- Soprano and Tenor Saxophone[39] are B flat instruments. Tenor sax parts are written an octave plus one step higher.

NOTE: Why are there transposing instruments? Sometimes this makes things easier on instrumentalists; they may not have to learn different fingerings when they switch from one kind of saxophone to another, for example. Sometimes, as with piccolo, transposition centers the music in the staff (rather than above or below the staff). But often transposing instruments are a result of the history of the instrument. See the history of the French horn[40] to find out more.

The transposition you will use for one of these instruments will depend on what type of part you have in hand, and what instrument you would like to play that part. As with any instrumental part, be aware of the range (Section 2.7) of the instrument that you are writing for. If transposing the part up a perfect fifth results in a part that is too high to be comfortable, consider transposing the part down a perfect fourth instead.

To Decide Transpositions for Transposing Instruments

1. Ask: what type of part am I transposing and what type of part do I want? Do you have a C part and want to turn it into an F part? Do you want to turn a B flat part into a C part? *Non-transposing parts are considered to be C parts.* The written key signature has nothing to do with the type of part you have; only the part's transposition from concert pitch (C part) matters for this step.

2. Find the interval between the two types of part. For example, the difference between a C and a B flat part is one whole step. The difference between an E flat part and a B flat part is a perfect fifth.

3. Make sure you are transposing in the correct direction. If you have a C part and want it to become a B flat part, for example, you must transpose *up* one whole step. This may seem counterintuitive, but remember, *you are basically compensating for the transposition that is "built into" the instrument.* To compensate properly, always transpose by moving in the

---

[35]"Clarinets" <http://cnx.org/content/m12604/latest/>

[36]"Trumpets and Cornets" <http://cnx.org/content/m12606/latest/>

[37]"The French Horn" <http://cnx.org/content/m11617/latest/>

[38]"Saxophones" <http://cnx.org/content/m12611/latest/>

[39]"Saxophones" <http://cnx.org/content/m12611/latest/>

[40]"The French Horn" <http://cnx.org/content/m11617/latest/#s2>

opposite direction from the change in the part names. To turn a B flat part into a C part (B flat to C = up one step), transpose the part down one whole step. To turn a B flat part into an E flat part (B flat to E flat = down a perfect fifth), transpose the part up a perfect fifth.

4. Do the correct transposition by interval (Section 6.4.3.2), including changing the written key by the correct interval.

Example 6.3:

Your garage band would like to feature a solo by a friend who plays the alto sax. Your songwriter has written the solo as it sounds on his keyboard, so you have a C part. Alto sax is an E flat instrument; in other words, when he sees a C, he plays an E flat, the note a major sixth (Major and Minor Intervals) lower. To compensate for this, you must write the part a major sixth higher than your C part.

Figure 6.21: In the top line, the melody is written out in concert pitch; on the second line it has been transposed to be read by an alto saxophone. When the second line is played by an alto sax player, the result sounds like the first line.

Example 6.4:

Your choral group is performing a piece that includes an optional instrumental solo for clarinet. You have no clarinet player, but one group member plays recorder, a C instrument. Since the part is written for a B flat instrument, it is written one whole step higher than it actually sounds. To write it for a C instrument, transpose it back down one whole step.

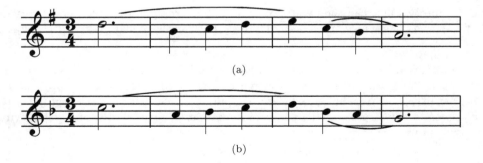

Figure 6.22: (a) Melody for B flat clarinet (b) Melody transposed for C instruments

Exercise 6.4:

There's a march on your community orchestra's program, but the group doesn't have quite enough trombone players for a nice big march-type sound. You have extra French horn players, but they can't read bass clef C parts.

Figure 6.23: Trombone line from a march

(Solution to Exercise 6.4 on p. 257.)

6.4.4.3 Playable Keys

Transposition can also make music easier to play for instrumentalists, and ease of playing generally translates into more satisfying performances. For example, transcriptions for band of orchestral works sometimes change the (often sharp) orchestral key to a nearby key with more flats. A guitar[41] player, given a piece written in A flat for keyboard, will often prefer to play it in A or G, since the fingerings for chords in those keys are easier. Also, instrumentalists, like vocalists, have ranges (Section 2.7) that need to be considered.

Example 6.5:

Your eighth grade bassoon[42] player would like to play a Mozart minuet at a school talent show with a flute-playing friend from band. The minuet is in C, but the melody is a little too low for a flute[43], and the bassoonist would also be more comfortable playing higher. If you transpose the whole piece up a minor third to E flat major, both players can hit the lowest notes, and you may also find that fingerings and tunings are better in the flat key.

---

[41]"Guitars" <http://cnx.org/content/m12745/latest/>
[42]"Bassoons" <http://cnx.org/content/m12612/latest/>
[43]"Flutes" <http://cnx.org/content/m12603/latest/>

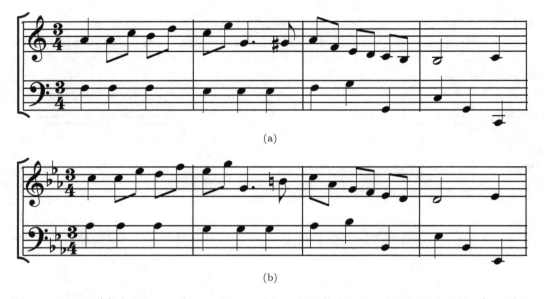

(a)

(b)

Figure 6.24: (a) An excerpt from a Mozart Minuet in C. The upper part is too low for a flute player. (b) Both young instrumentalists would be more comfortable playing in this key.

Exercise 6.5:

You've brought your guitar and your capo[44] to the sing-along because you'd like to play along, too. Going through the music beforehand, you notice that your favorite song is in A flat. The pianist isn't prepared to play it in any other key, but you really don't like those thin-sounding chords in A flat. You can use your capo to raise the sound of your instrument (basically turning it into a transposing instrument in C sharp, D, D sharp, or even higher), but the less you raise it the more likely you are to still sound in tune with the piano.

$$A^\flat \qquad\qquad B^\flat \quad E^\flat 7$$
$$\text{I}\quad \text{love you}\ \text{tru - - - ly,}$$

$$B^\flat \quad E^\flat 7 \qquad A^\flat$$
$$\text{Tru - - - ly,}\qquad \text{dear!}$$

Figure 6.25: Chords in the key of A flat major are not ideal for guitarists.

(Solution to Exercise 6.5 on p. 257.)

6.4.5 Transposing at Sight

Transposing at sight means being able to read a part written in one key while playing it in another key. Like any other performance skill, it can be learned with practice, and it is a skill that

---
[44]"Guitars" <http://cnx.org/content/m12745/latest/#p9c>

will help you become an extremely versatile instrumentalist. (Vocalists transpose at sight without even thinking about it, since they don't have to worry about different fingerings.) To practice this skill, simply start playing familiar pieces in a different key. Since you know the piece, you will recognize when you make a mistake. Start with pieces written in C, and play them only a half step or whole step lower or higher than written. When this is easy, move on to more challenging keys and larger intervals. Practice playing in an unfamiliar clef (Section 1.1.2), for example bass clef if you are used to reading treble clef. Or, if you play a transposing instrument[45], work on being able to play C parts on sight. You may find more opportunities to play (and earn the gratitude of your fellow musicians) if you can say, "we can change keys if you like", or "I can cover that bass clef C part for you, no problem."

6.4.6 Transposing Chord Names

If you are transposing entire chords, and you know the name of the chord, you may find it easier to simply transpose the name of the chord rather than transposing each individual note. In fact, transposing in this way is simple enough that even a musician who can't read music can do it.

Chromatic Circle

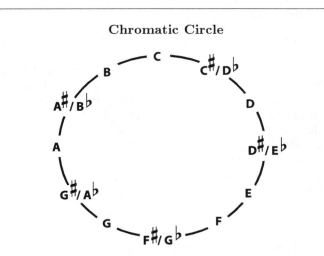

Figure 6.26: When transposing, you can use the chromatic (pg 123) circle both to change the name of the key (as above (Figure 6.14)) and to change chord names, because the basic idea is the same; the entire piece (chords, notes, and key) must move the same number of half steps (Section 4.2) in the same direction. If you're using a chromatic circle to transpose the names of all the chords in a piece, just make sure that you move each chord name by the same amount and in the same direction.

6.4.6.1 Step 1: Choose Your Transposition

Your choice of new key will depend on why you are transposing, but it may depend on other things, also.

- If you are transposing because the *music is too low or too high*, decide how much higher or lower you want the music to sound. If you want the music to sound higher, go around

---

[45]"Transposing Instruments" <http://cnx.org/content/m10672/latest/>

the chromatic circle (Figure 6.26) in the clockwise direction. If you want it lower, go in the counterclockwise direction. The further you go, the more it will change. Notice that, since you're going in a circle, raising the music a lot eventually gives the same chords as lowering it a little (and vice-versa). If some keys are easier for you to play in than others, you may want to check to make sure the key you choose has "nice" chords. If not, try another key near it.

- If you are changing keys in order to *make the chords easy to play*, try changing the final chord so that it names an easy-to-play-in key. (Guitarists, for example, often find the keys G, D, A, E, C, Am, Em, and Dm easier to play in than other keys.) The last chord of most pieces will usually be the chord that names the key. If that doesn't seem to work for your piece, try a transposition that makes the most common chord an easy chord. Start changing the other chords by the same amount, and in the same direction, and see if you are getting mostly easy-to-play chords. While deciding on a new key, though, keep in mind that you are also making the piece higher or lower, and choose keys accordingly. A guitarist who wants to change chords without changing the pitch (Section 1.1.3) should lower the key (go counterclockwise on the circle) by as short a distance as possible to find a playable key. Then capo[46] at the fret that marks the number of keys moved. For example, if you moved counterclockwise by three keys, put the capo at the third fret.

- If you are changing keys to *play with another instrumentalist* who is transposing or who is playing in a different key from you, you will need to figure out the correct transposition. For a transposing instrument (pg 248), look up the correct transposition (the person playing the instrument may be able to tell you), and move all of your chords up or down by the correct number of half steps. (For example, someone playing a B flat trumpet will read parts one step - two half steps - lower than concert pitch[47]. So to play from the same part as the trumpet player, move all the chords counterclockwise two places.) If the instrumental part is simply written in a different key, find out what key it is in (the person playing it should be able to tell you, based on the key signature (Section 1.1.4)) and what key you are playing in (you may have to make a guess based on the final chord of the piece or the most common chord). Use the chromatic circle to find the direction and number of half steps to get from your key to the other key.

6.4.6.2 Step 2: Change the Names of All the Chords

Using the chromatic circle to count keys, change the note names in all of the chords by the same amount (the same number of half steps, or places in the chromatic circle) and in the same direction. Change only the note names (things like "F" and "C sharp" and "B flat"); don't change any other information about the chord (like major, minor, dim., 7, sus4, add11, etc.). If the bass note of the chord is written out as a note name, change that, also (using the same chromatic circle).

Check your transposition by playing it to see if it sounds right. If you don't like playing some of the chords in your new key, or if you have changed the key too much or not enough, try a different transposition.

Example 6.6:

Say you have a song in the key of G, which is too low for your voice. If it's just a little too low, you can go up two keys to A. If this is still too low, you can go up even further (5 keys altogether) to the key of C. Maybe that's high enough for your voice, but you no longer like the chords. If that is the case, you can go up two more keys to D. Notice that, because the keys are arranged in a circle, going up seven keys like this is the same as going down five keys.

---

[46]"Guitars" <http://cnx.org/content/m12745/latest/#p9c>
[47]"Transposing Instruments" <http://cnx.org/content/m10672/latest/#intro>

Original Key	G	B♭	B♭6	B♭M7	E♭M7	E♭+	A7	D/A
2 keys higher	A	C	C6	C M7	F M7	F +	B7	E/B
5 keys higher	C	E	E♭6	E♭M7	A♭M7	A♭+	D7	G/D
7 keys higher (or 5 keys lower)	D	F	F 6	F M7	B♭M7	B♭+	E7	A/E

Figure 6.27

Example 6.7:

Now say you have a song in the key of E flat. It's not hard to sing in that key, so you don't want to go far, but you really don't like playing in E flat. You can move the song up one key to E, but you might like the chords even better if you move them down one key to D. Notice that if you are a guitar player, and everyone else really wants to stay in E flat, you can write the chords out in D and play them with a capo on the first fret; to everyone else it will sound as if you're playing in E flat.

Original Key	E♭	Gm	A♭	D♭	B♭7	B♭9	Cm	Gm
1 key higher	E	G♯m	A	D	B 7	B 9	C♯m	G♯m
1 key lower	D	F♯m	G	C	A 7	A 9	Bm	F♯m

Figure 6.28

Exercise 6.6:

Now say that you have a song that is in B flat, which is more than a little (more than one key) too high for you. Find a key a bit lower that still has nice, easy-to-play chords for guitar.

B♭ Gm Cm7 F 7   E♭   C 9 B♭9 Gm

Figure 6.29

(Solution to Exercise 6.6 on p. 258.)

Solutions to Exercises in Chapter 6

Solution to Exercise 6.1 (p. 239):

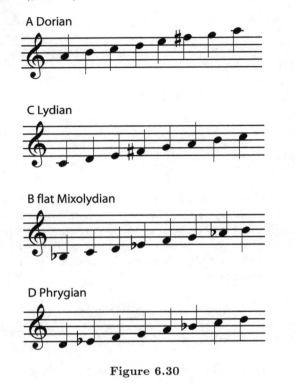

Figure 6.30

Solution to Exercise 6.2 (p. 246):
Play the part you have transposed; your own ears will tell you where you have made mistakes.

Solution to Exercise 6.3 (p. 248):

Transposing up a major third (Major and Minor Intervals), to E minor, puts the song in a better range for a soprano, with a key signature that is easy for guitars.

Figure 6.31: Moving tune up to E minor puts it in a better key for sopranos.

Solution to Exercise 6.4 (p. 251):

The trombone part is in C in bass clef; the horn players are used to reading parts in F in treble clef. Transpose the notes up a perfect fifth and write the new part in treble clef.

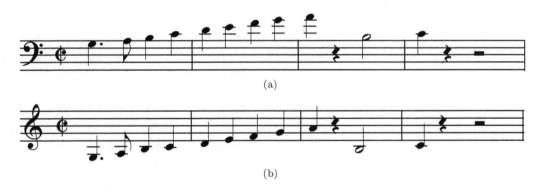

Figure 6.32: (a) This is the same part transposed up a fifth so that it is in F (b) Now write it in treble clef to make it easy for horn players to read.

Solution to Exercise 6.5 (p. 252):

Put the capo on the first fret to raise the sound by one half step. Then transpose the chords down one half step. You will be playing in G, a nice strong key for guitar, but sounding in A flat. For more on transposing chords, see the final section below (Section 6.4.6)

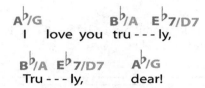

Figure 6.33: Giving guitarists the option of playing in G major (with a capo) can make things easier.

Solution to Exercise 6.6 (p. 255):

The best solution here is probably to put the song in the key of G. This is three keys lower, and has easy chords.

G   Em   Am7   D7   C   A9   G9   Em

Figure 6.34

Index of Keywords and Terms

Keywords are listed by the section with that keyword (page numbers are in parentheses). Keywords do not necessarily appear in the text of the page. They are merely associated with that section. *Ex.* apples, § 1.1 (1) **Terms** are referenced by the page they appear on. *Ex.* apples, 1

Attributions

Module: Interval
By: Catherine Schmidt-Jones

Module: Harmonic Series II: Harmonics, Intervals, and Instruments
By: Catherine Schmidt-Jones

Module: The Circle of Fifths
By: Catherine Schmidt-Jones

Module: Scales that aren't Major or Minor
By: Catherine Schmidt-Jones

Module: Triads
By: Catherine Schmidt-Jones

Module: Naming Triads
By: Catherine Schmidt-Jones

Module: Consonance and Dissonance
By: Catherine Schmidt-Jones

Module: Beyond Triads: Naming Other Chords
By: Catherine Schmidt-Jones

Understanding Basic Music Theory

An expanded version of "Introduction to Music Theory", this course includes a review of common notation and an introduction to the physics behind music theory, as well as the basic concepts of music theory and a few slightly advanced but very useful topics, such as transposition.

About Connexions

Since 1999, Connexions has been pioneering a global system where anyone can create course materials and make them fully accessible and easily reusable free of charge. We are a Web-based authoring, teaching and learning environment open to anyone interested in education, including students, teachers, professors and lifelong learners. We connect ideas and facilitate educational communities.

Connexions's modular, interactive courses are in use worldwide by universities, community colleges, K-12 schools, distance learners, and lifelong learners. Connexions materials are in many languages, including English, Spanish, Chinese, Japanese, Italian, Vietnamese, French, Portuguese, and Thai. Connexions is part of an exciting new information distribution system that allows for **Print on Demand Books**. Connexions has partnered with innovative on-demand publisher QOOP to accelerate the delivery of printed course materials and textbooks into classrooms worldwide at lower prices than traditional academic publishers.

CPSIA information can be obtained
at www.ICGtesting.com
Printed in the USA
BVHW070341280819
556726BV00009BA/197/P

9 781680 9215